BOURDIEU AND THE JOURNALISTIC FIELD

BOURDIEU AND THE JOURNALISTIC FIELD

EDITED BY RODNEY BENSON
AND ERIK NEVEU

Polity

First published in 2005 by Polity Press

Polity Press
65 Bridge Street
Cambridge CB2 1UR, UK.

Polity Press
350 Main Street
Malden, MA 02148, USA

ISBN 0 7456 3386 2 (hardback)
ISBN 0 7456 3387 0 (paperback)

A catalogue record for this book is available from the British Library.

Typeset in 10.5 on 12 pt Sabon
by SNP Best-set Typesetter Ltd., Hong Kong
Printed and bound in Great Britain by MPG Books Ltd., Bodmin, Cornwall.

For further information on Polity, visit our website: www.polity.co.uk

Contents

Acknowledgments

In the planning, writing, and editing of this book, we have incurred many debts, most of all of course to Pierre Bourdieu himself. Bourdieu took an active personal interest in introducing US scholars to his journalism research group at the Center for European Sociology (CSE), which laid the groundwork for the present collaboration. In 1998, he heartily endorsed our project of publishing an edited English-language volume on the journalistic field. Two years after his passing, Pierre Bourdieu's creative inspiration and gentle encouragement are still sorely missed.

During the spring of 1999, Eric Darras played a crucial role in advancing this project by organizing an application to the France–Berkeley Fund. We proposed to bring together French and American social researchers studying recent transformations of the relations between news media and politics. Our application was accepted, and a conference held on the University of California–Berkeley campus in May 2000 offered a first opportunity to collectively discuss field theory in relation to media research. Neil Fligstein, director of the Center for Culture, Organizations and Politics (University of California, Berkeley) and Rémi Lenoir, director of the CSE, generously offered to jointly host the conference, whose participants in addition to the authors of this volume included Timothy E. Cook, Thomas C. Leonard, and Theodore L. Glasser.

Through dozens of e-mail exchanges and meetings in Paris and Rennes between 2001 and 2003, we considerably refined the focus and organization of the book. Ad hoc brainstorming sessions – in Paris with Patrick Champagne and CSE colleagues, in Toulouse with

Eric Darras, in San Diego with Dan Hallin and Michael Schudson – inspired us and helped maintain our momentum. During this process, Craig Calhoun, Priscilla Parkhurst Ferguson, John B. Thompson, and Loïc Wacquant also offered encouragement and sage advice.

Chapter 2, "The Political Field, the Social Science Field, and the Journalistic Field" by Pierre Bourdieu is taken as an excerpt from a lecture delivered in Lyons, France, on November 14, 1995, "Champ politique, champ des sciences sociales, champ journalistique," Cours du Collège de France à la faculté d'anthropologie et de sociologie de l'Université Lumière, Lyon 2, with the guidance of Patrick Champagne. It is published with the kind permission of Jérôme Bourdieu and Marie-Christine Rivière, on behalf of the Bourdieu Estate, and was translated by Richard Nice.

Chapter 3, "The 'Double Dependency': The Journalistic Field Between Politics and Markets" by Patrick Champagne, originally appeared as "La double dépendance: Quelques remarques sur les rapports entre les champs politique, économique et journalistique" in *Hermès*, 17–18 (1995), pp. 215–29. It is published here in a slightly shorter form with the kind permission of the journal's editors, and was translated by James Ingram.

Chapter 4, "Subfields of Specialized Journalism" by Dominique Marchetti, originally appeared as "Les sous-champs spécialisés du journalisme" in *Réseaux*, 20, 111 (2002), pp. 21–56, and is published here in slightly adapted form with the kind permission of the journal's editors. It was translated by Kelly E. Benson.

Chapter 6, "The Contaminated Blood Scandal: Reframing Medical News" by Patrick Champagne and Dominique Marchetti, originally appeared as "L'information médicale sous contrainte: A propos du 'scandale du sang contaminé' ", in *Actes de la recherche en sciences sociales*, 101–2 (1994), pp. 40–62. It is published here as a slightly modified excerpt with the kind permission of the journal's editors. The main text was translated by Matthew R. Escobar; boxes were translated by James Ingram.

Chapter 7, "Economic Journalism in France" by Julien Duval, originally appeared as "Concessions et conversions à l'économie: Le journalisme économique en France depuis les années 80" in *Actes de la recherche en sciences sociales*, 131–2 (2000), pp. 56–75. It is published here as a slightly modified excerpt with the kind permission of the journal's editors, and was translated by James Ingram.

Chapter 8, "Media Consecration of the Political Order" by Eric Darras, was translated by James Ingram.

Chapter 10, "Bourdieu, the Frankfurt School, and Cultural

Studies: On Some Misunderstandings" by Erik Neveu, was translated by James Ingram. It features excerpts from "Sociologues des mythologies et mythologies de sociologues" by Pierre Bourdieu and Jean-Claude Passeron in *Les Temps modernes*, 211 (December 1963), pp. 998–1021, published here for the first time in English, and also translated by James Ingram. Kind permission to publish these excerpts was granted by Jean-Claude Passeron and by Jérôme Bourdieu and Marie-Christine Rivière, on behalf of the Bourdieu Estate.

Crucial support for the translation of French texts in this book was provided by New York University's Department of Culture and Communication and Steinhardt School, the Centre de recherches sur l'action politique en Europe at the Université de Rennes (CRAPE–CNRS), and the Institut d'études politiques de Toulouse. Kelly Benson, Julien Duval, Richard Kaplan, Eric Klinenberg, Dominique Marchetti, and David Swartz closely read various chapters and provided thoughtful suggestions and critiques. Polity editors Andrea Drugan, Sarah Dancy, and Felicity Marsh expertly guided us through the final stages and helped polish our phrasing and presentation. To all of those named above, we owe a debt of gratitude. As to any remaining flaws, the usual caveat applies.

RB and EN
New York and Rennes

Contributors

Rodney Benson is Assistant Professor in the Department of Culture and Communication, New York University. He has published widely on Bourdieu's field theory and on comparative media research in such journals as *Political Communication*, *Theory and Society*, *Journal of European Area Studies* and *French Politics, Culture, and Society*.

Pierre Bourdieu, 1930–2002, was Professor of Sociology at the Collège de France and is widely regarded as one of the most influential social theorists of the twentieth century. His major works in the sociology of culture, which form the basis for his analysis of the journalistic field, include *Distinction* (Harvard University Press, Cambridge, MA, 1984), *The Field of Cultural Production* (Columbia University Press, New York, 1993 and Polity, Cambridge, 1993), and *The Rules of Art* (Stanford University Press, Stanford, CA, 1995, and Polity, Cambridge, 1996). Well known for his work of popular media criticism, *On Television* (The New Press, New York, 1998), Bourdieu's comprehensive research program on journalism resulted in two special issues (101–2 in 1994 and 131–2 in 2000) devoted to the topic in the academic journal *Actes de la recherche en sciences sociales*.

Patrick Champagne is a researcher with the Centre de sociologie européenne (CSE), Ecole des hautes études en sciences sociales, Paris. He is the author of *Faire l'opinion* (Minuit, Paris, 1990) and numerous articles on journalism, politics and social movements. His recent works in English include “The View from the Media” and “The View from the State” in *The Weight of the World* (Stanford University Press, Stanford, 2000, and Polity, Cambridge, 2000) and “Pre-election opinion polls and democracy” in *Voices of France: Social, Political and Cultural Identity* (Pinter, London, 1997).

Eric Darras is Assistant Professor (Maître de conferences) in Information and Communication Sciences at the Institut d'études politiques, Université de Toulouse I. He is a former staff advisor to the Conseil supérieur de l'audiovisuel (CSA), the French counterpart to the US Federal Communications Commission, and has published widely on French media and politics.

Julien Duval is a researcher with the French National Center for Scientific Research (CNRS), Centre de recherches sur l'action politique en Europe (CRAPE), Rennes, and CSE, Paris. He is the author of *Critique de la raison journalistique: les transformations de la presse économique en France* (Éditions du Seuil, Paris, 2004).

Daniel C. Hallin is Professor in the Department of Communication, University of California–San Diego. His recent publications include *We Keep America on Top of the World: Television Journalism and the Public Sphere* (Routledge, New York, 1994) and, with Paolo Mancini, *Comparing Media Systems: Three Models of Media and Politics* (Cambridge University Press, Cambridge, 2004).

Eric Klinenberg is Assistant Professor of Sociology, New York University. He is the author of *Heat Wave: A Social Autopsy of Disaster* (University of Chicago Press, Chicago, 2002) and numerous articles on media in *Le Monde diplomatique*, *Theory and Society*, *Information, Communication and Society*, and other journals.

Dominique Marchetti is a researcher with the French National Center for Scientific Research (CNRS), Centre de recherches sur l'action politique en Europe (CRAPE), Rennes, and CSE, Paris. He is the co-author of a major demographic study of French journalists published by La Documentation française as well as numerous articles in such leading French media journals as *Hermés* and *Reseaux*.

Erik Neveu is Professor of Political Science, Institut d'études politiques de Rennes. He is the co-editor, with Raymond Kuhn, of *Political Journalism* (Routledge, New York, 2002) and the author of *Sociologie du journalisme* (La Découverte, Paris, 2001), and *Une* *des mouvements sociaux* (La Découverte, Paris, 1996) and *Une société de communication?* (Montchrestien, Paris, 1994). His most recent English-language articles have appeared in the *European Journal of Communication*, *Journalism Studies* and the *European Journal of Political Research*.

Michael Schudson is Professor in the Department of Communication, University of California–San Diego. His numerous books on the news media include *The Sociology of News* (W. W. Norton, New York, 2003), *The Power of News* (Harvard, Cambridge, MA, 1995) and *Discovering the News* (Basic Books, New York, 1978).

1

Introduction: Field Theory as a Work in Progress

Rodney Benson and Erik Neveu

The concept of the journalistic "field" as developed by Pierre Bourdieu and colleagues offers a new way of understanding and explaining the constraints and processes involved in news media production. Scholars and students already familiar with such spatial metaphors as Jürgen Habermas's "public sphere" or Manuel Castells's "media space" may find "field" not only a more empirically useful conceptual tool but also one that opens up new kinds of intellectual inquiries.[1] While Bourdieu is best known for his extensive and wide-ranging studies of education, art, and literature, news media have also been integral to his analyses of class and culture.[2] Journalism, however, became a central part of his research program – and that of his research team at the Center for European Sociology (Centre de sociologie européenne, or CSE) – beginning in the 1990s when a newly commercialized television sector so transformed social relations in France that it literally became impossible to speak of them without also speaking of the media.

Since *On Television*[3] appeared in English translation in 1998, public and scholarly interest in Pierre Bourdieu's approach to media research has grown. Taken out of the context of Bourdieu's immense oeuvre, the book is deceptively simple. As a result, some critics and readers have too hastily dismissed *On Television* as "the same old Frankfurt school" or "Althusserian," without really understanding what the book, and more importantly, Bourdieu's larger theoretical project, has to offer. This slim paperback is best understood as a provocation and an introduction: a provocation to a broader public debate about the social and intellectual effects of commercial television, but also an introduction to an innovative theoretical approach and empirical research program.

With the privatization of the largest French television channel in 1986, side effects long taken-for-granted by North Americans, British, Australians, and other "anglo-saxons" – sensationalized, depoliticized and trivialized news – quickly emerged, giving rise to Bourdieu's impassioned public intervention. *On Television* thus served as a wake-up call for many around the world that there was nothing "natural" about an advertising-saturated, audience-ratings-driven media culture. In addition, by virtue of its origins within a markedly distinct continental European context, Bourdieu's critique of commercialism provides a fresh perspective on a classic Anglo-American debate.

It is the second agenda, however, that of less politically-charged (though hopefully quite politically relevant) theory and research, that motivates this book, via which we hope to introduce Anglophone scholars to the broad scope of a "field theory" approach to media studies only hinted at in *On Television*.[4] In earlier books such as *Distinction*, Bourdieu wrote about the media, but he focused more on the consumption rather than production of news. In more recent books such as *The Rules of Art* and *The Field of Cultural Production*, Bourdieu elaborated more fully on processes of cultural production, but wrote little specifically about journalism.[5] This volume, featuring previously untranslated essays by Bourdieu and his close associate Patrick Champagne, is intended to fill this gap. By showcasing work from Bourdieu's colleagues at the CSE in addition to more distantly related but sympathetic researchers throughout France, we purposely seek to highlight the collective nature of the field theory research project. In addition, this volume demonstrates the growing interest in the field theory approach from leading US media scholars, including Daniel C. Hallin, Eric Klinenberg, and Michael Schudson.

In this introduction, we begin by situating Bourdieu's unique approach to media studies in the context of his broad theory of fields. We then compare and contrast Bourdieu's field theory to the dominant Anglo-American theories of news media. We conclude by discussing the challenges still facing field theory as a "work in progress" and highlighting the unique contributions to this project by the authors in this volume.

Field Theory and Journalism

Bourdieu's field theory follows from Weber and Durkheim in portraying modernity as a process of differentiation into semiautonomous and increasingly specialized spheres of action (e.g., fields of politics, economics, religion, cultural production). Both within and among these spheres – or fields – relations of power fundamentally structure human action. Individuals do not simply act to maximize their rational self-interest. For Bourdieu, the sources of competition go much deeper, via his extension of Saussurean linguistics to the social sphere. What is "real" is "relational"[6] and thus to exist socially is to mark one's difference vis-à-vis others in an ongoing process that is enacted for the most part unconsciously without strategic intention. "To think in terms of field is to think relationally," Bourdieu emphasizes, adding that "in analytic terms, a field may be defined as a network, or a configuration, of objective relations between positions."[7]

Fundamental to Bourdieu's understanding of structure and agency, that is the ways in which society shapes individual actions (and vice versa), is the notion of habitus. Habitus is defined as: "a structuring structure, which organizes practices and the perception of practices. . . . configurations of properties expressing the differences objectively inscribed in conditions of existence."[8] Or as he notes elsewhere, "To speak of habitus is to assert that the individual, and even the personal, the subjective, is social, collective. Habitus is a socialized subjectivity."[9] Such language may be off-putting to Anglo-American individualistic sensibilities. Nevertheless, the notion of habitus expresses a reasonable hypothesis: that individuals' predispositions, assumptions, judgments, and behaviors are the result of a long-term process of socialization, most importantly in the family, and secondarily, via primary, secondary, and professional education. Habitus is not unchangeable. In fact, it is constantly being modified. Nevertheless, early experiences and practices, shaped by one's location in the social class structure, shape those that follow.[10] By incorporating temporality, habitus combats naïve assertions of structural determinism. In other words, any explanation of attitudes, discourses, behavior, etc. must draw on an analysis of both structural position (within the field, the field's position vis-à-vis other fields, etc.) *and* the particular historical trajectory by which an agent arrived at that position (habitus). Two other important terms for Bourdieu are "illusio" which refers to an agent's emotional and cognitive "investment" in the stakes involved in any particular field, or simply, the belief that the game is worth playing. Agents who believe a given "game" is worth playing will also tend to share a "doxa," that is, a "universe of tacit presuppositions" (see p. 37) that organize action within the field.

In the ongoing struggle that is society, two forms of power, or what Bourdieu terms "capital," are crucial: economic and cultural.[11] By economic capital, he means simply money or assets that can be turned into money. Cultural capital encompasses such things as educational credentials, technical expertise, general knowledge, verbal abilities, and artistic sensibilities.[12] The social world, as a whole, is structured around the opposition between these two forms of power, with economic capital, on the whole, being more powerful; and with fields inside fields inside fields (like a series of Russian dolls) parallel to each other in their internal organization (see p. 55). This similarity within a difference is what Bourdieu means when he describes fields as "homologous."[13]

The specific form of economic and cultural capital varies within each field, however. Inside the journalistic field, economic capital is expressed via circulation, or advertising revenues, or audience ratings, whereas the "specific" cultural capital of the field takes the form of intelligent commentary, in-depth reporting, and the like – the kind of journalistic practices rewarded each year by the US Pulitzer Prizes. Each field is thus structured around the opposition between the so-called heteronomous pole representing forces external to the field (primarily economic) and the "autonomous" pole representing the specific capital unique to that field (e.g., artistic or scientific skills). Fields are arenas of struggle in which individuals and organizations compete, unconsciously and consciously, to valorize those forms of capital which they possess.[14] The resistance encountered when agents attempt to move from the heteronomous to the autonomous pole, before having paid all the necessary "dues" – as in the 2003 controversial awarding of an American literary prize to popular novelist Stephen King[15] – is a good indicator of the ongoing power of distinctions between a cultural "sacred" and economic "profane" to structure action within cultural fields. Nevertheless, many agents do succeed in amassing both forms of capital. In journalism, media outlets such as the *New York Times* or the *Wall Street Journal* have accumulated significant economic capital even as, and largely because, they embody professional excellence. Indeed, organizations or individuals who dominate a field are generally those who successfully convert one form into the other, and in so doing, amass both "social capital"[16] of friendship and colleague networks, and "symbolic capital"[17] through which their dominance is legitimated.

Spatial, relational metaphors are used by Bourdieu to express his conception of the ordering of journalism, other fields, and the broad social world, all of which he conceptualizes in "chiastic" (cross-like) terms.[18] The vertical axis measures the overall volume of capital, whereas the horizontal axis measures the proportion of cultural to economic capital (by convention, Bourdieu has located the cultural pole on the left and the economic pole on the right). As one moves from left to right in all social spaces, the proportion of (dominated) cultural capital decreases and the proportion of (dominant) economic capital increases. From bottom to top in the space of social classes, the overall volume of all forms of capital increases. Thus, at the "top" of the social space, one finds the "field of power" organized around the same basic cultural/economic opposition but with all actors possessing relatively high volumes of at least some form of capital.

The journalistic field is seen as part of the field of power; that is, it tends to engage with first and foremost those agents who possess high volumes of capital. Within this field of power, however, it lies within the "dominated" field of cultural production – a field within this larger field. At its "left" cultural pole, journalism is part of the field of "restricted" cultural production (produced for other producers – small literary journals, avant-garde art and music, etc.), while at its "right" economic pole, it belongs to the field of large-scale cultural production (produced for general audiences – mass entertainment, etc.). In its dominant tendency, the journalistic field belongs to the latter. That is, compared to other specialized fields within the broader field of cultural production, the journalistic field is "characterized . . . by a high degree of heteronomy" which is to say that "it is a very weakly autonomous field." Nevertheless, Bourdieu insists that even the journalistic field is best understood as a microcosm set within the macrocosm – it obeys "its own laws, its own nomos" (p. 33). Via this conceptualization of the field, Bourdieu thus attempts to avoid the "reductionist" danger – or what he calls the "short-circuit fallacy" – of directly reducing journalistic or any other process of cultural production to broad societal level processes, whether political, cultural, or economic.[19]

If cultural and economic resources structure fields along one dimension, the "old" and "new" represent the second major structuring dimension. Drawing here on the Durkheimian tradition of social morphology, Bourdieu posits that influxes of new agents into the field can serve either as forces for transformation or conservation. At the managerial or elite professional level, new agents can only establish themselves by marking their difference with those already in the field, and thus have the greatest incentive to found a new kind of press outlet or adopt a distinctive editorial voice. For example, Champagne and Marchetti show in chapter 6 of this volume how the changes in recruitment of medical journalists helped trigger dramatic changes in the reporting of medical news. A large mismatch between the quantity of new entrants relative to available positions, especially at the entry levels, may also have conservative effects. Increased competition for scarce jobs may make journalists more cautious and conformist, contributing to simple reproduction of the field.[20] Changes in the class composition of new entrants can be another source of dynamism in the field. Following from Bourdieu's notion of habitus, one can examine various characteristics of those entering the field – their social/economic origins, where they went to school and received professional training, and how they rose in the profession. According to Bourdieu, journalists from high cultural or economic capital backgrounds are most likely to have the motivation and capacity to change the field based on the experience of their "deviant trajectories."[21]

Despite the inherent dynamism and conflict inside fields, most of this activity will tend to largely reproduce the structure of the field, Bourdieu suggests, unless and until it is also subject to pressures from neighboring fields. Such external shocks could include new political orders brought about by democratic processes, dramatic changes in the overall legal and economic policy environment, as well as specific media regulations, social and cultural movements, and economic crises. Any of these shocks may transform the relative "attraction" of the autonomous and heteronomous poles of the journalistic field and other fields of cultural production. Bourdieu uses the metaphor of Einsteinian physics: "the more energy a body has, the more it distorts the space around it, and a very powerful agent within a field can distort the whole space, cause the whole space to be organized in relation to itself" (p. 43).

Transformations of the journalistic field matter, Bourdieu argues, precisely because of the central position of the journalistic field in the larger field of power, as part of an ensemble of centrally located fields – also including social sciences and politics (both state and parties or associations) – that compete to impose "the legitimate vision of the social world" (p. 36). Because fields are closely intertwined and because journalism in particular is such a crucial mediator among all fields, as the journalistic field has become more commercialized and thus more homologous with the economic field, it increases the power of the heteronomous pole within each of the fields, producing a convergence among all the fields and pulling them closer to the commercial pole in the larger field of power. This is the chief thesis of *On Television*; but it is not the whole of field theory – it is field theory used to describe one particular historical configuration and transformation of fields. Our aim with this book is to show how field theory may indeed be used to describe and account for a variety of other types of situations.

One final comment seems in order here. While field studies in recent years have primarily emphasized processes of cultural *production*, Bourdieu's theory clearly makes room for *reception* as well (see especially *Distinction*). Once again, Bourdieu sees these two processes as homologous or running parallel with one another. In other words, since both production and reception are shaped by the same processes of class distinction, without any overt coordination, they will in a sense end up at the same place. In the essay included in this volume, Bourdieu thus writes, "To understand a product like [the French newsmagazines] *L'Express* or *Le Nouvel Observateur*, there is little point in studying the target readership. The essential part of what is presented in *L'Express* and *Le Nouvel Observateur* is determined by the relationship between *L'Express* and *Le Nouvel Observateur*." And this is so, Bourdieu stresses, because "there is a homology between the space of the microcosms of production and the encompassing social space" (p. 45).

Structural homologies are both an explanatory tool and a testable hypothesis about producer–audience relations. It would be wrong to claim that such correspondences constitute a sort of iron law, since fieldwork reveals many situations with a less than tight overlap between the spaces of production and reception. "Omnibus" media, including national broadcast television channels and newspapers with a regional monopoly, potentially appeal to audiences across a variety of class backgrounds. In France, a growing number of sociologists argue, with strong empirical data, that class or education alone no longer make sense of the growing complexity of cultural and media practices: individuals possess a variety of so-called "highbrow" and "lowbrow" cultural tastes.[22] Far from being unstructured, however, reception processes continue to be patterned in significant, if increasingly complex, ways.[23] If Bourdieu's empirical findings on reception need to be updated, his conceptual tools are thus likely to continue to be useful in conducting such research.

Situating Field Theory

Field theory offers a new paradigm for the sociology of news, yet one that in many ways supplements rather than entirely supplants existing approaches. In what follows, we compare field theory to the predominant Anglo-American research paradigms – technological, political economy, hegemony, cultural, organizational, and new institutionalist.

Despite the use of a title that singles out a particular medium – television – Bourdieu is most emphatically not a "medium theorist," to borrow Joshua Meyrowitz's term. Bourdieu himself has clearly distinguished his approach from those of theorists, such as Régis Debray and others influenced by Marshall McLuhan, who have leaned towards technological determinism.[24] At the same time, he has acknowledged some important differences between television and print media, in particular, audience size, breadth and diversity, as when he distinguishes between "omnibus" media and more specialized, segmented media.[25] *On Television* raises many of the same concerns about the degradation of public discourse brought about by television, as does Neil Postman's *Amusing Ourselves to Death*. However, whereas Postman emphatically links these features to unique characteristics of the television "medium" – the "inherent bias" of this technology to promote a discourse that "abandons logic, reason, sequence and rules of contradiction"[26] – for Bourdieu, the problem is not television per se, but commercial television governed by the logic of the "Audimat" audience ratings (the French equivalent of the US Nielsen system).[27]

A more serious empirical technological critique would be that Bourdieu did not pay enough attention to the internet and other forms of "new" media.[28] To be fair, the internet's social penetration in France has been more gradual than in the United States. Bourdieu would doubtless be skeptical of claims that internet technologies represent a fundamental break with previous systems of communication. In any case, field theory could, and doubtless should, be enlisted in research that examines the complex interrelations between new media and old, in the context of their use in a range of fields of cultural production.

Theories concerned with economic power obviously provide a much closer point of comparison with Bourdieu's model, though the fit between traditional political economy models (especially the "Frankfurt School") and field theory is not nearly so close as some critics believe (see Neveu, chapter 10 in this volume). It is true that recent Bourdieu-inspired studies of journalism have emphasized increasing economic pressures, but this focus is certainly reasonable during a period marked by a dramatic rise of market power in France. Around the globe (and from across the ideological spectrum), media researchers and journalists alike have documented the same commercializing tendencies. While insisting on the power of the economic field in the contemporary historical context, Bourdieu distances his model from any form of orthodox Marxist teleology: "the relations between fields . . . are not defined once and for all, even in the most general tendencies of their evolution."[29]

Bourdieu's notion of the journalistic field can also be distinguished from Habermas's model of the "public sphere." Despite some modifications in his model,[30] Habermas's conceptualization of the mass media's relation to the public sphere largely revolves around the single variable of commercialization. Historically, Habermas argues, the "press itself became manipulable to the extent that it became commercialized," beginning in earnest in the mid-1800s; the public sphere was thus transformed from a forum for rational–critical debate into a "platform for advertising."[31] In contrast to Bourdieu's understanding of the journalistic field as possessing some autonomy, Habermas portrays the press as completely lacking in defenses against the market and the "mass-welfare state." Whereas Habermas writes in relation to democratic normative theory, Bourdieu maintains a more ambivalent or at least indirect relation to such concerns. Normatively, if Habermas wants to restore the possibility of attaining an "ideal speech situation," Bourdieu is interested foremost in maintaining the optimum social conditions for the production of specialized knowledge and modern forms of enlightened citizens. More crucial for our purposes, however, are the empirical and analytical affinities between the two. As we emphasize in the concluding section of this introduction, "public sphere" as an empirical concept would be much improved through the kind of detailed specification of structures and processes that field theory could provide.

Hegemony theory is sometimes seen as another variant of political economy, which on first glance bears some resemblance to field theory. The notion of hegemony derives from Antonio Gramsci, who called special attention to the role of intellectuals in shaping a society's "common sense." Stuart Hall, Todd Gitlin, Dan Hallin, and others were among those first to adapt the notion of hegemony to media research. Hallin argues that hegemony captures the "process by which a world-view compatible with the existing structure of power in society is reproduced, a process which is decentralized, open to contradiction and conflict, but generally effective."[32] Likewise, field theory is concerned with how macrostructures are linked to organizational routines and journalistic practices, and emphasizes the dynamic nature of power. But the field and hegemony models part company in their conceptions of power and the potential for its transformation. Hegemony analyses usually entail functionalist-style conclusions, that is, that media systems will tend to "hold . . . communication within limits relatively less threatening to the established order."[33] In field theory, journalistic fields do *not* always reinforce the power status quo, but under certain conditions may actually transform power relations in other fields. And because power is conceptualized as itself divided (between forms of cultural and economic capital, and, at least potentially, among various fields), the mechanisms by which transformation as well as reproduction can occur are laid out much more clearly.

In relation to political economy, broadly speaking, field theory thus explicitly rejects the Chomsky-style notion that the news media's behavior can be explained solely by reference to their capitalist ownership and control.[34] In contrast to such mechanical thinking, field theory is dedicated to understanding the web of mediations which intervene between Marx's "infrastructures" and "superstructures." For instance, Bourdieu has been attentive to the innumerable mismatches between individuals and the positions they hold, between dispositions and situations, as well as temporal incoherences (effects of "hysteresis") which lead persons to judge and act today according to dispositions previously acquired under quite different social conditions.[35] In contrast to the Marxist contention that the "dominant ideas are the ideas of the dominant class," Bourdieu explores the specific social worlds in which such ideas are actually produced with careful attention to their specific institutions, relationships, and material and symbolic stakes and functioning. Bourdieu thus underlines the possibilities for the autonomy of journalistic and other cultural fields, including the paradoxical manner in which such autonomy comes to be institutionalized, as in, for instance, statutes which serve to protect the university or public television, both institutions of the state, from the state itself.

If field theory cannot be simply labeled a variant of political economy models, it likewise rejects too close an association with cultural theories, at least those which portray symbolic systems as untethered from the social world. Bourdieu shares with Michel Foucault the relational understanding of language derived from Saussure "that a work does not exist by itself, that is, outside relationships of interdependence which unite it to other works." The problem, according to Bourdieu, is that Foucault refuses to acknowledge that there is something outside of such language games and that he thus "transfers into the 'paradise of ideas' . . . the oppositions and antagonisms which are rooted in the [social] relations between the producers and the consumers of cultural works."[36] One could offer a similar critique of Roland Barthes' semiology or more recently the culturalist sociology of Jeffrey Alexander.[37]

Methodologically, many field case studies seem closest to the Anglo-American tradition of newsroom organizational ethnographies (although any complete examination of the field necessarily involves historical and statistically-informed institutional analysis as well).

Organizational studies emphasize the bureaucratic constraints imposed on journalists by their employing organizations and by the official agencies who serve as their chief sources. Field theory shares with the organizational approach a highly empirical approach and interest in the everyday practice of journalism.[38] Where field theory, at least in principle, differs from the standard organizational literature is in its more systematic attempt to incorporate empirical data on individual journalists, newsbeats, and media organizations into progressively larger systems of power.

Here perhaps is where the distinct characteristics of field theory become most evident. If there is some evidence that bureaucratic characteristics of newsrooms vary, the most significant differences seem to be cross-national.[39] Thus, while organizational dynamics are important, they probably exert their most powerful semiautonomous effects not at the level of individual organizations, but at the mezzolevel of the interorganizational "field," which tends to be national. This concept of field would also incorporate influences arising from characteristics of journalists as individuals (social and educational background) and as a corporate group defending (and struggling to define) a professional identity. In short, the "field" opens up a new *unit of analysis* for media research: the entire universe of journalists and media organizations acting and reacting in relation to one another.[40]

In this sense, American "new institutionalism" and Bourdieu's field theory share many features in common. New institutionalists likewise argue that contemporary societies are composed of a number of competing and semiautonomous institutional orders or fields and that a focus on these "intermediate-level institutions . . . [helps explain] variation among capitalist countries."[41] For example, Timothy Cook shows how the media system may act as a "political institution" in its own right, in that journalistic "production values" linked to increased market pressures have not only shaped how journalists frame their news reports, but have led policy makers to increasingly create and shape policies *in order* to achieve media attention.[42] Like Bourdieu, Cook identifies elements that all actors within the field have in common, particularly the implicit codes and practices about what constitutes news. From where do these shared assumptions come? For both new institutionalist and field theories, there is no such thing as natural historical evolution; there is, however, "path dependency," in other words, the likelihood that the outcomes of past historical struggles will tend to have constraining effects on the future to the extent that these outcomes are transformed into implicit rules – common sense assumptions about how the world works that can scarcely be articulated let alone challenged.[43] Drawing on organizational sociology, new institutionalist Bartholomew Sparrow suggests another reason for homogeneity across media organizations: the desire to reduce risk amidst the uncertainty of the organizational environment.[44]

For Bourdieu, however, institutionalization is a *variable*; the extent to which rules and practices are "institutionalized" is one important way in which fields differ from one another (and over time).[45] And if both Bourdieu and his new institutionalist cousins emphasize some form of uniform field or institutional logic, Bourdieu's theory takes power dynamics more seriously, both within and among fields (or institutional orders). As a result, field analysis places greater emphasis than new institutionalism on competition and distinctions among journalists, and thus pays greater attention to such social phenomena as competition over scoops, the "revue de presse" in which journalists monitor the stories of their colleagues at other media outlets, struggles over access to sources, changes in the relative prestige of news organizations, in short, to the "relational" construction of journalistic identity. Moreover, Bourdieu's model places a greater emphasis on individual class (habitus) backgrounds (of both journalists and their audiences) in addition to the already noted morphological aspects of fields, that is, the number of agents seeking entry into a field relative to the number of positions available, the geographical concentration of those agents, etc.[46]

In sum, field theory positions itself precisely between those approaches (political economy or cultural) that commit the "short-circuit" fallacy and link news production directly to the interests of broad social classes or the national society, and those (organizational) that focus too narrowly on particular news producers. Field research thus calls for the examination of "institutional logics": the simultaneous analysis of social structures and cultural forms, as well as the complex interplay between the two.[47]

New Frontiers for Field Theory: Contributions of this Book

In this volume, we are fortunate to be able to include not only a never-before-translated essay by Pierre Bourdieu, but a range of empirical and theoretical papers by French and American media scholars who have found it extremely fruitful to think "with" (and even "against") Bourdieu – in the process, we hope, expanding and stretching field theory's capacity to explore and explain increasingly complex news media environments. Chapter 2 was originally a university lecture delivered by Bourdieu in Lyons, France. Since it was prepared to be spoken, the tone is informal and accessible. Bourdieu sought to deepen understanding of field relations and structural tendencies, and thus he downplayed subtle dynamics of human agency developed elsewhere in his writings. But this brief text clearly states several of the main elements of field theory: the notion that reality is both relational and hidden from ordinary intuition, "field" as a concept meant to be put to work empirically, how use of the concept helps avoid the excesses of either "internalist" or "externalist" readings of texts, and the meaning of "autonomy."

If Bourdieu's essay focuses on journalism's external relations with the political and social scientific fields, the chapter by Patrick Champagne looks more closely at the internal dynamics of the journalistic field. Taking as a starting point an increasing concern with ethics among French journalists, Champagne emphasizes how this "malaise" is no accident, but the result of the journalistic field's increasingly ambiguous and tenuous position in the field of power: "Journalists are structurally condemned to produce . . . under political and/or economic constraints" (p. 50). Champagne's essay is useful not only for the insight it gives us into the particular circumstances of the French journalistic field, but for the way it uses the French case as a means of illustrating general operations of journalistic fields everywhere, such as the process of "story pick-up" through which media outlets (some with more "consecrating power" than others) signal to each other what is important and what is not.

The following two chapters – Marchetti's and Benson's – attempt to draw out what is implicit but often underdeveloped in field theory: the element of variation. Dominique Marchetti's empirical concern is with the various types of journalistic specialties. Marchetti's focus on specific types of journalists, rather than journalists as a whole, follows from the basic relational insight of field theory that discursive disposition varies systematically depending on one's relative position in social space. As Marchetti explains, "Because specialized journalists have different characteristics and thus different categories of perception for the same event, the handling of news will sometimes be noticeably different according to the specialty mobilized" (p. 70). Marchetti's essay has the virtue of synthesizing the "thick descriptions" of dozens of individual case studies and then abstracting from these cases a number of variables that help account for differences among specialized subfields, e.g., "degree and forms of competition and collaboration," "journalistic demographic characteristics," and "mechanisms of professional socialization."

In chapter 5, Benson notes that Bourdieu-inspired French case studies of journalism have surprisingly little to say about what makes the French press distinctive. In the attempt to explain why a French "political/literary" journalism continues to differ from its American "informational" other, field theory is nudged in new directions. For instance, a French–American comparison powerfully calls into question Bourdieu's elision of economic and political constraints, as in the phrase the "pole of economic and political power."[48] This kind of compression of two analytically distinct forms of power provides no leverage to explain the different ways that US and French (not to mention British or other) state bureaucracies or elected bodies wield power over the news media, often in direct or indirect conflict with market logics. While national case studies emphasize how heteronomous economic pressures combined with morphological shifts have seemingly transformed journalism (and surrounding fields), Benson shows how cross-national research calls attention to the relative *lack* of change. In order to explain enduring cross-national differences in journalistic practice, field theory would do better to document *variations* in pressures (both enabling and constraining) from the political field, historical path dependent processes of field formation, and internal structural–ecological properties of the journalistic field.

In perhaps the classic illustration of a complete (if necessarily compressed)[49] field analysis, Patrick Champagne and Dominique Marchetti (chapter 6) examine the scientific, political, and journalistic construction of the "contaminated blood scandal" – charges that during the mid-1980s top government health officials knowingly distributed HIV-infected blood to thousands of French hemophiliacs. They show how this media event, which emerged and reemerged several times between the mid-1980s and early 1990s, both reflected and helped to bring about a new discursive order in medical information: moving from one in which specialists generally set the agenda and tone of medical information released to the public to one in which journalists, under increasing economic pressures, are willing to use drama, emotion and unconfirmed reports in order to maximize audience share. Champagne and Marchetti analyze the complex interplay between on the one hand long-brewing structural changes in the journalistic, medical/scientific, and political fields, and on the other, a range of historically-contingent events and actions. Their case study shows how field theory can contribute to the "social problems" research tradition in sociology, offering a "structural constructivism" that allows for the simultaneous analysis of changing media (and other) institutions along with changing social problem definitions, distinct research problematics too often separated by Anglo-American researchers.

In the next case study, a thorough mapping of the French subfield of economic or business reporting (chapter 7), Julien Duval analyzes the relative convergence and overlap among media outlets possessing various amounts of economic and professional capital. Overturning the conventional view that journalistic professionalism is opposed to commercialism, Duval finds that media outlets highly dependent on the economic field also tend to possess the most internal professional symbolic capital. Despite the centrality of correspondence analysis for so much of Bourdieu's empirical research (*Distinction* and *The State Nobility*, especially), Duval's study is in fact a rare and exemplary attempt to use this method to study the news media. Future research could build upon Duval's template by mapping fields during two time periods and then linking these structural characteristics to "before" and "after" news content analyses.

In chapter 8, Eric Darras examines the leading US and French political talk shows, *Meet the Press* and *L'Heure de verité* (Hour of Truth). Against the conventional wisdom of all-embracing media power, Darras shows that political talk shows serve as political institutions whose selection of guests and ideas is dictated far more by the logic of the political field (occupancy of powerful positions) than the journalistic/media field (appearance, self-presentation, etc.). Differences in the American and French shows are also best explained by differences in political systems and traditions rather than media systems. Darras's analysis shows that Bourdieu's field theory is clearly not a neo-Marxist dogmatism that always insists on the power of the economic field, but is rather an empirical tool to help examine the complex and varying relations and hierarchies of fields.

Eric Klinenberg (chapter 9) argues that field theory is especially useful for mapping the range of challenges facing youth media activists and other groups interested in effecting change within journalism. Bourdieu's concept of capital (cultural, economic, social, and symbolic) provides additional explanatory power, since the varying distributions of capital among different agents determine their capacity for effective action. For Klinenberg, field theory also helps to call attention to the structural and conjunctural conflicts and affinities that unite or divide similarly disposed actors, and in this case helps to show how competition for resources split potential allies.

Part III – Critical Reflections – highlights three major aspects of Bourdieu's field theory which are in need of further elaboration: audiences, autonomy, and intra- and interfield dynamics.

In chapter 10, in addition to helping situate field theory vis-à-vis the Frankfurt School and British Cultural Studies, Neveu argues that it is simply not true that Bourdieu or that field analysis in general has ignored audiences. Nor, given Bourdieu's complex understanding of structure and agency, is it true that Bourdieu portrays audiences as somehow passive or "cultural dopes." At the same time, as this volume shows, field analyses often do emphasize production over consumption. As Neveu concludes in chapter 10, field theory can and must be developed so that its unique spotlight more fully illuminates all three interdependent aspects of field (production), form (discourse), and reception.

Is there a naïve or overblown faith in the virtues of field autonomy present in Bourdieu's theory, if only implicitly? Michael Schudson's essay (chapter 11) directly confronts this important normative question, noting Bourdieu's own admission of the dangers of an "egoistic closing-in on the specific interests of the people engaged in the field" (citing Bourdieu, p. 45). Even more than the scientific communities which Thomas Kuhn criticized for their resistance to new ideas, journalism, Schudson argues, "has no systematic means for policing its own intellectual narrowness" (p. 219). Rather than attempting to preserve its autonomy, Schudson insists, journalism should remain open to the social, political, and even economic currents sweeping society. This normative issue certainly deserves further debate, and it may well be that autonomy is more desirable in some fields than others. We would only emphasize that such questions do not minimize what seems to us the unique empirical value of the notion of field autonomy: both objectively (the ways in which journalists are actually insulated from outside influences) and subjectively (journalists' professional self-understandings), autonomy offers a potentially significant and previously understudied variable shaping the practice of journalism.

In the closing chapter of this volume, Daniel Hallin praises Bourdieu's field theory for conceptualizing media as an institution within a wider social formation. As the co-author with Paolo Mancini in 2004 of an important work on comparative media systems,[50] Hallin systematically compares field theory with other models that have attempted to analyze media at the systemic level, in particular the neo-Parsonian differentiation theory of Jeffrey Alexander and Habermas's model of the public sphere. Hallin finds that field theory has certain advantages, avoiding the differentiation model's evolutionary assumptions and highlighting how markets as well as states limit autonomy. Whereas Alexander posits increasing differentiation, Bourdieu (and Habermas) see increasing de-differentiation of the press vis-à-vis the economy – which Hallin regards as a reasonable if incomplete assessment of current trends. Hallin also sees room for further development of field theory – to take more seriously cooperation as well as competition among journalists, to link more explicitly structural transformations with the systematic data on the discursive "representation of different social interests," and to better account for heteronomous interfield conflicts, especially between the political and economic fields.

Conclusion: Two Modes of Incorporation

Having argued that field theory and its associated terms – especially capital and habitus – offer a coherent and powerful analytical model for media research, we want to emphasize that we are not insisting that Anglophone researchers simply "take it or leave it." Just as French field researchers have borrowed fruitfully from Anglo-American political economy, organizational, and institutional studies, we would expect that non-French researchers will make their own judgments about what is new, interesting, insightful or useful. At the same time, we would caution against an "anything goes" approach: the better one understands the precise meanings of Bourdieu's terms, the more one is likely to be in a position to test, use, and actually improve upon them, as well as engage in a dialogue with the increasing numbers of other researchers also using the model. We conclude simply by noting two modes of appropriation that make the most sense to us.

The first, more modest incorporation of field theory would begin by building upon the categorizations of influences on news production offered by such media scholars as Herbert Gans, Todd Gitlin, Michael Schudson, Pamela Shoemaker and Stephen Reese.[51] These categorizations include both broad macrolevel factors (political, economic, and cultural) and microlevel factors including journalists' personal and professional characteristics and the organizational dynamics brought to light by the classic newsroom ethnographies of the 1970s. Influences emerging from the semiautonomous journalistic field – a mezzolevel organizational, professional and ideological space – represent an additional variable not previously considered. Future challenges, taken up by several authors in this volume, would thus include such questions as the following: How precisely do journalists and journalistic organizations exert influence on one another in ways that supplement or contradict constraints emerging within the single newsroom? And, to the extent that journalistic production is not the simple reflection of economic imperatives, or political pressures, or national cultural idioms, in what ways do (various kinds of) journalistic fields resist or reshape such outside pressures?

If incorporating field effects into existing models in the sociology of news can thus be seen as potentially quite productive, there are also benefits that would accrue from a more theoretically ambitious project. Advocating the concept of hegemony for media analysis, Todd Gitlin once wrote that it offers "not so much an alternative as a more ample theoretical domain."[52] While one can, as above, analytically separate the independent effects on news discourse produced by various kinds of structural factors, there are limitations to such an approach. Precisely because these effects are not independent, but act in relation to one another, the need for a more "ample" theoretical model remains. As Craig Calhoun notes, in reference to Habermas, what we crucially lack is an analysis of the "internal organization" of the public sphere, in other words, a mapping of the public sphere as a "socially organized field, with characteristic lines of division, relationships of force, and other constitutive features."[53] Leading scholars have anticipated or recently taken up this challenge, from Hilgartner and Bosk's "public arenas" to Åsard and Bennett's "marketplace" model to Hallin and Mancini's "media systems."[54] However, like Calhoun as well as Philip Schlesinger,[55] we are inclined to believe that field theory offers the best developed means of providing this comprehensive mapping not only of the media space, but of increasingly "mediatized" societies.[56]

In sum, whether field theory is used in a limited, or ample, form, we believe its virtues are numerous. First, field theory provides a means of incorporating history into the very heart of media analysis. Fields cannot be understood apart from their historical genesis and trajectory; likewise, individual agents' actions are not simply determined by social position, but are the result of a complex, always partially contingent interplay between one's social and educational trajectory and the position within a field where one finds oneself at any given moment. History is also behind whatever semiautonomous institutional logic a field offers up as a partial barrier against the varieties of heteronomous power (themselves also the cultural products of historically contingent struggles). Second, we gain a tool for relational and spatial social analysis. This relational approach helps us locate, situate, and explain the very real differences among media outlets according to their possession of different types and quantities of capital. Finally, field theory provides perhaps the best defense against Schlesinger's warning of "media-centrism," helping us situate journalism in its larger systemic environment. Against the fruitless question of asking whether the press is or is not "independent," research could help pinpoint the journalistic field's relative position vis-à-vis the range of other societal fields that compete to shape our vision of the social world. In enumerating these virtues, we are not unaware, as we hope this introduction demonstrates, of critiques and challenges of methods, empirical foci, and theoretical assumptions. As more and more researchers engage with the model, we expect that some of these challenges will be worked through, while new ones will emerge. Field theory itself will be tested and modified in the process. That is as it should be, for a theory that is and must remain a work in progress.

Notes

1 See Jürgen Habermas, *The Structural Transformation of the Public Sphere* (MIT Press, Cambridge, MA, 1989) and Manuel Castells, *The Power of Identity* (Blackwell, Oxford, 1997), ch. 6.

2 One of Bourdieu's earliest major articles was focused on media. See Pierre Bourdieu and Jean-Claude Passerson, "Sociologues des mythologies et mythologies de sociologues," *Les Temps modernes*, 211 (1963), pp. 998–1021, discussed with excerpts in chapter 10 by Erik Neveu. See also P. Bourdieu, "The Production of Belief: Contribution to an Economy of Symbolic Goods," *Media, Culture and Society*, 2/3 (July 1980), pp. 261–93 (republished in *The Field of Cultural Production* (Polity, Cambridge, 1993, and Columbia University Press, New York, 1993), pp. 74–111), which examines theater criticism in newspapers, and *Distinction* (Harvard University Press, Cambridge, MA, 1984), esp. ch. 8. Early Bourdieu-inspired research on news media was also conducted by Louis Pinto, *Le Nouvel Observateur, ou l'intelligence en action* (AM Métaillié, Paris, 1984) and Patrick Champagne, *Faire l'opinion: le nouveau jeu politique* (Minuit, Paris, 1990).

3 Pierre Bourdieu, *On Television* (The New Press, New York, 1998).

4 This chapter builds upon the authors' previous efforts to analyze field theory's unique contributions to media research. See Rodney Benson, "Field Theory in Comparative Context: A New Paradigm for Media Studies," *Theory and Society*, 28 (1999), pp. 463–98, and "Bringing the Sociology of Media Back In," *Political Communication*, 21 (2004), pp. 275–92; and Erik Neveu, "Field Theory as a Work in Progress," paper presented to the France-Berkeley Fund conference on Contemporary Media and Politics, Berkeley, CA, May 2000, and *Sociologie du journalisme* (La Découverte, Paris, 2001), esp. pp. 34–42.

5 See Pierre Bourdieu, *The Rules of Art* (Stanford University Press, Stanford, CA, 1995, and Polity, Cambridge, 1996), *The Field of Cultural Production*.

6 Pierre Bourdieu, "Social Space and Symbolic Space," in *Practical Reason* (Stanford University Press, Stanford, CA, 1998, and Polity, Cambridge, 1998), p. 3.
7 Pierre Bourdieu and Loïc J.D. Wacquant, *An Invitation to Reflexive Sociology* (University of Chicago Press, Chicago, 1992 and Polity, Cambridge, 1992), pp. 96–7.
8 Bourdieu, *Distinction*, p. 170.
9 Bourdieu and Wacquant, *An Invitation to Reflexive Sociology*, p. 126.
10 Bourdieu and Wacquant, *An Invitation to Reflexive Sociology*, p. 133; see also Pierre Bourdieu, *Pascalian Meditations* (Stanford University Press, Stanford, CA, 2000, and Polity, Cambridge, 2000), ch. 2.
11 "Social space is constructed in such a way that agents or groups are distributed in it according to their position in statistical distributions based on the *two principles of differentiation* which, in the most advanced societies . . . are undoubtedly the most efficient: economic capital and cultural capital" (Bourdieu's italics). See Bourdieu, "Social Space and Symbolic Space," p. 6.
12 Cultural capital may take multiple forms: embodied (manners of the diplomat), objectified (owning a Monet painting), or institutionalized (cultural capital as certified by an authority: the Pulitzer or Nobel prize). See Pierre Bourdieu, "Les Trois états du capital culturel," *Actes de la recherche en sciences sociales*, 30 (1979), pp. 3–6.
13 For the best explication of the concept of field, see Bourdieu and Wacquant, *An Invitation to Reflexive Sociology*, esp. pp. 94–115. See also David Swartz, *Culture and Power: The Sociology of Pierre Bourdieu* (University of Chicago Press, Chicago, 1997), pp. 117–42.
14 Is society composed entirely of fields? Bourdieu's choices of research topics suggest he primarily viewed fields as relatively elite realms of cultural, political or economic entrepreneurial activity. Moreover, the distinction that Bourdieu usually makes between "fields" and "social space" as a whole clearly implies there are spaces that are not fields. The term "field" seems to encompass at least a mezzolevel of social interaction and imply a certain amount of institutionalization and status competition. For example, there is little in Bourdieu's model to support the notion of "fields of domestic and intimate relations" as suggested by Louis McNay ("Gender, Habitus and Field," *Theory, Culture and Society*, 16, 1999, pp. 95–117).
15 "Told of Mr. King's selection [to receive the National Book Award's 'annual medal for distinguished contribution to American letters'], some in the literary world responded with laughter and dismay . . . [Said one cofounder of the award granting foundation] 'You put him in the company of a lot of great writers, and the one has nothing to do with the other. He sells a lot of books. But is it literature? No.' " From David D. Kirkpatrick, "A Literary Award for Stephen King," *New York Times*, September 15, 2003, Arts Section, p. 1.

16 Bourdieu defines social capital as follows: "Social capital is the sum of the resources, actual or virtual, that accrue to an individual or a group by virtue of possessing a durable network of more or less institutionalized relationships of mutual acquaintances and recognition." (*An Invitation to Reflexive Sociology*, p. 119). See also Pierre Bourdieu, *The Logic of Practice* (Stanford University Press, Stanford, CA, 1992, and Polity, Cambridge, 1992), pp. 112–21.

17 Bourdieu writes that symbolic capital is manifested through "the recognition, institutionalized or not, that [one] receive[s] from a group." See Bourdieu, *Language and Symbolic Power*, ed., John Thompson (Harvard University Press, Cambridge, MA, 1991, and Polity, Cambridge, 1991), p. 72. Thompson, in his introduction to that same volume (p. 14) defines symbolic capital as "accumulated prestige or honor." Recently, Nick Couldry offers the intriguing argument that media constitute a new form of symbolic power – "media meta-capital" (in essence, celebrity) – that increasingly trumps the power of symbolic capital emerging within specialized fields of cultural production. Couldry elaborates and extends the concept of "media capital" introduced by Champagne (*Faire l'opinion*, pp. 237 and 243 for example). See Nick Couldry, "Media Meta-Capital: Extending the Range of Bourdieu's Field Theory," *Theory and Society*, 32 (2003), pp. 653–77.

18 For visual representations of field relations, see Bourdieu, *The Field of Cultural Production*, p. 38, and Benson, "Field Theory in Comparative Context," pp. 466, 472.

19 For discussion of the short-circuit fallacy, see Bourdieu, *The Field of Cultural Production*, pp. 181 and 188.

20 Alain Accardo, *Journalistes précaires* (Le Mascaret, Bordeaux, 1998).

21 On this general question of deviant trajectories, see Pierre Bourdieu, *The State Nobility* (Stanford University Press, Stanford, CA, 1996, and Polity, Cambridge, 1996), pp. 183–7. In *Journalistes au quotidien* (Le Mascaret, Bordeaux, 1995), p. 48, Alain Accardo also posits that for working-class journalists the tension of living between two habitus can contribute to the formation of a critical perspective toward standard journalistic practices, though such potentially subversive elements are normally overcome by the overwhelming bourgeois character of the media field.

22 See, e.g., Olivier Donnat, ed., *Regards croisés sur les pratiques culturelles* (La Documentation française, Paris, 2003) and Bernard Lahire, *La Culture des individus* (La Découverte, Paris, 2004).

23 A recent study of French detective novels ("neopolars"), for instance, found that contrary to the received wisdom that their audience is largely composed of academics and intellectuals, working-class as well as upper-class readers are also quite common. Instead of concluding that readership is thus randomly distributed, a closer analysis has revealed that working-class readers tend to be former Left party or union

activists, while most upper-class readers have risen socially or culturally to that status (and thus, the detective novels, generally situated in working class milieu, constitute a sort of "remembrance of things past"). See Erik Neveu and Annie Collovald, *Lectures du roman policier* (BPI, Paris, 2004).

24 Bourdieu, *On Television*, p. 50. Régis Debray's notable history of French intellectuals, translated into English as *Teachers, Writers, Celebrities: The Intellectuals of Modern France* (Verso, London, 1981), owes much to Bourdieu's analysis of the increasing mediatization of the intellectual field; the same cannot be said of Debray's current approach, which he terms *médiologie*. See Régis Debray, *Media Manifestos: On the Technological Transmission of Cultural Forms* (Verso, London, 1996).

25 For Bourdieu, however, the category of "omnibus" extends to all media outlets which "maximize their clientele by neutralizing their product" (*Distinction*, p. 442), such as most regional newspapers as well as broadcast television. On the logic of (commercial) television, see also Patrick Champagne, "La Loi des grands nombres: Mesure de l'audience et représentation politique du public," *Actes de la recherche en sciences sociales*, 101–2 (March 1994), pp. 10–22.

26 Neil Postman, *Amusing Ourselves to Death* (Penguin, New York, 1985), pp. 84, 105. Elsewhere, Postman concedes that television is not everywhere the same; nevertheless, he insists, American commercial television is the expression of the medium's inherent "full potentialities as a technology of images" (p. 86).

27 In this sense, Bourdieu's analysis bears some resemblance to that of Raymond Williams's *Television: Technology and Cultural Form* (Routledge, London, 1974).

28 See, e.g., Couldry, "Media Meta-Capital," p. 673.

29 Bourdieu and Wacquant, *An Invitation to Reflexive Sociology*, p. 110.

30 See Jürgen Habermas, "Further Reflections on the Public Sphere," in *Habermas and the Public Sphere*, ed. Craig Calhoun (MIT Press, Cambridge, MA, 1992), pp. 421–61; and "Civil Society and the Political Public Sphere," in *Between Facts and Norms* (MIT Press, Cambridge, MA, 1996), pp. 329–87.

31 Habermas, *The Structural Transformation of the Public Sphere*, pp. 181, 185.

32 Daniel C. Hallin, *We Keep America on Top of the World: Television Journalism and the Public Sphere* (Routledge, London, 1994), p. 12

33 Hallin, *We Keep America on Top of the World*, p. 80.

34 Bourdieu, *On Television*, pp. 16, 39.

35 On the "hysteresis effect," see, e.g., Bourdieu, *Distinction*, p. 109.

36 Bourdieu, *The Field of Cultural Production*, pp. 178–9.

37 See Roland Barthes, *Mythologies* (The Noonday Press, New York, 1990 [1957]), and, for example, Jeffrey C. Alexander and Philip Smith, "The Discourse of American Civil Society: A New Proposal for Cultural

Studies," *Theory and Society*, 22 (1993), pp. 151–207. Barthes, unlike Alexander and colleagues, does suggest some link (if diffuse) between mass-mediated mythologies and social class relations.

38 See, for example, the two special double issues on journalism of Bourdieu's journal *Actes de la recherche en sciences sociales*: 101–2 (1994) and 131–2 (2000).

39 Frank Esser finds systematic differences in newsroom organization between British and German newspapers. See Esser, "Editorial Structures and Work Principles in British and German Newsrooms," *European Journal of Communication*, 13 (1998), pp. 375–405.

40 In practice, field studies tend to examine some (geographical or medium-related) sub-universe of a national journalistic field, but this still represents a clear break from the classic single newsroom study. See, e.g., Eric Klinenberg, "The Spectacular City," in *Heat Wave: A Social Autopsy of Disaster in Chicago* (University of Chicago Press, Chicago, 2002), pp. 185–224; Georgina Born, "Strategy, Positioning and Projection in Digital Television: Channel Four and the Commercialization of Public Service Broadcasting in the UK," *Media, Culture & Society*, 25 (2003), pp. 773–99; and Ida Schultz, "Relational News Values: Media Field, Journalistic Practice & Television News," unpublished manuscript (May 2004), Department of Communication and Journalism Studies, Roskilde University, Roskilde, Denmark. For a study that analyzes transformations (or the lack thereof) across the major news outlets of a national journalistic field – and how relations among outlets potentially shapes news coverage – see Rodney Benson, "The Political/Literary Model of French Journalism: Change and Continuity in Immigration Coverage, 1973–1991," *Journal of European Area Studies*, 10, 1 (2002), pp. 49–70. For an analysis of the British national journalistic field, see Jean K. Chalaby, *The Invention of Journalism* (Palgrave MacMillan, London, 2000).

41 Kathleen Thelen and Sven Steinmo, "Historical Institutionalism in Comparative Politics," in *Structuring politics: Historical institutionalism in comparative analysis*, ed. K. Thelen, F. Longstreth, and S. Steinmo (Cambridge University Press, Cambridge, 1992), pp. 10–11.

42 Timothy E. Cook, *Governing with the News: The News Media as a Political Institution* (University of Chicago Press, Chicago, 1998).

43 John Mohr terms this process "the inertial effects of institutionalized forms of knowing and acting." See Mohr, "Introduction: Structures, Institutions, and Cultural Analysis," *Poetics*, 27 (2000), p. 58.

44 Bartholomew H. Sparrow, *Uncertain Guardians: The News Media as a Political Institution* (The Johns Hopkins University Press, Baltimore, 1999), pp. 14–17.

45 In *The Rules of Art* (p. 382, fn. 22), in an analysis that could easily apply to the "journalistic field," Bourdieu insists precisely on this reason for preferring the term "field" over that of "institution":

> There is nothing to be gained by replacing the notion of literary field with that of "institution": besides the fact that it risks suggesting, by its Durkheimian connotations, a consensual image of a very conflictual universe, this notion causes one of the most significant properties of the literary field to disappear – its *weak degree of institutionalization* [Bourdieu's italics]. This is seen, among other indices, in the total absence of arbitrage and legal or institutional guarantee in conflicts of priority or authority and, more generally, in the struggles for the defense or conquest of dominant positions.

46 For an extended discussion of field theory and new institutionalism in relation to news media research, see Rodney Benson, "News media as a journalistic field: What Bourdieu adds to new institutionalism, and vice versa," *Political Communication* (under review).
47 Mohr, "Introduction," p. 64; see also Bourdieu, "Social Space and Symbolic Power," in *In Other Words* (Stanford University Press, Stanford, CA, 1990, and Polity, Cambridge, 1990), ch. 8.
48 See, for example, Pierre Bourdieu, *Homo Academicus* (Stanford University Press, Stanford, 1988, and Polity, Cambridge, 1988), p. 38, and p. 41 in this volume. See Benson, "Field theory in comparative context," pp. 482–3 for an earlier articulation of this critique relative to Bourdieu's writings on the news media. On the overall lack of attention by Bourdieu to contradictions in interfield relations, see Swartz, *Culture and Power*, p. 128.
49 For a more in-depth examination, see Dominique Marchetti, "Contribution à une sociologie des transformations du champ journalistique dans les années 80 et 90. A propos d' 'événements sida' et du 'scandale du sang contaminé,'" Paris, doctoral thesis in sociology (Pierre Bourdieu, director), Ecole des hautes études en sciences sociales, 1997.
50 Daniel C. Hallin and Paolo Mancini, *Comparing Media Systems: Three Models of Media and Politics* (Cambridge University Press, Cambridge, 2004).
51 See Herbert Gans, *Deciding What's News* (Vintage, New York, 1980); Todd Gitlin, *The Whole World is Watching: Mass Media in the Making and Unmaking of the New Left* (University of California Press, Berkeley, CA, 1980), esp. pp. 249–51; Michael Schudson, "The Sociology of News Production Revisited (Again)," in *Mass Media and Society*, ed. J. Curran and M. Gurevitch (Arnold, London, 2000), pp. 175–200; and Pamela J. Shoemaker and Stephen D. Reese, *Mediating the Message: Theories of Influence on Mass Media Content* (Longman, New York, 1991). See Benson, "Bringing the Sociology of Media Back In," for a more elaborated discussion.
52 Gitlin, *The Whole World is Watching*, p. 251.
53 Craig Calhoun, "Introduction," in *Habermas and the Public Sphere*, p. 38.

54 See Stephen Hilgartner and Charles L. Bosk, "The Rise and Fall of Social Problems: A Public Arenas Model," *American Journal of Sociology*, 94 (1988), pp. 53–78; Erik Åsard and W. Lance Bennett, *Democracy and the Marketplace of Ideas: Communication and Government in Sweden and the United States* (Cambridge University Press, Cambridge, 1997); and Hallin and Mancini, *Comparing Media Systems*.

55 See Calhoun, "Introduction," p. 48, fn. 57, and Philip Schlesinger, "Rethinking the Sociology of Journalism: Source Strategies and the Limits of Media-Centrism," in *Public Communication: The New Imperatives*, ed. M. Ferguson (Sage, London, 1990), esp. pp. 77–9. Schlesinger sees field theory chiefly as an advance on Stuart Hall's overestimation of the power of official "primary definers" to shape the news: "The main value of Bourdieu's schema . . . lies in conceiving of dominance as a continual struggle for position involving the mobilization of resources in a process of change. Putting it differently, primary definition becomes an achievement rather than a wholly structurally predetermined outcome." This fluidity is definitely a part of field theory, and clearly distinguishes it from Herman and Chomsky's propaganda model. But perhaps more than Schlesinger, we would emphasize field theory's structuralist credentials, that is, a structuralism of a particularly complex and nuanced sort.

56 On the notion of "mediatization," see John B. Thompson, *The Media and Modernity: A Social Theory of the Media* (Stanford University Press, Stanford, CA, 1995, and Polity, Cambridge, 1995).

Part I

Theoretical Orientations

2

The Political Field, the Social Science Field, and the Journalistic Field

Pierre Bourdieu

I aim here to satisfy two types of expectations: on the one hand, what could be called academic expectations, by trying to present the theoretical instruments which, it seems to me, can serve in a very general way to analyze social phenomena and, in particular, phenomena of cultural production such as literature, art, journalism, etc.; and, on the other hand, political or civic interests – I often say that sociology can be a kind of symbolic combat sport that offers a means of defense against the various forms of symbolic violence that can be exerted against citizens, in particular, and very often nowadays, through the field of the media. But first I would like to run very quickly through a certain number of definitions, around the concept of field.

I set out the intellectual genealogy of "field" in my book *The Rules of Art*[1] and in an article in the *Revue française de sociologie* which analyzed the religious field.[2] On some other fields – the scientific field, the political field, the legal field, etc. – there are also several articles in *Actes de la recherche en sciences sociales*. In *The Political Ontology of Martin Heidegger*[3] there is an analysis of the German philosophical field within which and in relation to which Heidegger's thinking was constituted. Finally, in *The Rules of Art* there is a detailed study of the functioning of the literary field.

I have chosen to present to you an object which is, it seems to me, a very important one both scientifically and politically, namely the relationship between the political field, the social science field, and the field of journalism. These three social universes are relatively autonomous and independent, but each exerts effects on the others that I should like to try to bring to light. When we watch television, when we read a book or a newspaper, we tend to judge and explain what we see or read by mobilizing the resources of spontaneous sociology, and to impute everything to the responsibility of individuals, the malign nature of institutions, etc. But, in my view, one can truly understand these things only through an analysis of the invisible structures that are fields, and, in this particular case, through an analysis of some particularly invisible structures, namely the relations between these three fields.

Here is a simple definition of the notion of field, a convenient one, but, like all definitions, a very inadequate one: a field is a field of forces within which the agents occupy positions that statistically determine the positions they take with respect to the field, these position-takings being aimed either at conserving or transforming the structure of relations of forces that is constitutive of the field.

In other words, in certain respects, the field (for example, the literary field as a microcosm bringing together the agents and institutions engaged in the production of literary works) is comparable to a field of physical forces; but it is not reducible to a physical field – it is the site of actions and reactions performed by social agents endowed with permanent dispositions, partly acquired in their experience of these social fields. The agents react to these relations of forces, to these structures; they construct them, perceive them, form an idea of them, represent them to themselves, and so on. And, while being, therefore, constrained by the forces inscribed in these fields and being determined by these forces as regards their permanent dispositions, they are able to act upon these fields, in ways that are partially preconstrained, but with a margin of freedom.

The concept of field is a research tool, the main function of which is to enable the scientific construction of social objects. That is why, to make clear what I mean by field, rather than paraphrasing what I have just said, or presenting a genealogy of the concept – by saying that the concept comes from Ernst Cassirer, through Kurt Lewin, etc. – or again, rather than showing the relationship – of both continuity and rupture – with equivalent notions in the work of Max Weber (the sociologist who came closest to the notion of field but who, because he did not construct it explicitly, was not able to complete the project on which he worked throughout his life), in short, rather than perform scholastic exercises around the concept of field, I should like to put it to work in a kind of exercise in object construction, with all the uncertainty, imperfection, and incompleteness that this entails.

In the contemporary social universe, there are, for the eyes of common sense, journalists, politicians, television journalists who interview politicians, sociologists who give interviews in the newspapers or who interview politicians and journalists, and so on. So there are visible, perceptible agents, who meet one another, who may do battle with one another, compete with one another, and so on. What is gained by substituting for this phenomenal vision, for this set of singular agents designated by proper names, the spaces of invisible relationships that are constitutive of what I call the field of the social sciences, or the journalistic field, or the political field? On an election night on television, for example, the fields I have just mentioned – the political field, the social science field and the journalistic field – are present, but they are present in the form of persons. You will see a well-known historian, a specialist in political history; he will comment on the results, alongside a journalist and the director of the Paris Institut d'études politiques, who is a member of the academic field and the social science field through the polling organizations which he also advises. One could produce an interactionist description, that is, a description limited to the interactions between individuals, or a discourse analysis looking at the rhetorics deployed, the procedures, the strategies, and so on. What I am proposing is quite different: I postulate as a hypothesis that when the historian addresses the journalist it is not an historian who speaks to a journalist – which is already a start in the construction of the object – it is an historian occupying a determinate position in the field of the social sciences who speaks to a journalist occupying a determinate position in the journalistic field, and ultimately it is the social science field talking to the journalistic field. And the properties of the interaction – for example, the fact that the journalist defers to the historian as a kind of transcendent arbiter situated above the strictly political debate, the authority who can have the last word – express the structure of the relationship between the journalistic field and the social science field. And, for example, the statutory objectivity that is granted to the historian is not linked to any intrinsic properties of the person but to the field of which he or she is a part, which is an objective relationship of symbolic domination, in a particular respect, over the journalistic field (while the latter may also exert a symbolic domination over the social science field in another respect, for example that of mastery of access to the public). In short, a TV panel, when looked at through the concept of the field, delivers a host of properties that do not present themselves to intuition.

The field that I am thus offering for analysis is an expanded form of what is ordinarily called the political world, the political microcosm. The word microcosm goes some way to suggest that the political universe, with its institutions (the parties), its rules of functioning, its agents selected in accordance with certain (electoral) procedures, etc., is an autonomous world, a microcosm set within the social macrocosm. The political microcosm is a kind of small universe caught up in the laws of functioning of the larger universe, but nonetheless endowed with a relative autonomy within that universe and obeying its own laws, its own *nomos* – in a word, autonomous.

One has to take note of this relative autonomy in order to understand the practices and works that are generated within these universes. Thus, traditionally, most studies devoted to law, literature, art, science, philosophy, or any cultural productions, are distributed between two major forms of approach. One of them, which can be called internalist, posits that in order to understand law, literature, etc., it is necessary and sufficient to read texts without necessarily referring to the context, that the text is autonomous and self-sufficient, that there is therefore no need to relate it to external factors (economic or geographical ones, for example); the other approach, by contrast, a much rarer, and dominated, approach, undertakes to relate texts to their social context. In a general way, this externalist reading is considered sacrilegious and is looked on with great suspicion by the caste of commentators, the *lectores*, the priests of commentary, who have the monopoly of legitimate access to the sacred text. Against the internalist vision, which is very powerful in philosophy (philosophy and law are the two disciplines that have managed to retain the monopoly of their history to the present day), I always invoke a very fine text by Spinoza, who, in the *Tractatus theologico-politicus*, discussing the classic problems of exegesis that have given rise to hermeneutic traditions – Hans-Georg Gadamer, Paul Ricoeur, and others – asks a series of questions: how can you understand the sacred texts, those of the prophets, of the Bible, if you do not know who wrote them, when they wrote them, how they wrote them, in which language, who defined the canon – that is to say, the *corpus* of sacred canonical texts, the texts that deserve to be regarded as sacred?[4] Spinoza raises all these questions about the sacred texts of the religious tradition, and, curiously, the philosophers who claim allegiance to Spinoza, or some of them at least, still consider it sacrilegious to ask these questions of Spinoza in reference to philosophical texts as well: "Who wrote them?" – that is, what were they doing, how were they trained, where did they study, whose pupils were they, who were they writing against, in other words, what was the field in which they were embedded? The concept of field had the initial function of offering a route out of this forced choice, of refusing the choice between an internal reading of the text which consists in considering the text in itself and for itself, and an external reading which crudely relates the text to the society in general. Between the two there is a social universe that is always forgotten, that of the producers of the works, the universe of philosophers, the universe of artists, the universe of writers, and not only writers but also literary institutions, journals for example, the universities where writers are educated, and so on. To speak of the field is to name this microcosm, which is also a social universe, but a social universe freed from a certain number of the constraints that characterize the encompassing social universe, a universe that is somewhat apart, endowed with its own laws, its own *nomos*, its own law of functioning, without being completely independent of the external laws.

One of the questions that has to be asked about a field is that of its degree of autonomy. For example, among the three fields that I have mentioned, the journalistic field is characterized, in comparison with the field of sociology (*a fortiori* in comparison with the field of mathematics), by a high degree of heteronomy. It is a very weakly autonomous field, but this autonomy, weak though it is, means that one cannot understand what happens there simply on the basis of knowledge of the surrounding world: to understand what happens in journalism, it is not sufficient to know who finances the publications, who the advertisers are, who pays for the advertising, where the subsidies come from, and so on. Part of what is produced in the world of journalism cannot be understood unless one conceptualizes this microcosm as such and endeavors to understand the effects that the people engaged in this microcosm exert on one another.

Much the same goes for the political field in the narrow sense. Marx says somewhere that the political universe, identified with the parliamentary world, is a kind of theater, offering a theatrical representation of the social world, the social struggle, one which is not entirely serious, but derealized, because the real stakes, the real struggles, are elsewhere. In doing so, he points out one of the important properties of the political field, the fact that this field, however little autonomy it may have, does have a certain autonomy, a degree of independence, so that, in order to understand what goes on there it is not sufficient to describe the agents as being in the service of the steel producers, or the beetroot growers, as people once used to say, or the big employers, etc. To say that politicians – parliamentarians or ministers – are inscribed in a field is to say that the stakes for which they strive, the motivations that drive them, have their principle in the microcosm and not directly in the macrocosm. In other words, to understand the political positions that a representative takes, it is not sufficient to consider the ordinary variables, such as class membership and social position in the overall social space. It is not even sufficient to know relations of dependence vis-à-vis this or that external power, such as the fact that he or she is the former employee of a bank – a fact that does not escape mention in electoral battles – or to characterize the social agent by his or her external determinants, which may derive from social origin, occupation, or economic or social connections, direct or indirect. One also has to take into account the position occupied in the political game, the fact that the agent is located on the side of the more autonomous pole of the field or, on the contrary, on the side of the more heteronomous pole, the fact that he or she is a member of a party situated on the more autonomous or the less autonomous side, and, within that party, has a more or less autonomous status.

In fact, the amount that can be explained by the logic of the field varies according to the autonomy of the field. The political field, although apparently subject to a constant pressure of demand, to constant control by its clientele (through the electoral mechanism), is nowadays very strongly independent of that demand and more and more inclined to close in on itself, on its own stakes (for example, those of competition for power among the parties and within each party). It is a kind of vague intuition of this closing-in on interests specific to the mandate-holders that is expressed in diffuse antiparliamentarianism or in the more or less overtly declared hostility to politicians, denunciations of corruption, and so on. Some sociologists, known as neo-Machiavellians, such as Robert Michels, a German theorist of social democracy, or Gaetano Mosca, an Italian theorist, have identified the logic – they call it the iron law of oligarchy, in particular that of political oligarchies – which favors this separation and this closure by leading even the parties that ostensibly speak for the most disadvantaged strata to end up authorizing authoritarian forms of representation, with a small minority of representatives eventually monopolizing the social energy delegated to them by their electors. There is a logic whereby the power democratically acquired by the representatives of a party is in some sense concentrated in the hands of the leaders, who little by little cut themselves off from their base and eventually act as a kind of oligarchy, thriving on the power of the dispossessed mandators. The iron law of political oligarchies is the equivalent of the "tendency of the clerical corps" to take upon itself, as Weber says, "the legitimate monopoly of the handling of the goods of salvation." This tendency towards the concentration of political means, which is the equivalent of the concentration of access to the means of salvation, takes the form of the concentration of speech, for example: the electors delegate to the parliamentarians, who delegate to spokespersons, etc., and, given the role of the contemporary media, four or five spokespersons, permanently present on television, take on a kind of monopoly of access to the means of legitimate manipulation of the vision of the world (which is the definition of political action).

So the political field is a kind of game apart, within which specific stakes are defined and which, in its limiting case, can function rather like a field of poets or mathematicians, in almost total autonomy. To understand what happens in contemporary poetry – and this is what makes people think that sociological analyses are impotent – one can seemingly dispense with knowledge of what happens in the political world, external readings being in this case very reductive. A study of nineteenth-century French music which tries to relate the music of Fauré directly to the strikes at Fourmies, and other contemporary social dramas, sees it as a form of "escapism,"[5] in other words a means of escaping the harshness of social conditions, forgetting the strikes, the revolts of the working class, etc. These readings are obviously ridiculous. In very advanced, very autonomous literary or artistic fields, the attempt to make a direct connection between what happens in the field and external events, such as a war, an epidemic or an economic crisis, is clearly ineffectual, and one can imagine states of political fields in which the same would be true, that is to say, with populations that are very poor culturally and economically, and so on, and therefore totally dispossessed of the means of political opinion – political microcosms that would function as closed vessels exactly like the universe of poets, so that, in order to understand what happens in such a universe, one would only need to know what stakes were generated within it. To understand the currents, tendencies, fractions or factions in a very autonomous political space, one only has to know the relative positions within the microcosm of the agents concerned. It is within the field that the differences are engendered, which does not mean that they are purely personal differences; they are differences with a social basis, but the social basis is not where people think it is, in the overall social space, but rather within the political microcosm.

I have taken examples of subfields within the field, but one would need to take some broader examples, where it would be seen that a very significant part of what is engendered in the political field (and this is what the populist intuition grasps) has its principle in complicities linked to the mere fact of membership in that same political field. Retranslated into the antiparliamentary, antidemocratic language of fascist or quasi-fascist parties, these complicities are described as participation in a kind of corrupt game. In fact, these kinds of complicities are inherent in participation in the same game, and one of the general properties of fields is that there are struggles within fields for the power to impose the dominant vision of the field, but these struggles are always based on the fact that the most irreducible adversaries have in common that they accept a certain number of presuppositions that are constitutive of the very functioning of the field. In order to fight one another, people have to agree on the areas of disagreement. There is a kind of fundamental complicity among the members of a field, and the interests inherent in belonging to a field are the foundation of complicities that are, in part at least, hidden from the participants themselves by the conflicts of which they are the principle, complicities which, in other words, engender conflicts that have the effect of concealing the very principle of those conflicts.

I started out on the description of the political field without spelling out what it has in common with the field of the social sciences and with the journalistic field. If I have brought these three universes together so as to try to shape an idea of their relationships, this is because they have in common the fact that they all lay claim to the imposition of the legitimate vision of the social world, they have in common the fact that they are the site of internal struggles for the imposition of the dominant principle of vision and division. All social agents have principles of vision and division. We go out into the social world with categories of perception, principles of vision and division, that are themselves partly the product of the incorporation of social structures. We apply categories to the world – for example, masculine/feminine, high/low, rare/common, distinguished/vulgar – adjectives which often function in couples. In dictionaries, one can discover the vast universe of the adjectives (heavy/light, bland/spicy, etc.) that we use daily, in the practical state, to judge a picture, a student's work (brilliant/workmanlike), a hairstyle, and so on. And these adjectives that we use, which function in couples that are partly independent, partly superimposed, are categories in the Kantian sense, but categories that are socially constituted and socially acquired.

The *homo academicus* of the social-science variety has his or her head full of couples of oppositions (explaining/understanding, theory/practice, for example), implicit schemes of classification that we master in the practical state, that we know how to use in situations, but of which we do not have explicit mastery. Many judgments of taste are situated somewhere between the adjective and the exclamation. They most often have as their principle practical schemes which make it possible to organize the world, but which remain implicit, and which are very hard to make explicit (think of dissertations on "quantity and quality," or "quantitative methods and qualitative methods"), and yet very deeply rooted in thought and even in the body: an American sociologist has made a very fine study of the opposition between "hard" and "soft," showing that "hard" is more masculine and "soft" more feminine and that they correspond to the distribution by sex of the various disciplines and specialities. These seemingly vague, "fuzzy" oppositions are very fundamental in that when a whole society has them in its head, they end up defining reality.

These practical schemes – implicit, tacit, very hard to make explicit – are constitutive of the *doxa*, as the philosophers call it, in other words the universe of the tacit presuppositions that we accept as the natives of a certain society. But there is also a specific doxa, a system of presuppositions inherent in membership in a field: when we belong to the sociological field, we accept a whole series of scientific or semi-scientific oppositions that are often oppositions belonging to the encompassing social world, slightly adjusted, reordered and euphemized (to take one example among countless others, the opposition between "individualism" and "holism" is a barely transformed form of the opposition between "individualism" or "liberalism" and "collectivism" or "totalitarianism," and that is the source of its most guaranteed symbolic effects).

Those who deal professionally in making things explicit and producing discourses – sociologists, historians, politicians, journalists, etc. – have two things in common. On the one hand, they strive to set out explicitly practical principles of vision and division. On the other hand, they struggle, each in their own universe, to impose these principles of vision and division, and to have them recognized as legitimate categories of construction of the social world. When a bishop declares, in a newspaper interview, that it will take twenty years for French people of Algerian origin to be regarded as French Muslims, he is making a prediction that is charged with social consequences. This is a good example of the claim to legitimate handling of the categories of perception, of symbolic violence based on a tacit, surreptitious imposition of categories of perception endowed with authority and designed to become legitimate categories of perception, which is of exactly the same type as the symbolic violence performed by those whose labels slip imperceptibly from "Islamic" to "Islamicist," and from "Islamicist" to "terrorist."

Those whose profession is the making explicit of the categories of construction of reality and the imposition of those categories first have to transform the schemes into explicit categories. "Category" comes from the Greek verb *kategorein*, which means to accuse publicly: the acts of categorization to which we have recourse in daily life are often insults ("You're just a . . .," "Typical teacher . . ."), and insults, racist ones, for example, are categoremes, as Aristotle called them, that is to say acts of classification, based on a classificatory principle that is often implicit, that does not need to set out its criteria, in order to be consistent with itself. So a first task is to make the schemes explicit, to transform them into explicit categories, into discourse, and perhaps to draw up systematic tables of categories, since a good part of ideological work consists in transforming the implicit categories of a class, a stratum, into taxonomies that have a coherent and systematic air to them. I refer you to the analysis of the philosophical field in the time of Heidegger, which I carried out in *The Political Ontology of Martin Heidegger*:[6] there I try to show that beneath a certain number of central philosophical theses in Heidegger's work, there are commonsense taxonomies such as the opposition between "unique" or "rare" and "common" or "vulgar," between the "authentic subject," which is "unique," etc., and *das Man*,[7] "they," the "common," the "vulgar," etc. These oppositions drawn from ordinary class racism – "distinguished" people and "vulgar" people – is converted into a misrecognizable philosophical opposition, likely to pass unnoticed before the eyes of a philosophy professor, who may himself be perfectly democratic, and who will comment on Heidegger's famous text on *das Man* without realizing that it is the irreproachable expression of a sublimated racism.

So, those who are engaged in the three fields that I have sketched strive to make explicit principles of qualification that are initially implicit, practical, to systematize them, to give them coherence (or, as in the religious field, a quasi-systematic character). Then, and in that very process, they struggle to impose them, and the struggles for the monopoly of legitimate symbolic violence are struggles for symbolic royalty. I refer you here to the etymology of the word *rex* (king) which Emile Benveniste offers in his very fine book *Indo-European Language and Society*.[8] *Rex* comes from the verb *regere*, which means to regulate, to direct, and one of the king's main functions is to *regere fines*, to delimit the frontiers, like Romulus with his plough. One of the functions of taxonomies is to say who is "in" and who is "out," who are the citizens and who the foreigners. For example, one of the dramas of the political struggle in France today is that, through the irruption into the field of a new player, the *Front national*, the principle of division between "citizens" and "foreigners" has imposed itself very generally on all agents in the field at the expense of a principle which once seemed dominant, the opposition between "rich" and "poor" ("Proletarians of all countries, unite!").

Having rapidly outlined the common stakes, I turn to the specific logic of each of these fields. The political field explicitly asserts that it makes it its aim to say what the social world is. In a discussion between two politicians who bombard each other with statistics, what is at stake is to present one's vision of the social world as being well founded, grounded in objectivity, because it is endowed with real referents, and also grounded in the social order through the confirmation it receives from all those who adopt it for themselves, who adhere to it. In other words, what starts as a speculative idea becomes a "powerful idea," what we call in French an *idée-force*, through its capacity to mobilize people by leading them to adopt for themselves the principle of vision that is proposed. The imposition of a definition of the world is in itself an act of mobilization which tends to confirm or transform power relations. My idea becomes an idée-force through the force that it manifests by imposing itself as a principle of vision. A true idea can only be countered by a refutation, whereas an idée-force has to be countered by another idée-force, capable of mobilizing a counter force, a counter manifestation.[9] Politics is a struggle to impose the legitimate principle of vision and division, in other words the one that is dominant and recognized as deserving to dominate, that is to say, charged with symbolic violence.

To recapitulate, what are the properties that emerge from the fact that the political universe is a field? First, the fact that the principle of the visions put forward for popular judgment, for approbation outside the field, lies to a large extent within the field, in the competition among the individual and collective agents engaged in the field. It follows, for example, and this always surprises people, that the most violent political struggles take place between parties or sects or tendencies or movements that are particularly close to each other in the political space. Given that, in the political field, the aim is to accumulate a symbolic power to impose beliefs, recognized principles of vision, and that, to impose these principles of belief, one needs to be credible, to command credit, to have accumulated a capital of belief, of specific authority, an authority which comes in part from the effect that it produces, and finally that the symbolic capital that an agent possesses in a political field is in part a distinctive, differential capital, nothing is more threatening for the holder of a symbolic capital than the alter ego, the rival who puts forward a program capable of depriving the capita holder of his very existence.

To exist in a field – a literary field, an artistic field – is to differentiate oneself. It can be said of an intellectual that he or she functions like a phoneme in a language: he or she exists by virtue of a difference from other intellectuals. Falling into undifferentiatedness – the constant problem of the center in the political space – means losing existence, and so nothing is more threatening than the look-alike who dissolves your identity. This explains why the two extremes maintain each other by their mutual opposition; in the limiting case, they may have no other content than the relationship of opposition. (In the same way, states of the literary field can be observed in which there is no opposition left except old/young, seniors/newcomers, an almost empty opposition.)

I said rather rapidly that the three fields in question had the same stake: to impose the legitimate vision of the social world. Willy-nilly, whether they realize it or not, sociologists intervene in this game. If, for example, I intervene in a regionalist struggle – one of the "rex" types of struggles, in Benveniste's terms, in other words about defining a frontier: does Occitania exist or not? – instead of taking it as an object, if I take up a position in the struggle for the existence or nonexistence of the Occitan region, I may think I am stating a scientific verdict, but, in fact, whether I want to or not, I am intervening in a political debate.[10] And part of the heteronomy of the sociologists and other social scientists arises from the temptation to intervene as effective umpires in the political struggle ("Let me explain: there aren't three classes, as Marx says, there are four; let me explain: Occitania is a pseudo-region, because there are four conditions for the existence of a region, and Occitania only fulfills three of them; let me explain, in the suburbs, you don't find Islamicists, but assimilated *beurs*,"[11] and so on). Sociologists then take on the role that journalists expect of them. A sociologist who responds to a survey on the existence or not of Occitania will be awarded a certificate of scientificity if he tells the journalist, and beyond him the reader of the paper, what he expects to hear and read ("He's a real sociologist because he really says what I think is really true"). And sociologists find it very difficult to resist this role of ratification.

The field of the social sciences does not aim to intervene in the struggle for the imposition of the dominant vision of the social world. It nonetheless does so, in as much as its findings immediately become instruments in the struggle. On the one hand, like all fields, the field of the social sciences is organized according to the degree of autonomy of the institutions and agents that are engaged in it, so that the "epistemological break" that has been so much discussed since Bachelard is fundamentally a break with social demands, with social expectations that contain problematics. For example, if a social science researcher signs a research contract, this is a very serious and delicate operation, an epistemological operation that is not often perceived as such. In particular, a state contract for sociological research – a very significant proportion of the funds that sociologists work with comes from the state – like a patron's commission to a painter in the *quattrocento*, contains a whole program. Painters had to fight for centuries to break free of patronage and assert their autonomy: the right to use colors as they wanted, the right to choose the manner; if the color was forced on them, the right to choose the subject, the right to depict the patron or not, to depict him kneeling or standing, large or small, and so on. Unfortunately, sociologists and historians have not all, and not always, achieved the level of self-consciousness that painters had reached by the *quattrocento*, and they have not yet learned how to negotiate contracts so as to defend their control over the object, their specific competence, which is the condition of their autonomy. Sociologists have to learn how to defend their freedom to construct their object as they see fit, to define the program themselves. The instruments that I have described, such as the notion of the field, are the instruments for an epistemological break, but also for a social break.

As for the field of journalism, why does it seem to me important to talk about it? Because (and here the civic function arises alongside the scientific function) it seems to me that for a number of years now the journalistic field has exerted an increasingly powerful hold – and we are not talking here about "the power of journalists" – on other fields and, in particular, as regards symbolic productions, on the field of the social sciences and the political field. One could also add the philosophical field in France, and also the scientific field in as much as, through the desire to gain the notoriety that is becoming increasingly indispensable in order to win grants and contracts, scientists are also obliged to enter into competition for the notoriety that only the media can give. Like most fields, the journalistic field, which, as we have seen, has very low autonomy, is structured on the basis of an opposition between these two poles, between those who are "purest," most independent of state power, political power, and economic power, and those who are most dependent on these powers and commercial powers. The hypothesis that I would advance – and which is very strongly demonstrated – is that the journalistic field, which is increasingly heteronomous, in other words increasingly subject to the constraints of the economy and of politics, is more and more imposing its constraints on all other fields, particularly the fields of cultural production such as the field of the social sciences, philosophy, etc., and on the political field.

Why is it important to talk about the journalistic field and not about journalists? Because so long as one talks about journalists, one is talking within a logic of personal responsibility: one is looking for people to blame and, on the other hand, one oscillates between the positive image that journalists continue to propagate (against all the evidence), with the theme of journalism as a countervailing force, a critical tool (no democracy without journalists), etc., and the opposing vision which sees journalism as a relay of the structure of oppression, etc. Journalists are set up as responsible, and, because the problem is posed in terms of responsibility, the visible agents become scapegoats, whereas if one talks in terms of a field one substitutes for these visible agents – who, in Plato's metaphor, are the puppets whose strings have to be found – the structure of the journalistic field and the mechanisms that operate within it.

I have stressed the fact that it seems to me that the journalistic field is losing more and more of its autonomy, and it is not difficult to see why this is so: through "audience research," economic constraints are increasingly weighing on production as advertisers distribute their budgets, the finance without which television cannot live, according to the size of the audience delivered by "ratings." In other words, through "audience ratings," which bear particularly heavily on the most heteronomous sector of journalism – television – and on the most heteronomous sectors of the subfield of television, the weight of the economy within the field is constantly growing. But (proving that journalism is indeed a field), the model of the most heteronomous area of the field, that of television, is little by little spreading to the whole field, including its "purest" regions. There are obvious signs of this: the growing place devoted to television in the newspapers, including *Le Monde*, or the fact that television journalists have more and more weight in the journalistic world, even in the management of the press. Having said that, the domination of the commercial pole is not uncontested and here too one sees a chiastic structure homologous with that found in the field of power (with the opposition between "artists" and "bourgeois") or in the literary or artistic fields (pure art/commercial art). Cultural capital remains on the side of the "purest" journalists of the print press, and they are often the ones who launch the critical debates that television picks up. The heteronomy linked to the pressure of advertisers, through audience ratings, is intensified by the current situation of precarious employment that is linked to the existence of widespread underemployment within the intellectual professions. The overproduction of university graduates creates, around the fields of cultural production, a cultural reserve army equivalent to the old "reserve army of labor" in industry. The pressure of this reserve army on the universes of cultural production facilitates a policy of precarious employment in which censorship can be exercised through political or economic control.

In the media, a growing proportion of the specific cultural producers are in a somewhat precarious state, on short-term contracts and so on. Naturally this precariousness implies a form of constraint and censorship. The autonomy of the professors and teachers who sided with Zola in the Dreyfus affair was partly linked to the fact that they were tenured – paradoxically, privilege is the precondition of freedom in that case. So precarity of employment is a loss of liberty, through which censorship and the effect of economic constraints can more easily be expressed. One could say the same of the state.

The journalistic field is increasingly heteronomous, increasingly dominated by its most heteronomous pole. The newspaper *Le Monde* – not that I would see it as an island of purity, by any means, but everything is relative – is subjected to the weight of a television network like TF1, in other words the commercial pole. To be an agent within a field is to exert effects there which increase with the specific weight that one has. As Einsteinian physics tells us, the more energy a body has, the more it distorts the space around it, and a very powerful agent within a field can distort the whole space, cause the whole space to be organized in relation to itself. The process we are witnessing at the present time is one in which the forces of commercial heteronomy, incarnated by the most commercial television, are progressively gaining ground to such an extent that all fields – journalism, publishing, etc. – are governed by what could be called an "audience ratings mentality." Only 30 years ago, the temporal success of a book was a kind of condemnation: as in religions based on the idea of salvation, success in the marketplace was suspect from the point of view of inner values. Nowadays, even in a publicly financed research body such as the Centre national de la recherche scientifique (CNRS), the media or market success of a publication is taken into account. In other words, sales values, against which all specific autonomies have been constructed – all microcosms are constructed against the commercial, they all have this in common, including the legal field – become, if not dominant, then at least threatening, in every field.

To understand what is happening in the journalistic field, one has to understand the degree of autonomy of the field and, within the field, the degree of autonomy of the publication that a journalist writes for. There are indices of this: for example, in the case of a newspaper, the proportion of its income that comes from the state, from advertisers, etc. For a journalist, the degree of autonomy will depend on one's position in the journalistic field, which means, for example, on one's authority. So one can establish indices of autonomy, which, it can be assumed, would enable one to predict the way that agents will behave, particularly in their capacity to resist the impositions of the state or the economy. Freedom is not a property that falls from the sky; it has its degrees, which depend on the position occupied in the social games.

This journalism, increasingly dominated by commercial values, is expanding its domination over other fields. In other words, journalism is tending to strengthen the most heteronomous zone in each of the fields – scientific, legal, philosophical, etc. To put it briefly, in the philosophical field, it strengthens the "new philosophers," the media philosophers. By valorizing what has most value in external markets, it affects the internal relations within the field.

A field is a field of forces and a field of struggles in which the stake is the power to transform the field of forces. In other words, within a field, there is competition for legitimate appropriation of what is at stake in the struggle in the field. And, within the field of journalism, there is permanent competition to appropriate the readership, of course, but also to appropriate what is thought to secure readership, in other words, the earliest access to news, the "scoop," exclusive information, and also distinctive rarity, "big names," and so on. One of the paradoxes is that competition, which is always said to be the precondition of freedom, has the effect, in fields of cultural production under commercial control, of producing uniformity, censorship and even conservatism. One very simple example: the battle between the three French weekly news magazines, *Le Nouvel Observateur*, *L'Express* and *Le Point*, results in their being indistinguishable. To a large extent this is because the competitive struggle between them, which leads them to an obsessive pursuit of difference, of priority and so on, tends not to differentiate them but to bring them together. They steal each other's front page stories, editorials, and subjects. This kind of ferocious competition is spreading from the journalistic field to other fields. One example is the field of literary prizes, which is a small subfield of the institutions of literary consecration. Two prizes were given to the same person, because the Prix Médicis, which was formerly relatively independent and was awarded later in the year, after the Prix Goncourt, brought forward its date to get ahead of the Goncourt; in exasperation, the Goncourt jury gave its prize to the same author. Another battle typical of what happens in the journalistic field is that *Le Nouvel Observateur* and *L'Express* each in turn brought forward their publication date by one day. What is very important in understanding a field is that the direct producer–client relationship is mediated by the relationship between the producers. To understand a product like *L'Express* or *Le Nouvel Observateur*, there is little point in studying the target readership. The essential part of what is presented in *L'Express* and *Le Nouvel Observateur* is determined by the relationship between *L'Express* and *Le Nouvel Observateur.* Ultimately the readers of *L'Express* may be to the readers of *Le Nouvel Observateur* what the journalists of *Le Nouvel Observateur* are to the journalists of *L'Express*. This is not at all because the producers of each magazine are adjusting to their respective readerships, but because there is a homology between the space of the microcosms of production and the encompassing social space.

Journalists are caught up in structural processes which exert constraints on them such that their choices are totally preconstrained. Through these processes there is exerted a kind of overall threat for the autonomy of all the fields of cultural production, that is to say, for all the universes within which the things we attach the most value to are produced – science, law and so on – including the political field, which, however heteronomous it may be, however subordinated to external constraints, has an alchemical function.

Demagogy, incarnated in "ratings," destroys the conquests of autonomy. This having been said, there is an ambiguity in autonomy which stems from its social conditions of possibility. Autonomy can lead to an "egoistic" closing-in on the specific interests of the people engaged in the field. But this closure can be the condition of freedom with respect to immediate demands and demagogy. Mallarmé, contrary to what is often thought (in his youth, he wrote some dreadful things about the "crowd," the "people"), spent his life asking how one can save what is only possible in autonomy, in the privilege of esotericism, while trying to transmit it to the largest possible number. The relationship between the conditions of production, that is to say, rarity, privilege, and the conditions of diffusion is a complex one. What is at stake is not the opposition elitism/democracy, but autonomy/heteronomy. Clearly, to do mathematics, one needs leisure. For Plato, *skholè*, which means "school," also means "free time." But journalism is immediacy, it is the clepsydra. You cannot do mathematics in front of a TV camera, nor sociology either. You cannot do anything there. People say – it has happened to me countless times – "Do you want to come on the evening news and talk about the crisis? You'll have three minutes." Autonomy presupposes a price for entry: to enter the game of advanced mathematics nowadays, you have to have accumulated some specific capital of mathematical culture; otherwise you don't even see where the problems are. To enter the sociological field nowadays – most sociologists don't realize this, still less the nonsociologists – you also need a lot of capital. It's only when you have this capital, which enables you to cross the barrier to entry, that you can attain autonomy with respect to crass social demands. It's because one has read Max Weber – and so many other authors that one resists crass social demands of the kind: "Are you in favor of television for a wide audience or an elitist cultural television?" – that one is able to say: "The problem is ill-posed, I won't answer that question." To defend the price of entry is not to defend elitism but to defend the social conditions of production of things that are only accessible in certain conditions. This price of entry may also be a barrier, protecting privileges, but not necessarily. There is a problem of getting in, but there is also a problem of coming out: these fields, these microcosms, are something you have to get into, but also something you have to come out of. What did Zola do? The Dreyfus affair is the story of a man who, being within the autonomous literary field, which had at last achieved autonomy (a process that had taken several centuries), came out of it to say: in the name of the values of purity, freedom, truth, and so on, which are those of the literary field, I enter the political field while remaining a writer (he did not become a politician).

The real question is that of autonomy, in other words the question of the right to enter and the duty to emerge. One can thus raise in a quite new way a problem in which all political reflection on the intellectual world has been enclosed: how can one simultaneously defend the conditions necessary for the production of certain kinds of specific, specialized works, without abdicating all democratic concern?

Notes

1 Pierre Bourdieu, *The Rules of Art: Genesis and structure of the literary field,* tr. S. Emanuel (Stanford University Press, Stanford, CA, 1995, and Polity, Cambridge, 1996).
2 Pierre Bourdieu, "Genèse et structure du champ religieux," *Revue française de sociologie*, 12 (July–September 1971), pp. 294–334, translated as "Genesis and Structure of the Religious Field," *Comparative Social Research*, 13 (1991), pp. 1–44.
3 Pierre Bourdieu, *The Political Ontology of Martin Heidegger* (Polity, Cambridge, 1991, and Stanford University Press, Stanford, CA, 1991).
4 B. Spinoza, "Tractatus Theologico-Politicus," in *The Chief Works of Benedict de Spinoza*, tr. R. H. M. Elwes (George Bell and Sons, London, 1905), vol. I, p. 103.
5 In English in the original – TRANS.

6 Bourdieu, *The Political Ontology of Martin Heidegger*.
7 See M. Heidegger, *Being and Time*, tr. J. Macquarrie and E. Robinson (Basil Blackwell, Oxford, 1962), 111 ff. – TRANS.
8 E. Benveniste, *Indo-European Language and Society* (Faber & Faber, London, 1973).
9 The French word *manifestation* also means a political demonstration. – TRANS.
10 Occitania refers to the south of France. During the Middle Ages, the Latin-based language of this region differed from that spoken in central and northern France. Since the 1970s, Occitania – whose borders are blurred and contested – has served as the rallying cry for a sort of regionalist identity politics. – ED.
11 *Beur*: the second-generation child of immigrants from North Africa. – TRANS.

3

The "Double Dependency": The Journalistic Field Between Politics and Markets

Patrick Champagne

It is certainly no accident that for some time French journalism has seemed preoccupied with problems of professional ethics.[1] Caught between the competing imperatives of "freedom of the press" and the "laws of the market," few professions are represented in such starkly opposing ways. The social profile of the journalist tends in effect to oscillate between the prestigious role of the great reporter, who sometimes pays with his life to cover conflicts, the investigative journalist, who uncovers scandals and thus serves democracy, or the political commentator, who censures or celebrates the nation's officials, and an opposite, highly negative pole: the corrupt journalist who writes puff pieces, profits from the world's miseries, or even, like the *paparazzi*, tries to invade people's privacy, making news for purely mercenary purposes. In short, the journalist is an uneasy awkward figure, capable of good as well as bad, who has to come to terms with the political and economic constraints that weigh on him, rendering his position unstable and uncomfortable.

An Ambiguous Position

The considerable symbolic power the media possess today – especially radio and television, owing principally to their wide diffusion and the impact their images seem to have on the "general public" –

no doubt explains why this tension is now tending to become quasi-permanent. If there is a properly journalistic exploitation of this malaise insofar as journalists employ formulas to win large audiences, it nevertheless remains that the profession is unarguably traversed by a sort of endemic crisis. This is shown by, among other indicators, the recent spate of books written by journalists on the news and its vagaries, as well as on the current transformation of the profession. Some evoke the gap in the education of journalists, which is seen as too weak with respect to the power they now hold simply by virtue of technological progress; others denounce an all-powerful "mediacracy," which rules unchecked; still others point, on the contrary, to the manipulation of journalists by political authorities (as during the first Gulf War and Kosovo), or, more generally, to the proliferation since the mid-1970s of public relations consultants of all kinds, who produce "ready-made events" and "media campaigns" for all who can pay their exorbitant fees.

This malaise, which affects a not insignificant part of the journalistic scene, in fact expresses in its way all the ambiguity of the journalistic field's position in the field of power. This position is very powerful in its effects (which explains why some speak, a bit naïvely, of the press as the "fourth estate"), but, at the same time, by reason of this very power finds its operation strongly dominated and controlled by other fields, especially the economic and the political. In other words, to paraphrase a well-known expression, many social actors, especially those who belong to various fractions of the dominant class, think that the press is too serious a matter to be left to journalists.

This situation is far from radically new, however, and cannot in itself explain the recent boom in critical discourse about the news professions. The autonomy of the journalistic field has always been threatened; one has no difficulty finding numerous alarmist discourses of the same kind at the end of the nineteenth century, at the time of the rise of the popular press, or later, episodically in response to events or limit-situations such as wartime censorship, which places journalists in the position of victims, or, conversely, media excesses, which put them in the position of the accused (so-called media lynchings). Despite the journalistic milieu's incontrovertible efforts to professionalize its activities, to submit only to intellectual imperatives and techniques of information production – evinced, among other things, by the creation of the first school of journalism at the end of the nineteenth century and their proliferation over the past few decades – it seems that journalists' search for autonomy runs up against two limits: on the one hand, the strictly political requirements of press outlets which have been, in France at least, deeply implicated in broader political struggles; on the other, the increasingly strong relations which connect them to the real or imagined expectations of the public, from which, in the last instance, they earn their living. In other words, journalists are structurally condemned to produce – variably, depending on the period and outlet – under political and/or economic constraints. If, now as ever, the purely moral barriers some try to erect are almost necessarily destined to fail in view of the strength of the external constraints on journalism and the weakness of the profession's will to effectively impose such codes on itself, the ethics codes and journalistic charters remain of interest in how they draw up the list of obstacles typically faced by the news professions. The principal function of the reflections on "journalistic ethics" which periodically reemerge could well be to update the list of these "excesses," which are, as it were, inscribed in the very practice of a profession situated at the frontiers, in the position of mediator.

If we consider just the recent period, most debates about journalistic ethics and practice seem to be organized mainly around three themes. First of all, many journalists worry about the growing weight of economic considerations in the media sector, which has in fact become a major focus of financial investment. In the second place, television and radio journalists note and deplore the excesses of a pronounced acceleration of journalistic work, which tend to intensify competition and above all the speed of communication techniques. Finally, all agree on the major impact of modern means of communication (especially television) on the general public, which at the same time changes the relation of forces between different types of media, modifying both the types of viewpoints that are diffused and the very process of their circulation.

The journalist between politics and the economy

The history of journalism could well be in large part the story of an impossible autonomy – or, to put it in the least pessimistic way, the unending story of an autonomy that must always be re-won because it is always threatened. Journalistic production is always strongly dictated by the social, especially political and economic, conditions in which it is organized. Schematically, we can distinguish two major types of press: one that is strictly dependent on the state and thus destined to serve the powers that be (this was the case, for example, of the press in Communist regimes or of television news in France during the Office de radiodiffusion–télévision française [ORTF]);[2] and another that is constituted on the model of the for-profit commercial enterprise (this is the case in France for the daily press and, since 1985, the privatized sector of television news). Practically speaking, no major general news organization can heed only purely intellectual considerations. Competition, urgency, sales considerations, and political constraints always weigh on the production and diffusion of news, in different proportions according to the outlet. That the press is no longer controlled by the political powers that be does not imply the complete freedom of journalistic expression (on what grounds would journalists have this privilege?); there are other, equally strong constraints on journalistic production, notably those imposed by profitability. Many publications in the former Communist countries of Eastern Europe had to close, and those that survived paid the price of a profound transformation of content that did not strictly speaking appear as an improvement. Some journalists even preferred the era of political censorship, which was too visible not to be perceived by all and was embodied by a few more or less naïve bureaucrats who could be fooled without much trouble. Economic censorship, which occurs through the paper's sales, is stronger and much more merciless. It is anonymous and can appear legitimate to many: if the paper doesn't sell, or sell enough, whose fault is it but that of the journalists themselves, who don't know how to interest their readers?

The major contradiction within the operation of the journalistic field lies in the fact that the journalistic practices that best conform to journalists' ethical codes are very often simply not profitable. The journalist ideally wants to be the stalwart servant of the truth at any price, but he belongs to a paper that bears a price and is situated within an economic enterprise with its own exigencies, which are not all of the mind. The popular press, or "gutter press" as they say in England, thrives while the "serious" press barely survives. In Europe, legislative frameworks that regulate journalistic activity have recognized this contradiction and tried to attenuate it. These laws generally consist of two main arrangements: on the one hand, repressive measures that aim to protect private individuals from the excesses of the press, especially regarding defamation and the protection of privacy; on the other hand, forms of economic assistance, journalistic activity being recognized as a true public institution necessary for the proper functioning of democracy. We greet the birth of a new newspaper of whatever kind as progress for democracy, and ritually deplore the disappearance of a paper as an attack on pluralism, a voice falling silent.

If journalistic activity in democratic regimes seems to be little subject to political power, today it is, to the contrary, incontestably dominated by the economic field. On the one hand, newspapers can only survive in their rather luxurious present-day form (color photos, long editions, etc.) thanks to advertising (which pays up to half of the cost of the paper, often more), which is borne by businesses. But the risk of declining advertising revenue in an economic downturn can seriously threaten newspapers' financial equilibrium. Beyond this general pressure, we know that firms, especially the larger ones, can exert pressure individually by withdrawing (or threatening to withdraw) their advertising budget from certain newspapers that have published (or want to publish) unfavorable articles. But this type of direct pressure, often denounced by journalists themselves, conceals a much stronger pressure with much more important day-to-day effects: the fact that newspapers themselves are economic enterprises and are thus directly subject to economic laws which often come into conflict with the imperatives of intellectual production.

The effects of this economic domination on journalistic production can be seen in the often similar histories of a number of newspapers.[3] At the origin of a new paper is generally a small group of young journalists. Fresh out of school and without material means (hence with nothing to lose), they bring a noble vision of their profession and an activist approach; they are outraged by the media scene as it is and denounce the compromises of the "establishment press." They draw up a generous editorial policy, at the center of which is almost always the concern to tell their readers the truth, no matter the cost. Set up in a small office at the back of a courtyard, the newspaper only carries on thanks to volunteer and activist work, with very low salaries distributed among a small number of all-purpose editors who produce the paper out of sheer enthusiasm. Then success comes for some (fewer and fewer) papers. The newspaper modernizes, hires more journalists, pays them better and better. Gradually, through a process of routinization, the activist enterprise becomes just another economic enterprise. It has to ask banks for advances, figure out how to raise capital, settle its accounts, pay its debts. Journalism becomes an activity much like any other, undertaken to make money and make a career. Sales are monitored with mounting concern. Editorial content changes imperceptibly, following an internal crisis that pits the founders against the new generation of journalists. The newspaper less and less embodies the idea of *journalisme pur et dur* (pure, hard journalism). Often, this evolution is perceived as a *political* slide from left to right, from generous utopianism to cold realism: as the transition from an activist paper to a general interest paper, from a serious paper to a more frivolous one (see, for example, in France the case of weeklies like *L'Express*, *Le Nouvel Observateur*, *Le Point*, and *L'Evénement du jeudi* or dailies like *Libération* and *Le Monde*). In fact, the principle behind this change, which is quite real, lies in large part in the new dependencies the journalists face precisely as soon as their project succeeds. What changes are the structures of producing news. The recruitment of editors changes more or less quickly, the originally badly paid editors giving way to credentialed young people in search of a career. The newspaper's operation no longer involves only those who created it, but a growing number of people (investors, administrators, newly hired journalists, etc.) who are as attached to the economic success of the business as to its founding ideals. Through a sort of inversion, political weeklies which initially carried mostly articles interrupted by rare advertisements become lush advertising catalogues into which a few political articles are inserted (it is sometimes necessary to leaf through page upon page of ads). The paper becomes a business and can be sold as such to financial groups who buy it for business purposes. From then on, news production finds itself caught in a production logic characterized principally by intense competition and speed.

Technological transformations of the profession

Among the second group of problems mentioned by professionals at the dominant media outlets (whose effective weight within the journalistic field is determining) are the conditions within which the profession is practiced. New technologies lead journalists in the national media to work under constant time pressure, and increasingly to make news "direct" and "in real time." Television journalists produce "continuous news" and have to decide rapidly, among the uninterrupted flux of images, which portions they will use and produce instant commentary for. As a French television journalist remarked of CNN, producing the news increasingly consists of "putting the camera in the halls of power where something is happening." In the end, it is the very idea of journalistic work that is partially called into question here; the ability to react quickly and to produce instant commentaries become the qualities most sought in journalists. But the growing speed of covering the news places journalists in a position of weakness: far from being able to listen and comprehend, which is necessary for those who want to understand the events thrown up by the present, they are forced to mobilize ready-made explanatory schemes and look for reference points in precedent.

Small news agencies that try to cultivate another conception of journalistic work, and in particular want to prioritize long investigations (over three months) and subjects beyond the most topical, have great difficulty selling their work to the mainstream media. The small number of press groups creates competition that is that much stronger since the economic interests at stake have become considerable. On television, entertainment programs that are also news (televised news broadcasts, political programs, news magazines) are perceived and conceived as occasions to attract the maximum market share, the public being drawn to watch the ads that run before, during, and after each program. The cost of each program has to be paid by the advertising it generates, which depends on the audience.

Another, no less important, obstacle to the practice of journalism stems from the very fact that so much power is attributed to the media. This has the effect of making specialized "public relations strategists" proliferate and prosper. These specialists design highly elaborate "events" and increasingly sophisticated "media campaigns" for clients whose requests are often rather naïve – "we want to be on the front page," "we want to be on the evening news," "we want our picture in the paper," "we want to hold a press conference: get us a dozen journalists!", and so on. Results are then measured by type of media, topic, district, etc., supported by statistics and graphics. The problem is not whether or not, faced with these new enticements, journalists become complacent or even act out of material interest. They are generally taken in by this game in the best of faith because it is explicitly designed to take them in; public relations agencies really do put themselves in the journalists' place, doing real news work for these always hurried social actors who are constantly going from topic to topic. The real question is who pays for the services of PR specialists and benefits from their expertise and the sort of "symbolic added value" it produces.

This rationalization of the use of the media not only involves businesses or national political authorities. It tends to spread to all levels of the social universe and to all spheres of activity. Even those who cannot afford the services of an agency try more or less awkwardly to be "media friendly." Few street demonstrations today, for example, are not prepared and designed to "get on television"; the organizers negotiate the route and the time and place of dispersal with public officials according to the imperatives of television news; public relations specialists – many of whom are, moreover, former journalists – even advise union officials, who, in a sort of mirror game, try to interest journalists by finding out what interests them. It is much too simple to say, as is often said, that journalists are manipulated manipulators, since what is commonly called "news" or an "event" is a particularly complex collective product that partly escapes the control of journalists themselves. No doubt, in the process of producing news there are explicit efforts to manipulate, which journalists recognize and denounce without necessarily always being able to escape. On the one hand, there is active manipulation: "news spectacles," the fabrication of phony scoops, exaggerated or sensationalized reporting – in short, the massive use of formulas intended to produce larger runs for the newsweeklies or raise television ratings. On the other hand, there is passive manipulation: the constant efforts of mystification aimed at journalists (press files, organized visits, etc.), with the borders which formerly separated news from public relations becoming increasingly fluid and uncertain. But this vision of manipulation obscures the incommensurably greater effects generated by the journalistic field in its most ordinary functioning, beyond any explicit effect to manipulate, when the journalist only listens, we could say, to his professional conscience.

The dual structure of the journalistic field

The last point on which most analysts agree is the growing weight of the mass media in the manufacture of news, and hence of "social problems." When we invoke the vagaries of journalism today, we are in fact mostly talking about television news, since it has the largest audience and thus the greatest political effects. To understand the impact of this evolution, it is advisable to take leave of the journalist and consider the structure of the journalistic field as a whole. A number of its characteristics in fact belong to the market for what are called mass-market symbolic goods in general, as opposed to the limited market of creators (artists, scientists, writers, and others) who tend to produce in specialized journals or short-run books for a much more restricted public of other intellectual producers, who are also competitors. But this fundamental structure, which opposes "producers" to "vulgarizers" or "reproducers," or symbolic goods produced according to internal intellectual imperatives to symbolic goods produced to respond to external demand, is found again within the mass market field, especially the journalistic field, and so on at all levels, like a series of Russian dolls. If the mass media produce standardized products on a large scale, designed to respond to pre-existing, external demand – which can now be measured in a very sophisticated way by marketing techniques – it remains that not all media outlets are equally subject to this desperate search for the largest possible public. Thus, the print media taken as a whole may be contrasted to audiovisual mass media: the press, which requires an act of sale, only reaches publics that are highly segmented both geographically (Parisian versus provincial dailies) and socially (the popular press versus the more political and "highbrow" press), whereas television and radio directly reach a much larger and more diversified public on a national level, without regard to residence. But even within the television sector, although it is the most dependent of the mass media on the supposed expectations of the public, the constraints of ratings vary according to the channel (a completely private channel like TF1 as opposed to, for example, an entirely public channel like Arte)[4] and, for each channel, time of broadcast (prime time as opposed to late night, for example) – and so on.

We can see distinctions of the same order within the print media. Certain recent publications aimed at a popular readership (for example, *Voici* or *Gala*) are almost entirely conceived according to a strict marketing logic that in effect eliminates the journalist as autonomous intellectual worker as such, demand being measured with such precision that it predetermines the character of the product. On the other hand, newspapers like the big Paris dailies make it a point of journalistic honor to maintain a relative autonomy in relation to the most immediate demands of the public and support certain forms of journalism that are not economically profitable (like major investigations) but good for the brand name or "positioning" of the paper. Among the papers that claim to produce serious news, the tendency toward autonomization is constant; good advertising revenue and plentiful classifieds suffice, so that journalists forget that they are supposed to write for the readers and not for one another, which they tend to do more or less unconsciously. One finds this dual structure within one and the same paper, different areas offering greater or lesser degrees of relative autonomy according to the paper and the section. It manifests itself in degree of specialization (like sports, science, or the financial markets as opposed to miscellaneous news or crime) and in which subjects make it on the front page, that is, are of more "general interest" than others or are likely to become so. And if the mass-market papers sometimes deal with serious subjects, albeit most often in the inside pages, conversely, the so-called serious papers are not above putting catchy headlines or salacious topics on the front page from time to time to maintain or increase circulation.

Thus we see that it is hardly possible to speak of journalists in general, despite a number of common traits that characterize the profession (such as dependence on relations with audiences, the speed of work and writing, and the existence of subjects imposed by current events). Generic discourse on "the journalist" is in fact a major obstacle to understanding the field of relations within which this actor is situated and thus plays the game. Depending on the outlet and news department, journalists are nearer to or farther from the intellectual pole, they are more or less integrated into the strictly economic necessity of seeking to maximize circulation, they are more or less competent concerning the topics they cover, and they write their articles thinking more or less about the intellectuals they vulgarize or the other journalists who write in the area and are at once colleagues and competitors. Since journalism is a highly specific intellectual activity that can only exist and endure by being economically profitable in the short term, we see that all outlets and all journalists are, to varying degrees according to their position within the field and the editorial structure, more or less divided against themselves. They are torn between the contradictory demands of economic profitability, taking political positions, and the imperatives proper to intellectual work.

The structure of the journalistic field is homologous to that of the field of the dominant class, which is also characterized by a tension between an intellectual pole and an economic pole. These two social spaces have their own relatively irreconcilable laws of operation. Economic success in many respects opposes intellectual consecration: the first is of a purely material order and can be rapid and ephemeral, while the second is more symbolic and requires time for the slow recognition by the peer group, but is durable. As an intellectual enterprise (in the economic sense), as intellectual activity under external constraints, in practice the journalistic field has to reconcile these two antagonistic social universes. Within the dominant class, it tends to exert, via its own power of diffusion, a particular effect of mixing up boundaries – among other reasons, because it has an interest in mixing them up, especially that which separates the economic and the intellectual poles. This is embodied, as it were, in the hybrid, impossible figure of the media intellectual (or, more precisely, the intellectual-for-the-media). An economically successful journalistic enterprise always also seeks properly journalistic, which is to say intellectual, success. And if large circulation does not always make a great newspaper, poor circulation is always perceived as failure.

The power proper to the journalistic field and its capacity to weigh on other social fields can be seen in particular in the fame it creates, which falls more within the logic of the economic or political pole than in that of the intellectual field. If the journalistic field consecrates people already consecrated by the social spaces from which they come (by interviewing a Nobel Prize winner, for example) – figures whose fame owes nothing to the media and remains beyond ephemeral mediatization – it also possesses its own power of consecration by introducing the figures it presents to the general public as important. The latter owe their fame essentially to the media: they are basically media personalities, and often derive quick material profits from this. But this pure media fame, which is very often nothing but a thinly disguised form of commercial promotion, is in itself ephemeral and, in the case of intellectuals-for-the-media, requires the ongoing maintenance work of journalists in a sort of struggle against oblivion.

Two Principles of Legitimacy

The media field's immanent power of consecration – the power to say who and what is important, and what we should think about important things and people – is based on its own legitimacy, which journalists have collectively accumulated in the course of history. In fact, this social space is traversed by not one but two competing principles of legitimacy, which face off to define journalistic excellence. The principle of this competition is the profound duality of journalistic activity, which is at once intellectual and economic. In France, the good journalist is first of all, to put it briefly, one who writes for *Le Monde* or, to a lesser degree, for *Libération*, or one who conforms to the principles taught in journalism school (some of which are moreover run by former *Le Monde* journalists). He or she is a news professional who tries to ward off the two major threats that constantly weigh on the intellectual autonomy of journalistic production: on the one hand, political partisanship; on the other, the quest for circulation at any price one sees in the scandal sheets. This first – we could say intellectual – principle of legitimacy was incarnated in the emblematic figure of *Le Monde* founder and editor-in-chief Hubert Beuve-Méry. An austere figure to himself, his coworkers (who were, legend has it, badly paid), and his readers (he scorned photos and demanded that his journalists *faire emmerdant* – "be boring"), he was particularly uncompromising with news: he rejected "scoops" and made the exactitude of the factual information published in his paper a point of honor. This moral and intellectual rigor brought high symbolic profits, so that *Le Monde* quickly became the paper of managerial and influential circles; but it did not pay from an economic point of view due to relatively low circulation and advertising revenues. Having set up a system whereby the journalists effectively controlled the newspaper's financial capital (by creating the "Society of Editors"), and thus having in a way "neutralized" the economic dimension of the enterprise, the newspaper's founding editor was little concerned with such matters. Since the mid-1980s, *Le Monde*'s editors have not been so reluctant to expand the newspaper and assure its profitability. Nevertheless, the original model maintained its force, and in the early years of the twenty-first century the Society of Editors is marked by the clash between Beuve-Méry loyalists and those who favor expanding the newspaper.[5]

The second principle of legitimacy is embodied in the anchor of the evening news on the national private television channel TF 1 or, to a lesser extent, the public (but partially advertising-funded) channel France 2. It is of an economic–political order, even if it presents itself as a form of professional excellence. Although it aims at a general public, television or radio news wants to be serious, professional, demanding, beyond reproach. More strongly subject to the laws of competition than the print press, since the resources of the big media come largely, even exclusively, from commercial advertising, radio and television journalists, many of whom also come from journalism schools, have to try to reach the broadest possible public. To this end they employ a simple vocabulary and powerful images, covering topics that are meant to interest everyone. Their power does not reside in the intrinsic quality of the journalistic work, since they are in essence "pick-up media" – they essentially take stories originally covered by the print media and repackage them by adding voices and images. Their specific power resides in the influence they can have on a public that is practically coextensive with the entire population, that is, in the decisive contribution they make to creating public opinion. The audience of these programs is perceived as a sort of public vote of confidence, the "best" journalists being those who get the highest ratings, those who are in a way elected by the viewers – which is to say, those who in effect contribute the most to the channel economically in the form of advertisements.

Thus, between *Le Monde* and the TF1 eight o'clock news, we pass from a principle of internal legitimacy to a principle of external legitimacy, from peer judgment to a viewer plebiscite – in short, from the logic of the intellectual field to that of the political field. Even if these media enterprises are situated at two antipodes, since both participate in the process of producing news and are in some kind of competition, they cannot ignore one another. The celebrity television anchor is constantly judged by his colleagues in the written press, who are quick to denounce his professional failings, above all when they are perceived as concessions to ratings. Conversely, as individuals, the journalists at *Le Monde* can ostensibly mark their distance from television news, which, in their eyes, is not made by "true journalists" but only by "presenters." *A fortiori*, they can refuse to participate directly in such and such a news program (even if refusals tend to be increasingly rare). This cannot be the case for the editor-in-chief of a newspaper, who is responsible for the general interests of the paper and therefore cannot totally ignore the imperatives of circulation: this editor is generally pleased, even flattered, to see a story "broken" by his or her paper picked up and cited by the television channels; furthermore, he or she cannot completely ignore in the columns of the editor's own paper the subjects addressed on television, even those that seem trivial, since a story on national television news, by virtue of its broad diffusion and the impact of images, tends in itself to be an event. (We should say "television news programs" instead of "television news" in general, but the logic of this type of media tends to exert a powerful effect of uniformity, so that the same stories run on the news programs of different channels, often in the same order).

If the opposition between the limited-circulation and the popular press is not new – it was clearly established by the end of the nineteenth century with the appearance of the penny broadsheet (still represented by London's *Sun* and *Mirror*, or the New York *Post*) – it remains the case that the generalized diffusion of television from the mid-1970s onwards has profoundly changed the general economy of news production, and in particular the relation of forces between the two types of press. The popular press has never had the legitimacy that television tends to have today, especially since the privatization of television (or loosening of state controls in the case of public television), the professionalization of the work of television journalists (some of whom come from the print press), and above all the visibility and reach of this medium, which makes it central for all political action. Thus, the functional weight of the audiovisual sector in the total process of news production tends to be greater and greater, the strong position occupied by *Le Monde* even a few years ago being progressively taken over by, or at least shared with, television news programs.

There is an objective hierarchy among the different media outlets that can be seen not only in the laws regulating the circulation of information, but also in what we can call the phenomena of story pick-up. The press is first of all read by all journalists looking for story ideas. Starting each day with the already existing news, they thus try to distinguish themselves from competing papers by bringing, sometimes according to a logic of one-upmanship, "a plus" (as they say at *Libération*) or an original angle of attack. Important news is thus news that is considered important by the whole of the media and picked up as such, certain outlets nevertheless having more "consecrating" power within the field than others. A story that, for example, appears in the satirical weekly *Le Canard enchaîné* and is not picked up by another outlet remains a *Canard enchaîné* story and has only a very limited political effect.[6] Being picked up by *Le Monde*, however, changes the status of the story, transforming an item of gossip into an issue worthy of political debate. And being picked up by television news makes it into a national issue. If each outlet and each journalist is attentive to, not to say obsessed by, this process of story pick-up, this is because, on the one hand, it constitutes a sort of sanction proper to the journalistic milieu (all journalists experience a certain pride at seeing one of their articles picked up by other outlets, especially the most prestigious, which is seen as proof of the intrinsic importance of the story they originally broke). On the other hand, it is because a story's political efficacy, its capacity to upset and impose itself as a current event that cannot be ignored, depends on its being picked up by other media, especially the most prestigious or efficacious insofar as they give it symbolic value added: the Parisian daily press is "higher" than the provincial dailies, with *Le Monde* and to lesser extent *Libération* on the one side, and the television news programs on the other.

The most prestigious media outlets thus have greater weight in the production of news because they are read more, their stories are picked up more often by other outlets, and because they exert a true power of consecration on other papers by virtue of whether they pick up their stories. There has long been a separation between the mainstream popular press and the so-called serious press, with the latter principally feeding public debates. The new weight of the audiovisual media in the production of major news has helped overcome this frontier, thereby changing the logic of public debate as well as the economy that governs the market of opinions. It is no doubt here that the greatest source of anxiety among those who reflect on the evolution of the profession lies.

Notes

1 During the 1980s and 1990s, French television and print journalists were widely criticized for various violations of ethical or professional norms,

such as charges of secretly altered television news footage, overly close relations between prominent journalists and leading politicians, and systematic ideological biases in coverage of foreign affairs (the first Gulf War) or subsequently, the popular "social movement" that arose in December 1995 to protest against government plans to cut public retirement and health programs. During this period, this critique manifested itself in such regular forums as Daniel Schneidermann's *Arrêt sur images* on public television Channel 5 and a flurry of books by journalists themselves, offering varying degrees of critical distance, culminating most recently with Pierre Péan and Philippe Cohen's *La Face cachée du "Monde"* (*The Hidden Face of "Le Monde"* [Fayard, Paris, 2003]) as well as through the films of Pierre Carles, the interventions of academics and intellectuals, and the creation of websites and hosting of public discussions by activist media organizations such as Action-Critique-Médias (ACRIMED). – ED.

2 ORTF was the acronym for the state's monopoly television and radio system that underwent successive reforms but essentially remained in place until 1981. – ED.

3 Champagne is describing in general terms the post-World War II history of the French press. Immediately after the ending of the Nazi occupation, a politically and culturally diverse press thrived in France. Prewar publishers who had collaborated with the Nazi-dominated French Vichy regime were prohibited from participating in the new press system, and generous state subsidies helped journalists start their own newspapers. Between 1945 and 1960, most of these post-Liberation publications closed for economic reasons, but during the late 1960s and early 1970s, new alternative and noncommercial press voices emerged, most notably the daily *Libération* founded by Jean-Paul Sartre and other intellectuals and activists, which survives (much transformed) to this day. – ED.

4 TF1, or Télévision Française 1, is France's most watched television channel and since 1986 has been wholly privately owned and funded. Arte is a joint Franco-German government funded cultural channel with no advertising. Whereas TF1 features a range of entertainment programming, including "reality TV" and other game shows, Arte focuses on documentaries, critically-acclaimed films, and other arts. – ED.

5 For a more in-depth analysis of recent changes at *Le Monde*, see P. Champagne, "Le Médiateur entre deux *Monde*", *Actes de la recherche en sciences sociales*, 131–2 (2000), pp. 8–29. – ED.

6 For more background on this unique French journalistic institution, see L. Martin, *Le Canard enchaîné ou les Fortunes de la vertu: Histoire d'un journal satirique, 1915–2000* (Flammarion, Paris, 2001) and C. Thogmartin, *The National Daily Press of France* (Summa, Birmingham, AL, 1998), pp. 284–9. Founded in 1915, *Le Canard enchaîné* is a vehicle for satire and humor, including political cartoons, as well as serious investigative reporting. While accepting no advertising or state assistance, the

weekly has been highly profitable with circulation generally exceeding 500,000 in recent years (Martin, pp. 465, 496–7). The title literally means "the duck in chains," but *canard* also means "lie" and serves as a colloquial term, among journalists, to refer to one's own newspaper. Thogmartin suggests that the title could be justifiably interpreted as "just one lie after another" (p. 285). – ED.

4

Subfields of Specialized Journalism

Dominique Marchetti

The notion of field allows us to draw out both that which unifies and divides the journalistic space of cultural production. Previous research has emphasized the tensions among leading newspapers, or between television and the print press. But another important organizing distinction in an increasingly fragmented media environment is thematic specialization, what in the context of US journalism one usually calls a "beat." As with other field characteristics, however, the role that specialization plays in structuring journalistic production may only be grasped relationally. This essay offers a systematic categorization of the variable features of the subfields of specialized journalism, with the hope that this model might be adapted for use in identifying and analyzing other properties of cultural fields.

An analysis of this type begins with the discovery that the journalistic field is structured around an opposition between a "generalist" pole and a "specialized" pole, and that the degree of specialization varies depending on the media outlet and the journalist. In this regard, recent transformations in recruitment and the consequent effects on the struggle to define journalistic excellence are shown to demonstrate the growing weight of the specialized pole.

The specialized pole is far from uniform, however. Six variables help account for differences among the specialized subfields: (1) position occupied in the journalistic field, (2) structure of the relationship of internal forces to explain how the weight of different media outlets with respect to the production of specialized information varies from one specialty to another, (3) degree and forms of competition and collaboration, (4) circulation of specialized journalists within the journalistic employment market, (5) journalistic demographic characteristics, and (6) mechanisms of professional socialization.

Shifting then to an outward focus, four additional variables help account for different relations between journalistic specializations and those social spaces which they mediatize: (1) degree of interrelation between their respective economies, (2) degree of political control of their activities, (3) degree to which one or the other imposes its problematic and its principals of hierarchization, as well as (4) social characteristics of both the journalists and their interlocutors.

From Generalists to Specialists

The articulation of the journalistic field around the two poles "generalist/specialist" reflects, on the one hand, the characteristics of the publics to whom media outlets are addressed, and, on the other hand, those of the outlets and of the journalists themselves. Though only the second aspect is the focus here, it is linked to the first, that is to say, to the transformations of the public and their styles of life.[1]

Degree of specialization varies strongly, at least according to the type of media outlet (generalist/specialized, audiovisual/print press, small/large outlet), the specialties, and the position that the latter occupy in the internal hierarchy of the media outlet. Thus, to take an example from the mainstream news media, in moving from the numerous media outlets of the daily national or regional press toward audiovisual or small general media outlets, specialized departments or journalists become increasingly rare. Likewise in the mainstream news media very often one finds profiles of journalists who eventually become specialists after having started as generalists, or, just as often, specialists who are only moderately so, since they do not stay long with the same topic. In the specialized media, paradoxically, the higher one goes in the internal hierarchy, the more likely one is to be a generalist. To understand even more specifically the degree of specialization of departments and journalists, one can study the mobility of professionals within the journalistic field. While some of them have internal mobility in the sense that they remain either in the same department or in departments of the same specialty (sciences, sport, etc.), others circulate between employment markets, going from specialized media to generalist media, or the inverse.

Recruitment as revealing the structure

The massive arrival of young journalists in France during the 1980s and 1990s is marked by two trends that correspond to the restructuring of the business market. On the one hand, there is an increase in the number of journalists whom one might qualify as multicompetent generalists, in the sense that they are capable of working for different media and/or of carrying out very different tasks, or of covering different sectors of activity. On the other hand, there is a more significant phenomenon of the ascendancy of journalists who are more and more specialized, and of nonjournalist experts having undergone lengthy and very specialized post-secondary studies.

This trend of relative professionalization may be traced via the hiring requirements of employers from very different types of media.[2] The most generalized media seek, first, journalists who are immediately "operational," that is, who have training in a certain number of practices and techniques. The increase in the number of graduates of France's eight accredited journalism schools within the media outlets of generalist media is a good indicator of this requirement. Though such graduates only represent 12 percent of the total number of professional journalist cardholders,[3] their numbers are growing among the personnel of the most prestigious national newspapers and television channels. A multicompetent generalist should also possess sufficient general cultural knowledge and analytic ability acquired through a relatively long education (three or four years after the "high school" baccalauréat examination). In France, a degree from a university (history, law, literature) or, especially, the Paris-based Institute of Political Studies (Institut d'études politiques), is considered a guarantee of such general competence. Put another way, knowledge of the specific area to be covered is in some cases perceived as less important than the certified ability to deal with all subjects.

But this development should not obscure another that is much more significant; that is, the reinforcement of the specialized pole of the journalistic field, as shown by the ceaseless growth of the specialized magazine press (public, technical, professional) which now employs 32.7 percent of cardholding professional journalists.[4] Some specialized media outlets seek experts with journalistic skills, rather than generalist or even (relatively) specialized journalists, simply because such outlets are addressed to a professional or specialized public. What is sought then, is thus not only a capital of specialized knowledge but also a "proximity to the readership," as the editor in chief of one professional magazine specified.[5] Within the generalist media, the fastest growing area of recruitment has been for specialized professionals to write about business, science, health, and other topics. Both university communications programs and the postgraduate journalism schools have established thematic options in science, agriculture, sports, business, and European affairs, to name a few. In the specialized press, and for certain specialized subjects, it is not unusual to find journalists who have begun or completed a PhD, or have on-the-job experience as engineers, lawyers, or medical doctors.

Media organizations recruit specialists for both professional and commercial reasons. "Knowledge of the issue" is crucial to establishing journalistic credibility both with specialized (source) and generalized (reader) publics, as Jean Padioleau's study of French educational reporters showed.[6] Such knowledge is perceived as particularly important by publishers and owners when it comes to politically sensitive topics. Even so, most specialist journalists are only relatively specialized. Even journalists with medical degrees or MBAs can only have a limited knowledge of the many highly specialized subfields of medicine or business finance. But it is precisely this type of limited journalistic specialization that complements the advertising-driven growth of back-of-the-book sections on personal investing, health, science, and a variety of practical news ("news that you can use").

Split identities

Such morphologic transformations do not occur without exacerbating recurring identity debates over the definitions of journalistic excellence. Specialized journalists are often stigmatized as having been captured by their sources or even of serving as de facto spokespersons for the organizations they cover: political journalists or those that write about social issues like immigration are sometimes characterized as "activists," sports journalists are seen as "fans." Specialists are thus portrayed as having a narrow, incomplete vision, too partial and technical, that is to say, more inclined to underline continuity rather than the latest news.

From the generalists' point of view, in short, journalists simply do not need a priori knowledge of the topics that they cover. What really counts is mastery of journalistic techniques: resourcefulness, rapidity, brashness, ability to get there first, independence vis-à-vis sources. With these abilities, the best journalists are seen as those capable of handling any topic on short notice, and of writing about it in a way that the general public can easily understand. This widely shared professional standard places specialized journalists working for omnibus media (oriented toward large, heterogeneous audiences, especially television) in a particularly difficult position. They need to acquire credibility before their peers as a specialist in a field, particularly before the editor-in-chief of the media outlet for which they work, yet also to demonstrate the qualities demanded of journalists in general. Likewise, they seek to address a broad audience without being discredited before a more limited specialized audience. This is the dilemma faced by all but the most specialized journalists working for the most specialized publications: they are specialists who nevertheless want to be recognized as journalists "like the others."

Variable Characteristics of Journalistic Subfields

Having drawn out the model of a general structuring of the journalistic field and its recent transformations, one can imagine a second, more refined level of analysis, that is to say, a comparative study of the different specialized subspaces. The latter enjoy very little autonomy with respect to the journalistic field if one compares them, for example, to their equivalent in the scientific field, the various disciplines.[7] Journalistic specialization is obviously not comparable to academic disciplines, not least because there are no formal entry requirements such as possession of a diploma. Even so, as with the disciplines, one finds significant differences as one moves from one specialized journalistic space to another. Tunstall's pioneering study of specialized journalists in major British media showed significant variations in the constraints, the careers and earlier experiences, the status accorded a specialty, and the manner in which journalists conceive their role.[8] Taking relational sociology further, I have thus sought to compare different specialties in order to better understand their own logics and their specific properties, identifying in the process six major variables.

Position of specialization in the professional hierarchy

A specialization's position in the journalistic field can be measured through at least two sets of indicators: biographical trajectories of journalists and general economic/professional indicators. For example, a study of the professional trajectories of managing editors of nationally distributed newspapers in France would probably demonstrate the primacy of the political specialization, since most of them come from this beat. In the same way, reconstructing the pyramid of the ages of specialized journalists for a topic in order to compare it to journalists as a whole would probably show the dominated position of those connected to national general news or social issues (immigration, poverty, racism), who are generally younger than their colleagues in the more prestigious domestic or foreign political beats.

A second set of indicators is at once economic and professional. Space allocated to the topic, whether for audiovisual time or for written pages, the place in the distribution hierarchy or in the publication of subjects (notably, presence on page one or in newspaper headlines), the budget allocated, the salaries and status of the journalists (portion of permanent full-time, full-time temporary, freelance, etc.) are some of the elements permitting understanding of the position of a specialty. But it would be wrong to consider these aspects from an exclusively economic aspect. In fact, one should combine in the analysis both internal hierarchies, which reflect professional prestige, and external hierarchies, which are linked to social, economic, or even political logics. Thus, certain specialties that are relatively low with respect to professional reputation, such as sports or entertainment, can be strategic because they contribute strongly to the revenue (distribution, advertising, classified ads) of the media outlet, or because they reach a large audience or a targeted public (e.g., individuals with strong purchasing power, youth). From this, one can better understand the importance of the number of sports journalists in France (about 2,600 in 2001) who represent more than 8 percent of all cardholding journalists.[9]

In contrast, foreign and domestic politics, which tend to bring in less advertising than other topics, nevertheless occupy a high status position in the journalistic field. Specializations do not all fulfill the same objectives, and one must distinguish those which attract the audience ("circulation goal"), from those that attract ads ("advertising goal"), or both at the same time ("mixed goal"), or those that bring more prestige ("non-revenue" or "prestige goal").[10] The importance of internal hierarchies is particularly visible during major news events which create, by their breadth, competition between beats and departments. In a work on the mediatization of the "contaminated blood" issue in France (see chapter 6 in this volume), it was shown that the more important an event becomes, the more medical specialists tended to be replaced by generalists, legal specialists, and particularly political journalists and political editorialists. Obviously, these hierarchies have very concrete effects on the production of news. Thus, one is left thinking that the less strategic a beat is determined to be within the internal hierarchy, then the more autonomous it is with respect to news management control in its choice of subjects, hierarchies, "angles," even mode of writing. For example, one could hypothesize that the forms of writing are less standardized in the cultural beats than in the political or legal beats.[11] Because specialized journalists have different characteristics and thus different categories of perception for the same event, the handling of news will sometimes be noticeably different according to the specialty mobilized.

But the comparison of the two sets of indicators (biographical and economic/professional) in order to specify the position of a specialty in the professional hierarchy has a limited interest if it does not take into account the variations of the position over time and according to media outlet. In fact, positions are not fixed, and the creation of new specializations can upset old hierarchies. Researchers have documented the progressive decline since the 1970s of the social or labor news specializations, but one could also show how these issues (to the extent that they were taken up at all) came to be increasingly covered by business or political reporters.[12] Likewise, beginning in the 1980s, investigative journalism contributed to the devaluation of the legal column in France, previously considered one of the most distinguished beats in French journalism.[13] Other specialties such as religion, theatre and literary criticism, or international news, today occupy lower positions than in the journalistic field of the 1950s through the 1970s, as demonstrated by the generalist media's decreased interest in these topics. In contrast, the business beat, which has the advantage of attracting new, more strategic audiences and advertisers, has steadily increased in power, as attested to by indicators as diverse as the elevated salaries of business journalists, the existence of specialized degrees or training in this area, or the increasing prevalence of former business reporters among the ranks of top news executives.

In addition, each media outlet is at once a field of forces and of struggle between specializations and journalists. In other words, the same specialty does not necessarily occupy the same place in different outlets. For example, only at a regional newspaper with a large farming readership, such as the Brittany and Normandy-based *Ouest-France* would the agricultural beat be among the most prominent.[14] The relative weight of each specialty (and of its subspecialties) is linked to the types of public of the media outlet.

Position of media outlet

In addition to the position of the specialties in the internal hierarchies, the structuring of the specialized subspaces constitutes a second indispensable variable in comparative work. These are articulated more or less around two oppositions that have already been referenced: intellectual v. commercial and specialist v. generalist. In the case of the specialization "media and communication" one sees clearly the opposition between those media outlets closest to the intellectual pole (*Le Monde* or *Télérama* in France, the *New York Times* in the United States, the *Guardian* in Great Britain, etc.) and those which embody the more commercial pole (*Le Parisien/Aujourd'hui*, *USA Today*, or the *Mirror*). In the same way, the treatment of news differs when one goes from the pole of generalist media toward that of the specialized press. The relationship of forces among media outlets near different poles also varies according to the specialized subuniverse. For example, with business news, the relative weight of certain specialized dailies (the *Wall Street Journal*, *Financial Times*, *Les Echos*) tends to be equal or superior to those of generalist dailies. In contrast, in the case of medical journalism, the specialized press occupies a dominated position and often arouses irony or even disparagement from specialists employed at the major national news media. In this domain, as in others (politics, education, and culture, especially), the daily *Le Monde* occupies the dominant position in France.

Journalistic capital, the functional influence within the field of the various press outlets, can be measured by indicators linked to the production of the news itself: the number of "exclusives," rate of articles "picked up" by other media outlets, size of the staff of specialized journalists, or the editorial space allocated to the topic. It is also based, in part, on dissemination, taking into account factors both quantitative (raw size of audience) and qualitative (not only high consumption households, but various economic and political opinion leaders).

Degree and type of competition or collaboration

Competition to be first, to bring out "exclusive news," tends to be relatively weak in the social issues or educational beats. As leading French and British scholars have shown, this great collegiality can have non-negligible professional advantages, particularly in responding to the criticism of managing editors regarding getting scooped.[15] In contrast, competition characterizes the French subspace of investigative and medical journalism. While such differences can be explained by variations in the perceived economic, political or professional importance of the specialization, they may also be linked to the history of the specialization and its evolving relationship with the social space(s) "covered."

Not only the degree but also the form of competition may vary across different specialized microcosms. With sporting events or music, for example, this is resolved, at least in the case of television channels, through economic transactions in the strict sense: the organizers of events regularly require payment for the exclusivity of images of the most important events. Likewise, celebrity interviews may only be granted after the formal or informal negotiation of topics to be discussed. In short, economic capital of media outlet is determinative in the competitive game, which explains the weight of big groups in the production of such news. In other strategic areas (crime, scandals, politics more broadly) or when the competition concerns the print press or radio, competition is not, or rarely, the subject of economic transactions in the strict sense; it is more symbolic. In order to obtain exclusives or otherwise scoop the competition, what is crucial above all is the professional reputation of the press organization or the journalists and/or their capital of relationships in the journalistic field.

Circulation of journalists in the employment market

Degree of turnover provides an indicator of the specialization's level of professionalization. More professionalized subfields will generally have a smaller turnover. The rate of rotation will also be likely to vary according to the type of company and its policies in this regard. Studies on scientific, medical, business, and sports journalism show the relatively closed nature of these markets. In contrast, journalists specializing in immigration or other social issues generally do not stay long in the same specialty and thus become "successive specialists," in the words of a managing editor of a Parisian daily.[16]

Journalist characteristics

Relevant characteristics could include social origins and trajectories (how one arrived at one's current position), volume and structure of cultural capital, age, gender, and employment status (intern, freelancer, temporary employee, full-time employee).

Effects from social origins and trajectory could take a number of forms. For example, as one moves from columnists (editorialists, cinema critics, etc.) toward "behind-the-scenes" reporters, or in general, from critical reflection toward purely informational journalism, class background is likely to be lower.[17] Data on journalists' origins and trajectories could be compared to those of the social agents they write about, thus providing another means to assess the journalistic subfield's relative position in the larger field of power. In France, some former left activists, in particular, have found in investigative journalism, especially in the uncovering of political financial scandals, a manner of practicing politics by other means. Moreover, these journalists' criticisms of the socialist government which came to power in 1981 were probably even sharper to the extent that they were so disappointed in its policies. In the same way, certain social (and geographic) trajectories of journalists' spouses help explain who tends to occupy the position of foreign correspondent. Comparing correspondents specialized in geographic areas and generalist journalists of the major US media,[18] one recent study showed that the likelihood of being married to a person from the region, or of having maintained in the past a relationship with the region, and of possessing specific language competence, is stronger for the former than the latter.[19]

Volume and structure of cultural capital is also clearly important, although at least in France this factor has generally only been measured in terms of education level. Especially in fields demanding scholarly over practical knowledge, such as medical or legal journalism, level of education has risen sharply, far more than that of the population as a whole.[20] And in these specialized realms, the arrival of new generations of more highly credentialed journalists has, at least in part, contributed to the ascendancy of a journalism that is more critical than that practiced in the past.

Age, or more broadly, longevity in the specialty is a third essential characteristic. Perhaps more than any other factor, the massive arrival of new generations of journalists has contributed to the transformation of specializations, especially those subfields in their formative stages. Whether it is coverage of social issues, business, medicine, or European affairs in Brussels, new entrants tend to implement subversive strategies designed to put in place criteria of journalistic excellence that are more "professional" and less "activist" compared with those of prior generations. Age may also be deployed as a commercial and professional strategy (thus potentially either expanding news coverage, or undermining critical distance), as British sociologist Jeremy Tunstall recounts for the case of youthful sports journalists hired to get closer to their equally youthful sources.[21]

Between 1981 and 1999, the percentage of French journalists who are women increased from 24.5 percent to 45 percent.[22] Certain expanding news beats, such as health, constitute a field of choice for these new entrants because health tends to be a subject that is perceived as more "feminine" than "masculine," in contrast to science, religion, sports, business or politics, for example. The gender division of specialties reflects in large part that of news consumers (the specialties defined as more masculine tend to be read by men, and vice versa) or the social sector covered. The increase since the 1980s in the development of the specialized magazine press has thus participated in the feminization of French journalists. Next, the overrepresentation of women in certain functional specialties (for example, 58.7 percent of copy editors in France are women)[23] or in certain subject areas is linked to the fact that they correspond to low positions in the social hierarchy of journalistic specialties. Lastly, the analysis of the gender variable of the producers of specialized news should be linked to other variables, such as technological medium (audiovisual versus print).

Forms of professional socialization

Socialization may vary sharply across journalistic specializations, playing a potentially significant role in accounting for differences in the form and content of information produced. At the same time, since it involves a myriad of formal and informal interactions over a long period of time, and in its deepest forms almost by definition excludes outside observation, socialization is among the least visible variables examined by researchers. As a starting point, we may suppose that type of socialization varies according to type of primary workplace (main newsroom, bureau, office subsumed within the institution covered, or freelance work at home) and type of informal meeting place (headquarters of associations, cafes, homes of colleagues or even primary sources, etc.).

Professional socialization in the newsroom is the classic case. To the extent that specialists work side by side and meet with other kinds of specialists, as well as generalist journalists, this broad newsroom culture may overwhelm any particular values upheld by the specialization.

As news outlets rely increasingly on freelancers, who often work at home, informal and intermittent socialization assumes an ever increasing role. Investigative journalists, critics, and columnists also are more likely to rarely come into the main office. Lacking the same regular contact with other journalists, solitary work practices may in some cases facilitate more "independent" or "alternative" journalism. Yet one could also hypothesize that the lack of regular reinforcement of professional norms would expose the solitary journalist even more strongly to the raw power of the marketplace or a range of nonjournalistic cultural influences.

Other journalists who live and work in close proximity to their sources are exposed to a different kind of heteronomous pressure. For journalists who cover the regular activities of political institutions (the European Parliament, the United Nations, the national parliament), the principal workplace is usually not the newsroom but rather the headquarters of the institution where they are often provided with an office. Legal columnists who cover the Paris city courthouse function as a "little family" accredited by the institution, often seeing each other in the same places, whether in the hallways or the cafeteria of the courthouse, the hearing rooms, or even in hotels and restaurants when they cover a trial outside the Paris area. In these situations, socialization vis-à-vis both their colleagues and, equally importantly, their sources operates through formal and informal means (e.g., mentoring of newcomers by old timers).

Finally, there is socialization via professional associations that transcend one's employer or usual workplace, as for example the prestigious Association of Legal Press created in 1885.[24]

Taking into account these very different modes of socialization allows a more refined description of the process of producing news, as well as competing conceptions of the profession.

The Journalistic Field in Relation to Other Social Spaces

Because of the widespread belief in the media's immense power, researchers may be misled into believing that the production of news can be understood solely via an "internal" analysis. Yet news is never just the product of the specific logic of the journalistic field. To avoid this kind of "media-centric" bias,[25] comparative research should always examine journalism in its complex relations with the other social spaces with which it relates.

Comparative research also brings to light the need to break away from homogenizing expressions about the "general" relationships between "journalists and their sources of information." In such expressions, not only is the notion of source not thought of in relational terms, presupposing that the information only circulates in one direction from the source to the journalist, but the relationship between journalists and their informants is conceptualized in a too narrowly interactionist form. That is, these interactions are described as if one could find, in the interactions themselves, the theory of the actions or of the discourse of the individuals. Ignoring "the structures (or the objective relationships) and the dispositions (most often correlated with the position occupied in these structures),"[26] this type of method tends to forget that the interactions between journalists and their interlocutors are meetings between different habitus and different positions in the field. To take a schematic example, one can easily see the difference that may exist between, on the one hand, certain specialized journalists, who as "locals" have very frequent and regular contact with the same interlocutors and, on the other hand, journalists "parachuted" abroad or generalist journalists who cover a subject only occasionally.

For these reasons, research on specialized journalism is most complete when it offers a joint genesis of the journalistic subspaces, of the field of activity at issue and also of their interrelations — as, for example, a study of agricultural news covered by *Ouest-France* showing the successive stages in the joint history of agricultural labor organizing and agricultural journalism.[27]

Variable aspects of journalistic relations with other fields

One can advance four variables, a list which is obviously not exhaustive, to analyze these relationships, and in particular the degree of autonomy between these different spaces. The first, and often the most visible, is economic. The degree of autonomy of a specialized subfield can be measured by the interdependence of its economy with that of the space of activity being covered. Indicators could include proportion of funding for media outlet originating in state aid, sales, and advertising, and the degree of concentration of advertisers. The interpenetration of journalism and various other sectors of cultural production (publishing, music, film) is especially deep. Journalism sometimes participates very directly in the economy of these fields of production, not only because news can help create a market for other cultural products, but because increasingly a few major economic groups control both the production of news and the cultural realms that journalists cover. Sports operate increasingly this way, with television channels involved both in the original broadcast of events (for which they pay dearly) and the subsequent news coverage.

The degree of autonomy of a specialized subfield can likewise be measured with the help of a second variable that could be deemed political, in the broad sense of the word. Though all of the social universes covered by specialized journalists are fields of contestation, it is still true that certain institutions control to a greater or lesser extent the process of their own mediatization.[28] Some fields, such as the legal, scientific, medical, or political fields (the latter, especially in the military arena), historically exercise a relatively strong control in several ways: access to the location is prohibited or subject to authorization (prison, hospitals, battlefield in times of war) or official comments by its agents are tightly restricted, as is often the case with judges.[29] The most autonomous universes, such as the legal and scientific fields, have come to take into account more and more the manner in which journalists cover their activities, since the media images thus created have effects both real and imagined on the public as well as on the functioning of these fields.

A third measure of a specialized journalistic subspace's autonomy is the degree to which it imposes its own logic and internal hierarchies, or not, upon the field it is covering. Agenda-setting and framing studies have shown how media participate in the hierarchization and definition of "social problems." In politics, however, any purely journalistic imposition is difficult to disentangle. Journalists come to share a number of beliefs in common with their interlocutors, and thus as they consecrate political actors they tend to consecrate themselves at the same time. Thus French political journalists, who generally share with politicians a view of politics that is relatively strategic, or even cynical, used these particular "glasses" to understand the struggle between "intellectuals" during the French social movements of December 1995.[30]

In fact, it is probably more accurate to say that the journalistic field through its different specialized subspaces tends less to impose its own logic than an external logic, especially economic-political logic, on the social fields of which it speaks. In a study of a "hit parade" of intellectuals offered by the French magazine *Lire* (Read), Bourdieu has shown how much the journalistic space attempts to impose on a limited field of production, a place of production for producers, the norms of production and consumption of the cultural products *against* which it is constructed.[31] This transfer of the technique of "hit parade," winner's lists, prizes, or best-sellers, once reserved for food or cars, operates today across the fields of cultural and scientific production and tends to introduce by ricochet new forms of consecration and hierarchization. It remains true that this power is very uneven and varies according to the social universe and even within the same universe. Countering the usual assumptions, field studies have shown that journalists largely tend to consecrate those who are already consecrated, particularly in the political arena where the weight of official sources predominates (see Eric Darras, chapter 8 in this volume). In contrast, in more heteronomous universes, journalists contribute to imposing other forms of consecration.

Finally, the relations that the specialized journalistic subuniverses maintain with the different social spaces that they mediatize should take into account a fourth variable: the social characteristics of social actors. In some social spaces, there may be a strong proximity, as was the case for theater critics from the turn of the century until the 1930s, who were both journalists and playwrights and were engaged in activities related to the administration of theaters. Another example is the political journalist turned politician, or vice versa (Pat Buchanan or George Stephanopoulos, in the United States), which if not the norm, certainly occurs in both France and the United States. Demographic research conducted during the 1990s shows particularly close relations (and "revolving doors") between French journalists and such cultural fields as public relations, publishing, radio, television, and other entertainment fields. Sometimes, the social actors circulate from one space to another or are in an in-between space. More broadly, one could investigate how this practical knowledge (or lack thereof) of certain activities affects relationships between the journalists in certain specialties and those of their privileged interlocutors in regard to the handling of news.

Put another way, it is not only the professional trajectories but also the educational and social trajectories that must be understood if one wants to compare how the differences (or similarities) of the characteristics allow one to understand the relationship between these universes and the production of news. The lifestyle of some journalists, who frequent social worlds to which they do not belong, is often higher than their salary allows.[32] The study of these inequalities in the type and amount of economic, political, or cultural capital would probably allow a better understanding of the phenomenon of fascination–revulsion of journalists with respect to politicians or CEOs, or even sports figures, whose incomes are much greater than their own.[33]

Effects of external transformations

Changes in news coverage of any particular issue is always necessarily a result of both internal transformations of the journalistic field and transformations external to that field.

Beyond these structural transformations, which can have effects on the creation and development of specialties, the positions of these specialties in the journalistic space may be very sensitive to the characteristics of the era. Because journalism, as with other fields of cultural production "is situated in the short term of symbolic, perishable goods," that is to say, it plays "regularly with temporal differences, thus with change,"[34] certain events sometimes contribute to transform, temporarily or permanently, the position of certain topical specialties or simply their content. For this reason, the creation and/or development of new institutions and changes in legislation could explain the ascendancy to power of legal affairs correspondents in the British media.[35] A journalist from the Agence France Presse also recounts how immigration essentially emerged as a "social problem" as a result of dramatic events. "For years, we tried to publish articles on immigrants. They were not accepted anywhere and we were told 'This isn't worth anything . . . Can't you see?' . . . [But] since the day when some immigrants set fire to a shanty town, everything has changed. Now, immigration is considered a 'good' topic."[36] In the social issues and general news departments, specialties are frequently redefined and new themes often emerge in accordance with the latest events.

A comparative analysis of specialized subspaces making up the journalistic field thus appears even more indispensable today since what is blithely called "journalism," "press," or "media," reflects logics that are increasingly diverse in terms of production and consumption. Nevertheless, it would be an error to construct a study of specialized subfields of news production as a completely independent object of research. As indicated here, in each case it would be necessary to cross the specific logic of the subfield with the various external logics: the logic of the media outlets or of the type of media which constitute, themselves, relational spaces, those of the journalistic field as a whole, and finally those of the social spaces that are mediatized.

Notes

1 Bourdieu insists that one must simultaneously take into account the "objective orchestration" of the logics of "the fields of production,"

and the "field of consumption." A complete analysis of any field or subfield clearly ought to include both aspects. See Pierre Bourdieu, *Distinction* (Harvard University Press, Cambridge, MA, 1984), p. 230.

2 Valérie Devillard, Marie-Françoise Lafosse, Christine Leteinturier, and Rémy Rieffel, *Les Journalistes français à l'aube de l'an 2000: Profils et parcours* (Panthéon, Paris, 2001); Dominique Marchetti and Denis Ruellan, *Devenir journalistes: Sociologie de l'entrée dans le marché du travail* (Documentation française, Paris, 2001).

3 In France, a specialized commission composed of news executives and journalists provides a professional identity card to journalists under certain conditions, chiefly that at least 50 percent of the applicant's income derives from work performed for a media enterprise. This card functions in some ways like membership in the United States' House and Senate Press Galleries, easing access to cover government activities; unlike any comparable journalistic status in the United States it also guarantees special tax abatements. The French "carte" is not mandatory, however, and many French journalists exercise their profession without having the card.

4 Devillard et al., *Les Journalistes français à l'aube de l'an 2000* pp. 56–7.

5 All quotations from journalists in this chapter, unless otherwise specified, are from interviews conducted by the author in France between 1998 and 2002.

6 Jean-G. Padioleau, "Systèmes d'interaction et rhétoriques journalistiques," *Sociologie du travail*, 3 (1976), pp. 256–82, esp. p. 267.

7 Pierre Bourdieu, *Science de la science et réflexivité* (Editions Raisons d'Agir, Paris, 2001), pp. 123–40.

8 Jeremy Tunstall, *Journalists at Work* (Constable, London, 1971).

9 "Un nouveau président pour l'Association des journalistes sportifs," Agence France Presse, November 10, 2001.

10 Tunstall, *Journalists at work*. See also Jeremy Tunstall, *Newspaper Power: The New National Press in Britain* (Oxford University Press, Oxford, 1996), pp. 156–61.

11 Concerning music journalism, see, for example, Eamonn Forde, "From Polyglottism to Branding: On the Decline in Personality Journalism in the British Music Press," *Journalism*, 2, 1 (2001), pp. 23–43.

12 Since the 1980s, labor and other social movements have been covered increasingly in a more distant manner by journalists with an expertise (rather than a political engagement) in the topic. At the same time, a special "social issues" section has been progressively dismantled at most French newspapers and newsweeklies, generally subsumed within the "politics" or "economics" pages, with the exception of the communist daily *L'Humanité*. See Sandrine Lévêque, *Les Journalistes sociaux: Histoire et sociologie d'une spécialité journalistique* (PUR, Rennes, 2000).

13 Rémi Lenoir, “La Parole est aux juges: Crise de la magistrature et champ journalistique,” *Actes de la recherche en sciences sociales*, 101–2 (1994), pp. 77–84.

14 Alain Carof, *La Production de l’information agricole: L’exemple d’Ouest-France* (Centre de sociologie rurale, Paris, 1972).

15 Padioleau, “Systèmes d’interaction et rhétoriques journalistiques,” pp. 261–2; Tunstall, *Newspaper Power*, pp. 158–9.

16 Immigration reporting in the United States is largely delegated to generalists, though in some cases facility with the Spanish language (given the predominance of Mexican and other South and Central American immigrants) is considered a requirement for the job. One of the rare reporters who had covered immigration almost exclusively for many years observed nevertheless that “specialization or knowledge of a subject is not that highly regarded.” From Rodney Benson, “Generalist and specialized journalism: The case of American immigration reporting,” paper presented to Research Seminar on Specialized Journalism, Institut Français de Presse, Université Paris II, June 2001.

17 Tunstall, *Journalists at Work*, p. 74; Sandrine Anglade, “Des journalistes au théâtre: Identité professionnelle et espace parisien (1880–1930),” in *Médias et villes (*XVIIIe–XXe *siècle), Actes du colloque des 5 et 6 décembre 1997 tenu à l’Université François-Rabelais* (CEHVI–l’Université François-Rabelais, Tours, 1999). Anglade’s study of the French theatre at the turn of the twentieth century contrasts a journalism of pure information, which she terms the criticism of information, “often menaced by the mercantile aspect of theatre and which tended sometimes to become an agent of publicity,” with a journalism of “criticism-reflection, closer to the creative side of theatre.”

18 See Ulf Hannerz, *Foreign News: Exploring the World of Foreign Correspondents* (University of Chicago Press, Chicago, 2004); Lars Willnat, “Through Their Eyes: The Work of Foreign Correspondents in the United States,” *Journalism*, 4, 4 (2003), 403–22; and Mark Pedelty, *War Stories: The Culture of Foreign Correspondents* (Routledge, London, 1995).

19 Stephen Hess, “The Culture of Foreign Correspondents,” in *Media Occupations and Professions: A Reader*, ed. J. Tunstall (Oxford University Press, Oxford, 2001), pp. 162–9.

20 In a study of 250 French scientific journalists, Françoise Tristani-Potteaux showed that 47 percent of them had a postgraduate degree. See F. Tristani-Potteaux, *Les Journalistes scientifiques, médiateurs des savoirs* (Economica, Paris, 1997), p. 27.

21 “Sometimes ‘experience’ is deliberately planned and cultivated in advance; for instance the youngest football specialist may be assigned to cover the England Under 23 team – in the expectation that some of these players will later be in the full England team.” See Jeremy Tunstall, “Correspondents and Individual News Sources,” in *Media*

Occupations and Professions: A Reader, ed. J. Tunstall (Oxford University Press, Oxford, 2001), p. 148.

22 Source : Commission de la carte d'identité des journalists professionnels.

23 Devillard et al., *Les Journalistes français à l'aube de l'an 2000*, p. 47.

24 Other associations of specialized journalists in France include: L'Union syndicale des journalistes sportifs français, l'Association française des journalistes agricoles, l'Association des journalists économiques et financiers, l'Association des journalistes parlementaires, and l'Association de la presse présidentielle.

25 Philip Schlesinger, "Rethinking the Sociology of Journalism: Source Strategies and the Limits of Media-Centrism," in *Public Communication: The New Imperatives*, ed. M. Ferguson (Sage, London, 1990), pp. 61–83.

26 Bourdieu, *Science de la science et réflexivité*, p. 46.

27 Carof, *La production de l'information agricole.*

28 Richard V. Ericson, Patricia M. Baranek, and Janet B.L. Chan, *Negotiating Control: A Study of News Sources* (University of Toronto Press, Toronto, 1989).

29 Lenoir, "La Parole est aux juges."

30 Julien Duval, Christophe Gaubert, Frédéric Lebaron, Dominique Marchetti, and Fabienne Pavis, *Le "Décembre" des intellectuels français* (Liber-Raisons d'agir, Paris, 1998).

31 Pierre Bourdieu, *Homo Academicus* (Polity, Cambridge, 1988, and Stanford University Press, Stanford, CA, 1988).

32 Tunstall, *Journalists at Work.*

33 For a study of sports journalism in Australia, New Zealand, and the United Kingdom, see David Rowe, *Sport, Culture, and the Media* (Open University Press, Buckingham and Philadelphia, 1999).

34 Pierre Bourdieu and Yvette Delsaut, "Le Couturier et sa griffe: contribution à une théorie de la magie," *Actes de la recherche en science sociales*, 1 (January 1975), p. 16.

35 Philip Schlesinger and Howard Tumber, *Reporting Crime: The Media Politics of Criminal Justice* (Oxford University Press, New York, 1995), pp. 147–8.

36 Edouard Boutros and Henri Tincq, *L'Information sociale et ses publics*, Colloque de l'AJIS (Thema Edition, Paris, 1974).

Part II

Comparative Perspectives

5

Mapping Field Variation: Journalism in France and the United States

Rodney Benson

Given that a field approach to news media research has emerged out of France, it is surprising that field studies tell us so little about the distinctive properties of French journalism.[1] In fact, the French "political/literary" press tradition is sharply opposed in many ways to America's "informational" model. Rather than being downplayed, this difference needs to be emphasized and explained. Mapping and tracing the origins of this French specificity – especially in relation to its US "other" – offers a powerful opportunity to advance the field theory project.

As French press historian Pierre Albert observes: "French journalism has always been more of a journalism of expression than a journalism of observation. . . . As much as the presentation of facts, it is always interested in the exposition of ideas."[2] A relatively greater mixing of "fact" and "opinion" in French journalism has been confirmed by a content analysis of political news in the leading French and US national newspapers between the 1960s and the 1990s.[3] Research on US and French news coverage of the immigration issue between the 1970s and 1990s shows that the French press displayed a broader ideological diversity and performed a greater civic "mobilizing" role, while at the same time French news was presented in a more dramatized fashion than is typical of mainstream American journalism.[4] Some of these differences also extend to television news in the two countries.[5]

I should quickly add that "different" does not imply either better or worse. Media scholars Ben Bagdikian, Mark Pedelty, and others have argued that the more openly interpretive, ideologically diverse, and politicized French (and other European) press represents a superior alternative to the American "ideology of objectivity."[6] A worthy debate could be held over the advantages and disadvantages of each national "model." But my concern here is not so much normative as analytical: *Why* do the two systems differ, and how can field theory help us answer such a question?

Of course, Bourdieu understood that fields and field configurations could differ cross-nationally.[7] My point is simply that, at least for the case of journalism, rather than problematizing and theorizing such differences, he ended up eliding them. In so doing, Bourdieu was able to stress certain *general* dynamics of fields that operate in all cases. In what follows, however, I want to suggest a slightly different use of field theory, one that would highlight cross-national differences in order to draw out the *variable* qualities of fields and field configurations. This kind of project needs to proceed carefully and be mindful of the scientific cautions that guided Bourdieu's work. After laying this epistemological groundwork, I will then critically revisit elements of fields that Bourdieu has identified as theoretically significant: relations of the field at hand to heteronomous pressures (primarily economic and political), initial formation and subsequent historical trajectory of the field, and the internal morphological/demographic composition of the field. In this attempt to map two national journalistic fields – situated in their respective fields of power – we will be forced to make explicit what has remained until now too often implicit in field theory, that is, the element of variation. In the conclusion, we will consider which of these field aspects best helps us explain the distinctive production of news discourse in France and the United States.

Variable Qualities of Fields: Old Cautions, New Questions

Field theory is tailor-made for cross-national research, as Daniel Hallin notes in this volume. I want to emphasize here how cross-national research in turn offers an especially powerful means to elaborate and stretch field theory. However, there are important theoretical and methodological reasons why field theory has, to date, not been much used comparatively, which must first be addressed.

The first concern follows from field theory's insistence that analysis of the social world should be comprehensive, simultaneously examining historical geneses and trajectories, structural relations among fields, and the practices and worldviews of social actors within fields. Such comprehensive "thick description" is difficult enough to accomplish for a single field within a single national context, let alone cross nationally. Yet, as noted, there is an irony here: without cross-national comparison, significant aspects of a national field may become naturalized and thus remain invisible to the domestic-bound researcher. Cross-national research offers a valuable tool to help field researchers effect that all-important epistemological break with the commonsensical and hence ideologically-charged conceptions of their object of study.[8]

A second concern relates to the availability of adequate data. For Bourdieu, quantitative indicators can be very helpful for social analysis, but the researcher must fully understand the process by which they were constructed. If it is difficult enough to intelligently use data within one's own national context, in one's own language, the difficulties multiply exponentially with cross-national research. For such research to be successful, Bourdieu suggests, one has to enlist the help of foreign colleagues with "primary familiarity with the universe to be analyzed."[9] This chapter, as well as this book, represents an effort to organize such scholarly cooperation. Data that adequately measure forms and volume of capital, field relations, and the social properties of agents can be quite difficult to obtain. In the meantime, one can only try to "offer a very worthwhile first pass . . . on the basis of a secondary analysis of data already compiled."[10] For this particular "first pass," indicators are more suggestive than definitive. The discussion will be necessarily schematic but will hopefully open up a methodological debate over the possibilities and limitations of quantitatively measuring field relations.

A final field theory hesitation to cross-national research relates to the very project of theory building. Bourdieu distinguished his approach sharply from any positivist-style accumulation of social laws, arguing that field dynamics can only be understood in relation to concrete historical circumstances.[11] Given this caveat, Bourdieu also seemed to aspire to generalizable theory, writing at one point that "a particular case that is well constructed ceases to be particular."[12] No matter how well-constructed, however, research that confines itself to a single nation-state is limited in scope. Certain types of variation – especially at the broad system level – only become visible via cross-national research.

In sum, while there are dangers to avoid, they are outweighed by the potential benefits of careful cross-national research. We can fruitfully use field theory to understand French and American journalism, and in turn, the comparison may help improve field theory. We now turn to a systematic comparison of the journalistic fields of France and the United States in terms of (1) their economic organization, both external and internal, (2) their relation to the state, (3) their historical formation and level of autonomy, and (4) their internal morphology and demography.

Economic Pressures and the Spatial Structure of the Journalistic Field

In Bourdieu's writings on the media and in most field case studies, heteronomous constraints on journalism are portrayed as primarily economic. But economic pressures are not all the same. Which matter most? Almost in passing, Bourdieu mentions ownership and advertising as "important to keep . . . in mind,"[13] and emphasizes that these offer only a partial explanation. The rest of the explanation, at least relative to economic pressures, seems to be there in Bourdieu's detailed discussion of competition within the field. Implicit in this description, I suggest, is the variable of field "internal organization," which can be more or less concentrated and centralized. (See table 5.1 for a complete listing of several basic economic indicators for the French and US news media.)

Advertising expenditures as a percentage of gross domestic product are more than twice as high in the United States as in France – about 1.4 percent versus 0.6 percent of GDP, respectively. It is true that France has a vital and growing commercially-oriented magazine sector;[14] the difference is most marked when one compares those media outlets which are at least partially concerned with political and national affairs. Compared to the United States' average of nearly 80 percent, French national daily newspapers earn just over 50 percent of their revenues from advertising (while advertising makes up slightly over one-third of earnings for French regional newspapers).[15] Some of the leading French dailies, such as *Libération* and *Le Monde*, have earned as little as 20 or 30 percent of their revenues from advertising. The conservative *Le Figaro* is the only major French newspaper to approach the United States' advertising average.[16] Advertising is also restricted to a greater extent on French television, and is barred completely during television news broadcasts, both public and private.

Another major difference is that French media companies are less likely than US companies to be publicly traded on the stock market.

Table 5.1 French and US national journalistic fields: economic indicators

Economic indicators	France	United States
Media advertising as a percentage of gross domestic product[a]	0.62	1.36
Advertising as a percentage of newspaper revenues	50	79
Subscriptions as a percentage of all newspaper sales	28	81
Average daily circulation and location of major national newspapers[b]	*Le Parisien/Aujourd'hui en France* 513,000 *Le Monde* 399,000 *Le Figaro* 359,000 *Libération* 160,000 *Les Echos* 141,000 *La Croix* 98,000 *L'Humanité* 52,000	*USA Today* 2,136,000 (no local circulation base) *Wall Street Journal* 1,801,000 (New York) *New York Times* 1,113,000 (New York) *Los Angeles Times* 1,006,000 (Los Angeles) *Washington Post* 747,000 (Washington, DC)
Percentage of public with cable television	15[c]	68
Local broadcast television channels	4	1,733[d]

Sources:

Media advertising as a % of GDP: figures are for 2003. ZenithOptimedia Press Release, April 23, 2004, www.zenithoptimedia.com/pubadexf.htm, and Organization for Economic Cooperation and Development (OECD) Main Economic Indicators, June 2004, www.oecd.org/home/.

Advertising as a % of Newspaper Revenues: US figure is for 1987, from C. Edwin Baker, *Advertising and a Democratic Press* (Princeton University Press, Princeton, NJ, 1994), p. 16; French figure is for 1998, from Valérie Devillard, Marie-Françoise Lafosse, Christine Leteinturier, and Rémy Rieffel, *Les Journalistes français à l'aube de l'an 2000: Profils et parcours* (Panthéon-Assas, Paris, 2001), pp. 28–9.

Subscriptions as a % of Newspaper Sales: French figure is for 1998, from Devillard et al., *Les Journalistes français*, p. 28; US figure is for 2001, from Newspaper Association of America, *2001 Circulation Facts, Figures and Logic.*

Average Daily Circulation and Location of Major National Newspapers: "Top 20 Daily and Sunday Paper Lists," (average daily circulation for six months ending September 30, 2002), *Editor & Publisher,* November 6, 2002; Diffusion totale [total circulation] (for 2003), Diffusion Contrôle, Association pour le Contrôle de la Diffusion des Médias (Paris).

Percentage of Public with Cable Television: French figure is from *Tableaux de l'économie française* (Collection "Références," INSEE, Paris, 2003–2004, pp. 28, 181); US figure is from Table No. 1103: Utilization of Selected Media, *Statistical Abstract of the United States*, US Census Bureau, 2002. No data on US satellite usage is provided.

Local broadcast television channels: French figure is for 1998, from Devillard et al., *Les Journalistes français*, p. 29. US figure is for 2003 and is from an FCC News Release, February 24, 2004 ("Broadcast Station Totals as of December 31, 2003").

notes are on p. 112

The publicly-traded corporation is the dominant organizational form in the United States for the 80 percent of newspapers that are chain owned, as well as radio and television channels, both network affiliated and "independent."[17] In contrast, only a handful of the leading French media outlets, such as the national commercial channels TF1 and M6, and the cable movie and sports channel Canal-Plus (owned by Vivendi), are listed on the French stock market. Public stock ownership of media companies has been hindered by a 1986 law that limits the amount of foreign investment, as well as a provision that specifically prohibits a newspaper company from being publicly listed.[18]

Lacking significant advertising revenues as well as stockholder-driven pressure, French newspaper companies tend to be less profitable than their American counterparts. Socpresse, with a recent net income/total revenues ratio of 8.8 percent, has been considered the best performer among French newspaper companies.[19] In contrast, the Tribune Company, which owns the *Baltimore Sun*, *Chicago Tribune*, *Los Angeles Times*, and several other papers, fired the *Sun*'s editor in 2004 because he was not doing enough to maintain the corporation's reported 2003 net earnings of 28.4 percent.[20] Since 2000, net income as a percentage of annual sales (a more conservative measure) has ranged from 13.1 to 27.6 percent at Gannett (owner of *USA Today*) to 9.4 to 14.7 percent at the New York Times Company.[21]

Conventional economic indicators thus portray a US journalistic field far more commercialized than its French counterpart. Yet if we stopped here, we would remain far from a complete understanding of our two cases. Although not fully developed by Bourdieu, a field analysis could take into account another set of economic factors, conceptualized in relation to the spatial and temporal structuring of journalists' relations to one another, and news outlets' relations to their audiences – aspects related to what Michael Schudson has termed the "structural ecology" of the public sphere.[22] A spatial analysis of the field would thus consider such supplemental factors as the extent to which the field is centralized or fragmented,[23] and the intensity of organizational and individual competition within the field.

The French national journalistic field is more concentrated than its American counterpart. In France, more than 60 percent of journalists live in the Paris metropolitan region (Ile-de-France); in contrast, American journalists are spread out far more evenly across the country.[24] At the level of elite journalism, even if New York is the media capital of the United States, it must at least partially share that honor with other cities (Washington, DC, Los Angeles, and to a lesser extent Boston and Chicago) in a way that Paris clearly does not. Audiences are also much more concentrated in France, especially for television news. France's TF1 evening news alone captures 40 percent of the television audience on any given night, and most of the rest of the news audience is split among the two public channels France 2 and 3, and to a lesser extent the commercial channel M6 (with only news shorts) and the Franco-German cultural channel Arte.[25] As of 1998, there were only four local broadcast television channels in all of France (though the France-3 public television channel tailors its local news broadcasts by region); only 15 percent of the French public subscribes to cable television. In contrast, the three American network evening news shows combined are watched on a regular basis by less than 30 percent of adults, and the US audience is split further among more than 1,000 local channels (most of which have news broadcasts) as well as several national cable television news channels.[26] Since the 1980s, with the rise of the *New York Times* national edition, *USA Today*, multiple cable news channels, and of course the internet, American journalism may have become more "nationalized,"[27] yet relative to France, the US journalistic field remains clearly more decentralized. In contrast with the situation for the *Washington Post*, the *Los Angeles Times*, the *New York Times*, *USA Today*, and the *Wall Street Journal*, which compete for readers only to a limited extent, the daily competition between *Le Monde* and its main competitor, *Libération*, can in fact be quite intense, and this competition also encompasses to a certain degree *Le Figaro*, *Le Parisien*, *L'Humanité*, *La Croix*, the business daily *Les Echos*, and the weekly *Le Canard enchaîné*. Direct economic competition among these daily newspapers is supplemented and amplified by professional competition from the two major national television news broadcasts (TF1 and France 2), as well as several nationally-distributed radio channels. Contributing to this more competitive environment for the French media is a different relationship between news outlets and their readers. Not only do most French newspapers rely on circulation rather than advertising for revenues, as noted, but in addition they depend on daily sales rather than long-term subscriptions. Whereas subscriptions make up 28 percent of all sales for French national daily newspapers, they constitute more than 80 percent of total sales for US newspapers.

French and American national journalists, not surprisingly, perceive their respective competitive environments differently, although there is, of course, significant variation within each national field depending on one's position in that field.[28] French journalists at the leading national newspapers and newsmagazines are intensely aware of their cross-town competitors, whose news decisions in turn may have immediate effects on sales or audiences; in contrast, the regionalized and subscription-based US press is more insulated from such pressures. As a managing editor of the *Los Angeles Times* told me, "There is competition among the major [national] papers, but it's not about business."[29]

In sum, thinking of field "ecology" in variable terms allows us also to conceptualize and measure commercial competitive pressures in a much more precise manner.[30] While the American journalistic field largely consists of multiple, partially overlapping local fields, the French journalistic field is highly concentrated socially, professionally, and economically. Despite lesser commercialization in aggregate terms, the French journalistic field is thus organized in such a way as to actually intensify commercial and other competitive pressures.

Reconceptualizing Autonomous Political Power

In Bourdieu's model, the cultural logic of any given field confronts heteronomous power, conceptualized as the (singular, if complex) dominant power in the society at large, and in this one respect, shares an unfortunate tendency in much of the sociology of news to lump together a variety of heterogeneous influences under the broad category of "external" factors.[31] Most often, this external pressure is described as purely economic; at other times, as in the text published in this volume, Bourdieu joins the economic and political (p. 41). Perhaps more than in the United States, French state and market power have traditionally been tightly interlinked; government officials and corporate managers alike are trained and form lasting social networks at the same elite *grandes écoles*. This situation nevertheless remains a particular variant of a general relation; it remains important to analytically distinguish political and economic power, and indeed all forms of power. Elsewhere Bourdieu has emphasized that all fields retain to a certain degree their own specific logics. And, if this is the case, the political field, as well as all other fields – particularly the scientific, artistic, religious, and literary (including philosophy, which exerts a significant moral power in France) – also have to be considered in their potential to exert cross-cutting heteronomous power in relation to each other, as well as over the journalistic field. Such a conceptual adjustment threatens the graphical clarity of the typical representation of a field in terms of two opposing poles: Coming to terms with this more complex, multivalent (but not necessarily broadly pluralist) conception of power represents a significant challenge for field theory.[32]

What then is the distinctive power of the political field? Bourdieu sees the political field in terms both broad (the entire field of power) and narrow (state agencies and elected bodies);[33] the focus here will be on the latter. In his essay, "Rethinking the State," Bourdieu lists multiple forms of capital: economic capital, informational (or cultural) capital, symbolic capital, and "capital of physical force." He expands upon Weber's definition of the state as that body which possesses a monopoly over the legitimate use of (physical) violence, preferring instead to emphasize that the state also monopolizes the use of "symbolic violence," primarily through its capacity to inculcate through the educational system and the legal system the dominant "classification systems" which in turn mold "mental structures and impose . . . common principles of vision and division."[34] This emphasis lies close to Stuart Hall's notion of the state as the "primary definer" of social problems and debates in the media, although cognitively, it goes much deeper than that. While the state clearly has an advantage in setting the journalistic agenda, empirical research has also shown that it does not monopolize symbolic power.[35]

In short, if the political field (defined narrowly as state bureaucracy) wields symbolic power, this is not what sets it uniquely apart from other fields. Something important is lost in Bourdieu's reformulation. Where Bourdieu emphasizes a basic divide between economic and cultural capital, in his *Treatise on Social Theory* W.R. Runciman sees power embodied in three distinct forms: like Bourdieu, economic (means of production) and cultural/ideological (means of persuasion), but also coercive (means of coercion),[36] the latter of which restores Weber's assessment of the state's singularity. In its dealings with the news media, at least in western democracies, coercion may not seem an apt description of the state's normal procedures. But what are laws and regulations concerning the media if not guidelines ultimately backed up by the government's power to fine or imprison those who fail to comply? One important task then for a generalizable theory of journalistic–political field relations is to classify and analyze the various forms of state coercive power over the media. At the broadest level, we can say that these roles are either "restrictive" or "enabling."[37]

Restrictive power sets limits on either access to or publication of certain kinds of information or opinion. In France, journalists are subject to criminal prosecution if they publish restricted government information, violate personal privacy laws, or engage in defamation; although enforcement varies, there has been no substantial weakening of these laws.[38] In contrast, the trend in US federal court interpretations of the First Amendment has been a decrease in the state's capacity to inhibit journalistic investigations of government agencies or politicians' private lives. Since the mid-1980s, the US Federal Communication Commission's jurisdiction over the television networks and cable systems has also been progressively weakened.[39]

The state is "enabling" when it literally enables the media to exist or thrive via indirect (technology, distribution networks) or direct financial aid; in contrast to limiting speech, it enables or expands the range of speech made available to the public.[40] Enabling arguably presents a hybrid form of power. To enable via subsidies is to exert a sort of economic power, and indeed, Bourdieu at one point categorizes government subsidies as just another form of "economic censorship" along with "the companies that pay for the ads."[41] However, funding from the state, in which profits and audiences are not as crucially at stake, indeed are often explicitly not at stake, is not the same as funding tied to market imperatives.

The French state clearly plays a more active enabling role vis-à-vis the media than does that of the United States. The Paris-based newspapers *La Croix* (Catholic), *L'Humanité* (Communist), *Présent* (far right) and *Libération* (left leaning) have all at various times met the requirements of low advertising receipts and circulation of less than 150,000 in order to receive direct subsidies in defense of "press pluralism." The French state also provides general subsidies to all newspapers, such as reimbursements for telephone and fax expenditures, postal shipping, etc.; furthermore a tax on television sets provides significant funding for the public channels.[42] It is important to acknowledge that US journalism has also long benefited from government subsidies, including cheap postal rates, regulations that stabilize the industry and a government public relations infrastructure that provides an "information subsidy" by facilitating the gathering of news.[43] However, the US government has generally not provided direct subsidies or benefits to particular news organizations and the overall level of state aid to the press is much lower than in France.

In sum, while state policies, both restricting and enabling, sometimes reinforce the power of the market, there is always the possibility that they may not. It is thus somewhat surprising that Bourdieu largely ignores media policy, because the French case (far more than the American case) powerfully highlights this realm of state autonomy from the market. For many years, the French state-owned radio channel France-Inter has offered daily "press reviews" (revues de presse) which included the non-mainstream media. As the host of the show commented in an interview: "I often cited *La Croix*, which is a remarkably well-done small newspaper, and I often cited *L'Humanité* because it would be a catastrophe if *L'Humanité* were to one day disappear, an ecological catastrophe, in the sense of ecology of ideas."[44] This passage illustrates a clear way in which the French state encourages a form of journalism that is not market oriented, and thus represents a distinct heteronomous power over the journalistic field.

Historical Formation of the Journalistic Field and Cultural Inertia

According to Bourdieu, the "rules of the game" that are established at a field's founding tend to endure. They are not inviolable – inevitably they are modified over time – but field and institutional theorists stress continuity as early contingencies become routinized and naturalized, thus establishing a "path dependency" that is difficult to modify.[45] As Bourdieu notes,

> the stakes of the struggle between the dominants and pretenders [within any given field of cultural production, including journalism], the issues they dispute . . . depend on the state of the legitimate problematic, that is, the space of the possibilities *bequeathed by previous struggles*, a space which tends to give direction to the search for solutions and, consequently, influences the present and future of production. (My italics).[46]

Analysis of the formation and partially contingent transformations of a national journalistic field thus adds an important historical, contextual explanation missing from most political economy, organizational, or cultural studies of news production. These distinct histories both illustrate and explain the endurance of distinct "informational" and "political/literary" approaches to journalism in the United States and France, respectively (see box 5.1).[47]

Since the early 1980s, both the American and French media have been subject to greater commercial pressures. In the United States, an intensification of profit pressures has produced alienation in the newsrooms and more superficial, lifestyle- and personality-oriented news coverage.[58] In France, the most dramatic transformations came

Journalism's journey in France and the United States

In both France and Great Britain's North American colonies, the earliest newspapers (Theophraste Renaudot's *Gazette* in 1631, Benjamin Harris's Boston *Publick Occurrences Both Forreign and Domestick* in 1690) emerged under monarchical rule, and were subject to strict political censorship. Early on, however, the French made a greater, and more normatively charged, distinction between "news" and "views." Some historians argue that because this early French press endured so much longer than its "Anglo-Saxon" counterparts under strict monarchical rule, its well-known self-censorship earned mere "information" a bad reputation.[48]

With the political upheavals of the late eighteenth century, newspapers in both France and the United States became much more openly politicized and played an important role in the formation and consolidation of their respective democratic republics.[49] In France, however, this politicization was joined to a more literary and "explanatory" approach to journalism. The full title of a prominent early, and enduring, journal testifies to this twofold allegiance: *Le Journal des debats politiques et litteraires*.[50] In contrast to the US First Amendment which simply asserts a general right of "speech . . . and of the press," the eleventh article of the French Declaration of the Rights of Man and Citizen explicitly emphasized "the free communication of thoughts and opinions." Thus, in the French case, freedom of the press was from the beginning justified and defended as the right to opinions rather than "mere" information.[51]

After 1793, the paths of the French and US press began to diverge even more sharply. With the 1799 coup d'état of Napoleon Bonaparte and the subsequent restoration of the monarchy in France, overt state censorship of the press became the norm over the next eight decades. Thus, the particular French notion of journalistic autonomy was crucially influenced by this long formative period in which the French press was highly censored, and the early journalistic heroes were of necessity also political dissidents, some of whom were imprisoned or killed for attempting to exercise their metier. If the American press also remained highly partisan (closely allied to the major political parties) through the nineteenth century,[52] the stakes were not nearly as high. Somewhat less elitist (and certainly less literary and stylized) than its French counterpart at the outset, the US press even while retaining its partisan allegiances became significantly more populist, information oriented – and commercially profitable – beginning in the 1830s with the advent of the so-called penny press.[53] These developments did not go unnoticed in France, and a few enterprising businessmen, particularly Emile de Girardin, France's major press baron who dominated the French press from 1828 until his death in 1881, looked toward the United States and England and saw in their rising popular, apolitical, and sensationalistic press a particu-larly profitable model of journalism that might also thrive even under the threat of censorship. This politically opportunistic advocacy of information-oriented newspapers only led many French journalists and intellectuals to celebrate all the more the virtues of a literary, opinionated, and politically engaged press.[54]

If this US–French distinction between a journalism of facts and one of ideas was thus established early on, a distinctive American justification of information-oriented journalism around the notion of "objectivity" was not consolidated until at least the 1920s. While it does seem to correlate with an increasing dependence on advertisers rather than readers for funding, as well as the creation of local monopoly newspaper markets, Schudson argues that the rise of the objectivity doctrine also had much to do with the broader Progressive political and intellectual movement in the United States which stressed the value of rationalized social scientific and public administrative expertise.[55] With the launching of journalism schools and professional awards such as the Pulitzer prizes, American journalists increasingly sought to rationalize their professional practice, set standards for journalistic excellence, and raise their public prestige.

Another prerequisite for this kind of "objective" nonpartisan (which is not to say nonideological) journalism seems to be a relatively high degree of elite political consensus in the society. Although the United States was certainly riven by regional, race, and even class differences, political opposition was relatively well maintained within a broad ideological acceptance of the governmental system and the capitalist economy. In France, however, a highly "polarized pluralistic"[56] political system made adopting a neutral position outside and above the fray virtually impossible. When it was finally granted a measure of autonomy from the state during the Third Republic, with the passage of a new press law in 1881, an "independent" French press found itself on the shaky ground of a tenuous republican political consensus still very much threatened by antidemocratic currents on both the right (Monarchists, and later Fascists) and to a lesser extent the left (Communists, after 1920). Among these factions there was very little mutual trust, and the press continued to be seen as an appropriate means, in which lies, bribes, and scandal were acceptable, to attain mutually exclusive political ends. Because the parties themselves differed so fundamentally, the press was not allowed to avoid choosing sides and thus remained politicized even as it became more commercialized.

This process repeated itself after World War II, when most of the major French newspapers were not allowed to reopen because of their collaboration with the pro-Nazi Vichy regime. In fact, the whole notion of a commercial press was once again discredited because of this collaboration, and this reopened a new era for an engaged, politicized press, which continued in its "purest" form at least through the mid-1970s, with Jean-Paul Sartre's founding of *Libération*. Postwar legislation sought to protect the French press's independence against capitalist concentration and commercial pressure, laying the groundwork as well for an entirely state-owned television sector that endured, more or less in the same form, until the early 1980s.[57]

Of course, the United States did not experience anything like this level of internal political upheaval during the twentieth century. Commercialization has proceeded steadily, as has widespread acceptance of the professional ideal of objective journalism.

with the adoption of a Nielsen-style audience rating system, the privatization of the largest public television channel (TF1), and the creation of new commercial channels, all during the mid-1980s. It was these barely decade-old changes that Bourdieu criticized in *On Television*, providing the basis for his argument that the journalistic field was not only being fundamentally transformed but was modifying the relations of power throughout French society.

While increasing commercialism (if perhaps somewhat overstated in the case of France) is a reality, comparative and historical research suggests continuity as much as change. Distinctive differences endure, certainly in French ways of practicing journalism (e.g., a lesser concern with "sourcing" every fact or opinion included in a story),[59] in the final presentation of the journalistic "product" (e.g., greater mixing of editorials, cartoons, interviews, and news stories on the same pages), and in the mixing of news and opinion within articles.[60] Even as *Le Monde* was solidifying a partnership to publish a weekly supplement of the *New York Times*, in English, *Times* journalists in Paris interviewed in 2002 generally echoed the views of foreign journalists stationed in Paris of an earlier generation: that French journalists were more concerned with "writing style" and "expressing their opinions" than in digging up "facts."[61]

To the extent that Bourdieu has overstated the extent of change in French journalism due to either increasing commercialism or American influence,[62] I want to suggest it is only because he did not take seriously his own admonition against committing the "short-circuit fallacy," that is, eliminating serious consideration of the intermediary social space of the field that operates according to "its own logic."[63] *On Television*, while paying close attention to internal dynamics of the journalistic field, primarily shows us how journalistic practices *reflect* or at least *accommodate* themselves to commercial imperatives. What is missing from this analysis is the crucial question of how these practices also serve to *refract* or even *resist* such external pressures.

Can we say no more than that field internal "logics" will tend to persist even when conditions external to the field change? Even if we were so limited, this discovery represents a significant improvement to existing theories of news production. Precisely because the sociology of news has failed to take note of the mezzolevel institutional environment of the field – a social space with its own specific logic and a potential capacity to resist external pressures – it has not been able to explain why widespread commercialization does not always lead to wholesale change. In other words, the precise form that a specific journalistic capital takes – e.g., the valorization of opinion and style in France, of information in the United States – *does* help explain continuity in cross-national variation. *Generally* speaking, this part of the puzzle must remain rooted in the historical particular.

However, this question can be reformulated in more general, variable terms, in terms of what has sometimes been called "cultural inertia"[64] : Under what conditions does the semiautonomous logic of fields prove more or less powerful in resisting external pressures? Drawing on Bourdieu's general model, one could posit that those national journalistic fields which have been able to institutionalize "negative sanctions" against heteronomous practices (those originating in an external institutional logic, whether the political, economic, or even religious or activist fields) and "positive incitements to resistance and even open struggle against those in power" will be more likely to maintain continuity in their professional practices over time.[65] Bourdieu mentions these aspects only as "indicators" of a field's autonomy; he does not explain how and why they might emerge. But one implication surely seems that reform movements such as that on behalf of "public journalism" in the United States or efforts to create and maintain journalism schools, awards for journalistic excellence, ombudsperson positions and/or critical journalism reviews may have a significant semiautonomous power to shape the news.[66] Likewise, in France, "journalists' corporations" which emerged out of a professional reform movement in the 1960s continue to sometimes exert a countervailing pressure against market or political pressures inside individual newsrooms.[67]

Such hypotheses must remain at this point only exploratory. The notion of field "inertia" needs to be developed so that it is not simply tautologous, that is, used as a catch-all explanation for those cases when change does *not* occur. Change obviously does occur sometimes; indeed, the set of practices and norms surrounding the ideal of "objectivity" in American journalism represents one such change (from a previous more openly partisan approach). The challenge remains to specify why some fields – in some national contexts, historical periods, or particular endeavors – are more resistant than others to changes induced by heteronomous pressures.

Morphological and Demographic Factors

For Bourdieu, individual morphological and demographic factors – number of agents entering the field in relation to available positions, social characteristics, education and training, etc. – are also central to understanding reproduction and change within fields. As noted at the outset, finding data from two national settings that accurately measure the same phenomena is a major challenge for cross-national research. It poses a particular problem for morphological data, since national categories of educational attainment, class, and other individual characteristics are rarely equivalent. With these caveats in mind, I present here a portion of the available statistics.

Bourdieu seems to make three kinds of morphological claims. First, he emphasizes processes of distinction. Since to exist in a field is to mark one's difference, every new generation of journalists (as with other cultural producers) has an incentive to "import innovation regarding products or techniques of production."[68] This process thus helps account for the appearance of constant change within the field, and indeed "appearance" is the key word here. This continual process of distinction is unlikely to transform the field, Bourdieu insists, unless aided by transformations in neighboring fields or in the society as a whole.[69]

A second claim is that a simple increase in the number of individual cultural producers in the field, as well as an increase in the volume of the "audience of readers and spectators" will have transformative effects.[70] For the journalistic field, one field study suggests that a massive increase in the sheer number of new entrants attempting to find positions contributes to increased job insecurity, thus strengthening the hand of economic power over journalists as a whole.[71] Various indicators show that competition for jobs within the journalistic field is quite high in both countries, and has intensified in recent years. In the United States, the gap between the number of journalism jobs and the number of students enrolled in university journalism/mass communication programs has significantly widened. While the number of mainstream news media jobs increased by only 10,000 between 1982 and 1992 (from 112,000 to 122,000), total enrollment of students in journalism programs during the same time period increased more than 50,000 (from 91,000 to 143,000).[72] Since the early 1990s, reflecting a shift toward more "flexible labor," US newspaper, television and radio newsrooms have engaged in mass firings, reducing the number of journalistic positions available. In France, research has also demonstrated a massive increase in journalistic "job precarity," that is, the percentage of journalists who are hired only on a part-time or freelance basis, from about 5 percent in the 1970s to 17.9 percent in 1999.[73]

Finally, Bourdieu has emphasized the particular class composition of morphological shifts. On the one hand, he suggests that "deviant trajectories" – in particular, individuals who experience downward mobility – are a major source of mismatch between disposition (habitus) and (field) position that may threaten to unsettle a field.[74] But since such deviant trajectories are quite rare, field theory largely emphasizes how the social and educational attributes of new journalists serve primarily to reproduce the field. Systematic, direct information about the class backgrounds of journalists is scarce for both France[75] and the United States – in part because of the difficulties inherent in asking such questions, in part, perhaps because of the doxic assumption of journalists and many social scientific researchers that class no longer matters. Educational background often serves as a rough proxy for class. According to the most readily available survey data, US journalists as a whole are more likely to have a university bachelor's degree (or its equivalent) than their French counterparts.[76] Relative to average societal education levels (in terms of years of study, at least), journalists in the two countries are more closely comparable.[77] At the elite national media outlets, moreover, American and French journalists are both disproportionately recruited from elite institutions of higher education, such as "Sciences-Po" in France and

Ivy League universities in the United States.[78] As an element in the formation of agents' habitus, specialized education or journalistic professional education offers another potential area for research. Julien Duval (see chapter 7) shows that specialized economic education contributes to decreased intellectual autonomy for business journalists. Of course, the converse can sometimes be true. In his study of foreign correspondents in El Salvador, Mark Pedelty found that journalists "trained in fields other than journalism," such as theology, or art, or even economics, often produced the most in-depth, critical reporting.[79] Conceivably, professional training in journalism could also contribute to field autonomy; however, because access to such training, especially at elite levels (Columbia Journalism School, the Ecole Supérieure de Journalisme in Lille, France), is so powerfully determined by class background, it may just as often reinforce the upper-middle class "bias" of the field.[80]

In sum, aggregate indicators of number and type of agents competing within a field are obviously an important aspect of the *mechanisms* of reproduction and change. But to the extent that such morphological and demographic factors tend to move in the same direction as external pressures, it seems that they provide little in the way of a crucial *additional* explanatory factor. To help us understand and explain cross-national differences in journalistic fields, it may be, in fact, that morphological factors tell us very little. Nevertheless, morphology effects offer a unique and intriguing hypothesis that deserves further testing.

Conclusion

In his field theory, Bourdieu has emphasized "general properties"; it seems reasonable to suppose that such properties may also encompass variation. Cross-national research, by comparing the broad systematic characteristics of fields and field configurations, brings this kind of variation to the fore. Moreover, it can help us begin to sort out which properties exert the most powerful effects on journalistic production. Of course, a comparison with an N of 2 that varies on multiple factors cannot provide definitive answers to such questions. But I have hoped to show how a French-American comparison extends field theory, and in the process, modifies many of the assumptions in the sociology of news.

We began by noting that the French and American press differed on several important dimensions. French journalistic discourse tends to include a greater mix of information and opinion, to feature a wider range of ideologies, and to do more to promote political participation. Conversely, despite the serious reputation of such newspapers as *Le Monde*, observers have noted the extent to which the French national press dramatically constructs a "political spectacle," to borrow Murray Edelman's term.

Distinctive political field constraints, both restrictive and enabling – and, contra Bourdieu, clearly distinguished from economic field constraints – help explain the more politicized and ideologically diverse character of the French press. The unique historical formations and subsequent trajectories of the journalistic fields in France and the United States created a set of practices and norms, both codified and uncodified, that would seem to provide some level of resistance against external (primarily economic) inducements for change, also helping to explain the persistent character of differences between the journalism of France and the United States.

Lesser dependence on advertising and lesser profit pressures could conceivably explain the French press's greater civic orientation and ideological diversity, although one could quickly name even less commercialized (and more state dominated) media systems that are not particularly civic or diverse. The relationship at best, then, is diffuse. Moreover, those French news outlets that are the most commercialized along the American "model" (*Le Figaro*, even TF1) retain many distinctive characteristics of French journalism, including a greater focus on ideas and a greater mixing of fact and commentary.

On the other hand, spatial and temporal properties of journalistic fields significantly extend the power of economic models, in effect, showing how a less commercialized French journalistic field (in terms of advertising and ownership structure) could actually produce a more dramatized, event driven political spectacle. Somewhat surprisingly, morphological factors, much emphasized in national field case studies, seem to provide little leverage to explain French–American press differences. To be fair, significant problems exist in constructing comparable statistical indicators for these factors. More research is needed to specify and test the effects of variable morphological properties.

In sum, to put the case most starkly: While previous field research has emphasized how heteronomous economic pressures combined with morphological shifts induce change in journalism (and surrounding fields), an even greater puzzle lies in explaining the limits of such change. The answer to this question seems to lie elsewhere in field theory – in a research project that has scarcely begun – namely, the elaboration of variable kinds of political (state) field pressures, structural–ecological properties, and historical path-dependent processes, which together produce more or less "cultural inertia" within the journalistic field.

Notes

1 In *On Television* (New Press, New York, 1998), Bourdieu rarely mentions the specificity of the French journalistic field, with the exception of a footnote in which he notes that the field was initially organized around an opposition between the "literary field," which placed the greatest emphasis on style, and the "political field," in which partisan engagements mattered most (p. 94, fn. 4).

2 Pierre Albert, *La Presse française* (La Documentation française, Paris, 1998), p. 41. See also Erik Neveu, *Sociologie du journalisme* (La Découverte, Paris, 2001), pp. 12–16.

3 Based on a paragraph by paragraph analysis by Rodney Benson and Mauro Porto of *Le Monde*, *Le Figaro*, and the *New York Times* (a total of 626 articles from the French press and 358 articles from the US press), 19 percent of paragraphs in the French newspapers offered interpretation and opinion versus 5 percent of paragraphs in the *New York Times*. French news stories also offered more background contextual information. The proportions changed little between the 1965–7 and 1995–7 samples. Other findings reported in Daniel Hallin and Paolo Mancini, *Comparing Media Systems* (Cambridge University Press, Cambridge, 2004), p. 99. See Daniel Hallin and Rodney Benson, "Two models of political journalism: the French and American news media, 1965–1997," unpublished manuscript (2003) available from authors.

4 See Rodney Benson, "Shaping the Public Sphere: Journalistic Fields and Immigration Debates in the United States and France, 1973–1994," PhD Dissertation in Sociology, University of California, Berkeley, 2000; and "The Mediated Public Sphere: A Model for Cross-National Research," Working Paper #2001–7, Center for the Study of Culture, Organizations and Politics, University of California, Berkeley, August 2001, available at http://ist-socrates.berkeley.edu/~iir/culture/papers.html. My argument that the French press is more "dramatized" is based on the more dramatic visual and headline formulas used by *Libération* and since the mid-1990s, by *Le Monde* (*Libération* editor Serge July once proclaimed that his goal was to capture the "emotion of the news") as well as by French

national newspapers' relatively strong "crisis orientation." See Jean-Claude Perrier, *Le Roman vrai de "Libération"* (Editions Juilliard, Paris, 1994), p. 201; and J.W. Freiberg, *The French Press: Class, State, and Ideology* (Praeger, New York, 1981), p. 223.

5 In their 1988 comparison of French and US television news coverage of presidential political campaigns, Gerstlé et al. found that French television news focused more than twice as often on comparing the candidates' positions on the issues and also offered slightly more general issues background. See Jacques Gerstlé, Dennis K. Davis, and Olivier Duhamel, "Television News and the Construction of Political Reality in France and the United States," in *Mediated Politics in Two Cultures: Presidential Campaigning in the United States and France*, eds. L.L. Kaid, J. Gerstlé, and K.R. Sanders (Praeger, New York, 1991), pp. 119–43.

6 See, e.g., Ben Bagdikian, *The Media Monopoly*, 4th ed. (Beacon Press, Boston, 1992), pp. 17, 204–5; and Mark Pedelty, *War Stories: The Culture of Foreign Correspondents* (Routledge, London, 1995), pp. 9–12, and 219–30.

7 See, e.g., Pierre Bourdieu, "Social Space and Symbolic Space," in *Practical Reason* (Polity, Cambridge, 1998, and Stanford University Press, Stanford, CA, 1998), pp. 1–14.

8 For a discussion of the importance of making this epistemological break with "immediate knowledge" in the construction and subsequent carrying out of any research project, a notion influenced by the philosopher Gaston Bachelard, see Pierre Bourdieu, Jean-Claude Chamboredon, and Jean-Claude Passeron, *The Craft of Sociology* (de Gruyter, New York, 1991). For an elaboration of how cross-national comparative media research "cosmopolitanizes, opening our eyes to communication patterns and problems unnoticeable in our own spatial and temporal milieux," see Jay G. Blumler, Jack M. McLeod, and Karl Erik Rosengren, "An Introduction to Comparative Communication Research," in *Comparatively Speaking: Communication and Culture Across Space and Time*, eds. J.G. Blumler, J.M. McLeod, and K.E. Rosengren (Sage, Newbury Park, CA, 1992), pp. 3–18.

9 Pierre Bourdieu and Loïc J.D. Wacquant, *An Invitation to Reflexive Sociology* (University of Chicago Press, Chicago, 1992 and Polity, Cambridge, 1992), p. 75.

10 Bourdieu and Wacquant, *An Invitation to Reflexive Sociology*, p. 75.

11 Bourdieu declares at one point, "I believe indeed that there are no transhistoric laws of the relations between fields, that we must investigate each historical case separately" (*An Invitation to Reflexive Sociology*, p. 109). But see David Swartz, *Culture and Power: The Sociology of Pierre Bourdieu* (University of Chicago Press, Chicago, 1997), who suggests conversely that "in his zeal to distinguish his work from grand social theory in the tradition of Parsons and Althusser, Bourdieu

downplays the systemic character of his own thought and work" (p. 135).

12 Bourdieu and Wacquant, *An Invitation to Reflexive Sociology*, p. 77.

13 Bourdieu, *On Television*, p. 16.

14 See Jean-Marie Charon, *La Presse magazine* (La Découverte, Paris, 1999).

15 Valérie Devillard, Marie-Françoise Lafosse, Christine Leteinturier, and Rémy Rieffel, *Les Journalistes français à l'aube de l'an 2000: Profils et parcours* (Panthéon-Assas, Paris, 2001), p. 28.

16 Albert, *La presse française*, p. 81 (1990 edition) and p. 83 (1998 edition).

17 See Ronnie Dugger, "The Corporate Domination of Journalism," in *The Business of Journalism*, ed. W. Serrin (The New Press, New York, 2000), pp. 26–56. Some US newspapers, including the *New York Times*, issue a second class of controlling voting stock limited to members of the publishing family precisely in order to preserve some independence from profit pressures.

18 See Ignacio Ramonet, "*Le Monde*, la Bourse et nous," *Le Monde diplomatique*, December 2001. However, legal loopholes exist. *Le Monde* director Jean-Marie Colombani secured the assent of the newspaper's journalists to allow a limited sale of public shares, a move which has now been postponed indefinitely (see Rodney Benson, "'La fin du *Monde?*' Tradition and Change in the French Press," *French Politics, Culture & Society*, 22, 1, spring 2004, pp. 108–26). Socpresse, the owner of *Le Figaro* and *L'Express*, was recently purchased by Dassault, a French electronics and aeronautics company traded on the US NASDAQ exchange. Notably, however, Serge Dassault, head of the company, has expressed his interest in owning newspapers in political/ideological rather than profit-oriented terms: "For me, it's important to own a newspaper in order to express my opinion as well as to be able to respond to certain [critical] journalists." From "Dassault prend le contrôle de la Socpresse," *Le Monde*, March 11, 2004.

19 "*Le Figaro* s'offre une nouvelle formule pour enrayer la baisse des ventes," *La Tribune*, November 29, 1999, p. 20.

20 Jacques Steinberg, "New Editor of the Baltimore Sun Becomes a Lightning Rod Again," *New York Times*, January 12, 2004, p. C-1. Figure refers to the US standard calculation of earnings before interest, taxes, depreciation and amortization.

21 Source: Hoover's Online company profiles, accessed January 30, 2004.

22 See Michael Schudson, "The 'Public Sphere' and its Problems: Bringing the State (Back) In," *Notre Dame Journal of Law, Ethics & Public Policy*, 8 (1994), p. 539. For a specific elaboration of these points in relation to the journalistic field, see Rodney Benson, "Bringing the Sociology of Media Back In," *Political Communication*, 21 (2004), pp. 275–92.

23 Bourdieu (*An Invitation to Reflexive Sociology*, p. 77) alludes to such spatial elements in a discussion of how one might go about comparing the academic fields in France and the United States: "one would need to take into consideration another difference: the specificity of the very structure of the American political field, characterized, very cursorily, by federalism, the multiplication of and conflicts between different levels of decision making."

24 Devillard et al., *Les Journalistes français*, p. 67. In comparison, the Northeast (with New York and Boston) is home to just 19.8 percent of all US journalists. See David H. Weaver and G. Cleveland Wilhoit, *The American Journalist in the 1990s: US News People at the End of an Era* (Lawrence Erlbaum Associates, Mahwah, NJ, 1996), p. 7.

25 Source: *Bilan de la société privée TF1* (Conseil supérieur de l'audiovisuel, Paris, 2000).

26 Nearly twice as many persons in the United States are regular viewers of local rather than network television news (56 versus 30 percent). Viewing of all forms of television news has decreased in the 1990s, while use of "online" news has increased, with 15 percent reporting daily use in 2000. See The Pew Research Center for the People and the Press, Survey Report, "Internet Sapping Broadcast News Audience," June 11, 2000.

27 See Michael Schudson, *The Sociology of News* W. W. Norton, New York, 2003, p. 110.

28 For instance, competition among newsmagazines like *Newsweek*, *Time*, and *US News and World Report* as well as among local television news programs and the national cable news channels may sometimes approximate the competitive conditions of the French national journalistic field. Conversely, France's regional press, the total circulation of which is much larger than the national press (though it tends to be insignificant in generating national news), is largely organized around local monopolies as is the rule in the United States, and audiences for the national press are partially segmented by class or political leaning.

29 My assessment of the "subjective" feel of the US and French journalistic fields is based on interviews with journalists and observations inside newsrooms at the *Los Angeles Times* and *Orange County Register* (spring 1998), *Le Monde* (spring 1997, 1998, and 2002), *Libération* (1997 and 1998), *Le Figaro* (1997), and France 2 (1997 and 1998).

30 As Swartz notes (*Culture and Power*, p. 215), Bourdieu's field theory largely ignores organizations or organizational dynamics per se. Yet such a focus would seem to be a logical extension of the individual-level morphological aspects Bourdieu often emphasizes. In a classic article in the social problems constructivist tradition, Stephen Hilgartner and Charles L. Bosk ("The Rise and Fall of Social Problems: A Public Arenas Model," *American Journal of Sociology*, 94 [1998], p.

71) posit that "the smaller the carrying capacity of an arena is (ceteris paribus), the more intense the competition." One could argue that because of lesser advertising, French newspapers print fewer pages and therefore have lesser carrying capacity than advertising-saturated, multisectioned newspapers.

31 Benson, "Bringing the Sociology of Media Back In."

32 See Rodney Benson, "Field theory in comparative context: a new paradigm for media studies," *Theory and Society*, 29 (1999), pp. 482–3. Elsewhere, I suggest that

> the journalistic field could be seen as structured around an opposition between a cultural/state–civic pole on one side and an economic/state–market pole on the other. Autonomous cultural power would thus be seen to be crucially dependent on state subsidies, direct or indirect. But likewise, the dependence of economic power on the state, as in the case of privatizations, tax and monetary policies, would also be crucially acknowledged. Such a change in the model would also express the extent to which the state itself is not a singular entity, and in a very real sense is divided among and within its various agencies and elected bodies. Journalistic autonomy would consist precisely in the professional and organizational balancing of these two opposing poles.

See Rodney Benson, "News Media as a 'Journalistic Field': What Bourdieu adds to New Institutionalism and Vice Versa," *Political Communication* (under review).

33 See Benson, "Field theory in comparative context . . ." pp. 482–3.

34 Pierre Bourdieu, "Rethinking the State: Genesis and Structure of the Bureaucratic Field," *Sociological Theory*, 12, 1 (March 1994), pp. 1–18, esp. p. 7. See also Pierre Bourdieu, *Propos sur le champ politique* (Presses universitaires de Lyon, Lyons, 2000) and David Swartz, "The Social Basis of Symbolic Power: Bourdieu's Political Sociology," Paper presented to the American Sociological Association national conference, August 2000.

35 On the state as "primary definer," see Stuart Hall, Chas Critcher, T ony Jefferson, Tony Clarke, and Brian Roberts, *Policing the Crisis* (Holmes & Meier Publishers, New York, 1978). For recent research (drawing upon Bourdieu's notions of multiple forms of capital) showing the limited capacity of the state and other powerful actors to impose their symbolic definitions upon "mediated" reality, see Aeron Davis, *Public Relations Democracy: Public Relations, Politics and the Mass Media in Britain* (Manchester University Press, Manchester, UK, 2002).

36 See W.R. Runciman, *Treatise on Social Theory* (Cambridge University Press, Cambridge, vol. 2, 1989) and the discussion of Runciman in Nicholas Garnham, *Emancipation, the Media, and Modernity* (Oxford University Press, New York, 2000), pp. 25–6.

37 In highlighting these two distinct types of state constraints, I draw upon and revise Raymond Kuhn's (*The Media in France*, Routledge, London, 1995, p. 49) fourfold typology of state roles. See also Hallin and Mancini, *Comparing Media Systems*, pp. 41–4.
38 See, e.g., Antoine de Tarlé, "The Press and the State in France," in *Newspapers and Democracy*, ed. A. Smith (MIT Press, Cambridge, MA, 1980); and Emmanuel Derieux, *Droit de la Communication* (LGDJ, Paris, 1994), pp. 424–40. For French journalists' own conception of state constraints, see Bertrand Le Gendre, "La Justice gendarme de la presse; Les Tribunaux sont de plus en plus sévères à l'encontre des journalistes poursuivis pour diffamation," *Le Monde*, November 20, 1991, p. 1.
39 See Hallin and Mancini, *Comparing Media Systems*, p. 230.
40 See C. Edwin Baker, *Media, Markets and Democracy* (Cambridge University Press, Cambridge, 2002), for a particularly lucid elaboration (and passionate defense) of enabling media policies.
41 Bourdieu, *On Television*, p. 16; see also de Tarlé, "The Press and the State in France," p. 146.
42 See Kuhn, *The Media in France*, esp. pp. 40–2.
43 See, e.g., Timothy E. Cook, *Governing with the News: The News Media as a Political Institution* (University of Chicago Press, Chicago, 1998); and Oscar H. Gandy, Jr., *Beyond Agenda Setting: Information Subsidies and Public Policy* (Ablex, Norwood, NJ, 1982).
44 From Charles Silvestre, "Ivan Levaï n'en finit pas de passer la presse en revue," *L'Humanité*, November 16, 1996.
45 See, e.g., Walter W. Powell, "Expanding the Scope of Institutional Analysis," in *The New Institutionalism in Organizational Analysis*, eds. W.W. Powell and P.J. DiMaggio (University of Chicago Press, Chicago, 1991), pp. 191–4.
46 Pierre Bourdieu, *The Rules of Art: Genesis and Structure of the Literary Field* (Stanford University Press, Stanford, CA, 1995, and Polity, Cambridge, 1996), p. 206.
47 See, in particular, Jean K. Chalaby, "Journalism as an Anglo-American Invention: A Comparison of the Development of French and Anglo-American Journalism, 1830s–1920s," *European Journal of Communication*, 11, 3 (1996), pp. 303–26.
48 Thomas Ferenczi, *L'Invention du journalisme en France* (Plon, Paris, 1993), p. 12.
49 See Thomas C. Leonard, *The Power of the Press: The Birth of American Political Reporting* (Oxford University Press, Oxford, 1986) and Michael B. Palmer, "Les héritiers de Théophraste," in *Les Journalistes*, eds. J.-F. Lacan, M. Palmer, and D. Ruellan (Syros, Paris, 1994).
50 Ferenczi, *L'Invention du journalisme en France*, p. 27.

51 See Richard Barbrook, *Media Freedom: The Contradictions of Communications in the Age of Modernity* (Pluto Press, London, 1995), pp. 10–11.
52 Richard L. Kaplan, *Politics and the American Press: The Rise of Objectivity, 1865–1920* (Cambridge University Press, Cambridge, 2002).
53 Michael Schudson, *Discovering the News: A Social History of American Newspapers* (Basic Books, New York, 1978).
54 See Palmer, "Les Héritiers de Théophraste," pp. 146–58.
55 See Schudson, *Discovering the News*.
56 See Hallin and Mancini, *Comparing Media Systems*, pp. 59–63.
57 On the postwar history of the French print and "audiovisual" press, see Benson, "La Fin du *Monde*?"; Clyde Thogmartin, *The National Daily Press of France* (Summa, Birmingham, AL, 1998); and Kuhn, *The Media in France*.
58 See, e.g., Doug Underwood, *When MBAs Rule the Newsroom* (Columbia University Press, New York, 1995) and Eric Klinenberg, "Media Convergence: Newsrooms, Technology, and Journalistic Production in a Digital Age," unpublished manuscript, 2004.
59 Denis Ruellan, *Le Professionalisme du flou: Identité et savoir-faire des journalistes français* (Presses Universitaires de Grenoble, Grenoble, 1993), p. 202.
60 Rodney Benson, "The political/literary model of French journalism: Change and continuity in immigration coverage, 1973–1991," *Journal of European Area Studies*, 10, 1 (summer 2002), pp. 49–70.
61 See Benson, "La Fin du *Monde*?" p. 119; and Jean G. Padioleau, "Le Journalisme politique à la française: Regards étrangers," *Esprit*, 74 (1983), pp. 147–55, as well as his classic comparative study, *"Le Monde" et le "Washington Post"* (PUF, Paris, 1985).
62 While Bourdieu does not explicitly argue that French journalism has changed due to the influence of American journalism, he implies as much at one point. For a field analysis to be complete, Bourdieu insists, "the position of the national media field within the global media field would have to be taken into account," and he then goes on to specifically cite the "economic-technical, and especially, symbolic dominance of American television, which serves a good many journalists as both a model and a source of ideas, formulas and tactics" (*On Television*, p. 41). Historians (e.g., Ferenczi, *L'Invention du journalisme en France*) have documented an extensive record of French admiration of American journalistic practices, yet invariably conclude that US influence has been only minimal.
63 Bourdieu and Wacquant, *An Invitation to Reflexive Sociology*, p. 69.
64 See Mark A. Schneider, "Does Culture Have Inertia?" *Culture* (Newsletter of the Sociology of Culture Section of the American Sociological Association), 15, 3 (spring 2001).

65 Bourdieu, *The Rules of Art*, p. 220.
66 On the public journalism movement, see Jay Rosen, *What are Journalists For?* (Yale University Press, New Haven, CN, 1999).
67 See, e.g., Thogmartin, *The National Daily Press of France*, pp. 195–203.
68 Bourdieu, *The Rules of Art*, p. 225.
69 Pierre Bourdieu, *The Field of Cultural Production* (Columbia University Press, New York, 1993, and Polity, Cambridge, 1993), pp. 57–8.
70 Bourdieu, *The Rules of Art*, pp. 225, 232.
71 Gilles Balbastre, "Une information précaire," *Actes de la recherche en sciences sociales*, 131–2 (March 2000), pp. 76–85.
72 Statistics from Weaver and Wilhoit, *The American Journalist in the 1990s*, p. 31. A significant portion of US university journalism students intend to and eventually do find jobs outside of journalism, primarily in public relations and advertising. See David H. Weaver, "Journalism Education in the United States," in *Journalism Education in Europe and North America: An International Comparison*, eds. R. Fröhlich and C. Holtz-Bacha (Hampton Press, Cresskill, NJ, 2003), p. 52.
73 Devillard et al., *Les Journalistes français*, p. 40.
74 Pierre Bourdieu, *The State Nobility* (Stanford University Press, Stanford, CA, 1996, and Polity, Cambridge, 1996), pp. 183–6.
75 Dominique Marchetti and Denis Ruellan, *Devenir Journalistes: Sociologie de l'entrée sur le marché du travail* (La Documentation française, Paris, 2001), p. 10.
76 Ninety percent of US journalists aged 25–34 in Weaver and Wilhoit's survey had a bachelor's degree or higher, whereas 61 percent of French journalists in Marchetti and Ruellan's study of "new" French journalists (62 percent of whom were 25–34; 78 percent of whom were 22–34) had a French license degree or higher. See Weaver and Wilhoit, *The American Journalist in the 1990s*, pp. 34–7; Marchetti and Ruellan, *Devenir Journalistes*, pp. 20, 25.
77 Eleven percent of the total French active population have a license degree or higher (Marchetti and Ruellan, *Devenir Journalistes*, p. 25), while about 25 percent of American adults have a bachelor's degree. This journalist–public gap suggests another line of field research, documenting the relationship between class demographics of particular news outlets and their publics. For instance, a 1999 French census study showed that regular readership of national newspapers (twice or more per week) varied sharply by educational background: While 30 percent of persons with more than two years education after the baccalauréat (somewhat more advanced than a high school degree) were regular readers, the figure dropped sharply to 5 percent for those with "no diploma" ("Le lectorat de la presse d'information générale," INSEE Premiere, No. 753, Dec. 2000).
78 See, e.g., Rémy Rieffel, *L'Elite des journalistes* (PUF, Paris, 1984).

79 Pedelty, *War Stories*, p. 229.
80 See Weaver, "Journalism Education in the United States," and Jean-Marie Charon, "Journalist Training in France," in *Journalism Education in Europe and North America*, pp. 49–64, 139–67.

Notes to table 89

[a] Percentages are calculated from raw data on 2003 domestic advertising expenditures in major media (print press, television, radio, cinema, outdoor, internet) and on Gross Domestic Product.
[b] All French major national newspapers are based in Paris.
[c] An additional 3.2 million households subscribed to satellite television (in part because cable is not available in their area), for a combined cable/satellite percentage of 27.4 percent.
[d] 1,352 combined UHF and VHF commercial stations, and 381 combined UHF and VHF "educational" stations.

6

The Contaminated Blood Scandal: Reframing Medical News

Patrick Champagne and Dominique Marchetti

New technologies and the increasing commercialization of news production have profoundly transformed the structure and functioning of the journalistic field. They have also increased the influence that the news media hold over a number of social universes. In particular, the miniaturization of news equipment and the speed with which information can be transmitted allow journalists to work "in real time" and therefore to be actors in as well as witnesses to the events that they cover. This omnipresence and increased power of the media have imposed themselves as an unavoidable given that each institution and group in society has had to confront, either by using the media, integrating its effects into the very functioning of these fields, or, conversely, by more clearly drawing the limits and attempting to reestablish the borders threatened by the intrusion of journalism.

A Very Media-Friendly Epidemic

Science news, and specifically health news, is in this regard a particularly interesting domain inasmuch as it obliges one to pose very forcefully the question of the limits of journalism. Who, in fact, is competent to speak in the mainstream media about science or medicine? Are there legitimate limits to the mediatization of this kind of information?[1]

Until the mid-1980s, medical information, whether clinical or research oriented, had been subject to certain controls by French medical authorities. It was seen as not suitable for "typical media treatment" not only because it requires at least some minimum specialized expertise, but also because premature publication of inaccurate information could upset doctor/patient relations. In the mid-1980s, however, AIDS, and its probably inevitable mediatization, fundamentally called into question the earlier institutions for handling medical information, that is, the tremendous control that recognized medical institutions held over its publication.

From the very beginning, what was at first only a marginal, bizarre illness attracted the curiosity of a few young medical reporters. This story about a strange sickness that began by selectively striking homosexuals in the United States included several elements that have always tended to fascinate both journalists and their publics: sex, mystery, and death. The gradual spread of the illness beyond the United States and the initially affected social groups, followed by the progressive awakening to the extent and gravity of what was becoming an epidemic, forced healthcare officials to implement new policies and to raise public awareness through media campaigns.

Then, several dramatic events began to dominate front page coverage in the mainstream press: the scientific controversy (with its economic implications) between professors Gallo and Montagnier concerning who had first discovered the virus, the "publicity effects" of supposedly effective vaccines or drugs, discussions around screening tests or prevention campaigns based on condoms, the emotional effects of the AIDS-related deaths of several celebrities (whose heretofore hidden homosexuality was thus suddenly revealed), and last but not least, the "contaminated blood scandal."

For several years during the early 1980s, before the HIV virus had even been identified and effective tests had become available, blood concentrates contaminated with HIV were distributed to about 3,500 hemophiliacs across France, as elsewhere. Yet, as early as 1984, new concentrates began to be sold by foreign companies which had been treated so as to deactivate the virus. By March 1985, the administration of the Centre National de la Transfusion Sanguine (national center for blood transfusions – CNTS) came to realize that all its concentrates were potentially contaminated, yet it continued to prescribe them (at least to some patients) until September 1985. Some patients considered that this constituted a scandal since the healthcare authorities distributed what they knew to be contaminated and thus potentially deadly concentrates. Since their efforts at governmental redress failed, they turned to journalists, who amplified and sometimes distorted the issues at stake.

To describe the scandal as a social construction is in no sense to deny the tragedy experienced by French hemophiliacs. It is only to acknowledge that the specific form that this problem took in the media was crucially shaped by other factors, as well as the fact that magnitude of the problem is no guarantee of press and thus public attention. In other European countries, like Spain, blood transfusions caused the infection and death of hundreds of hemophiliacs, yet the tragedy did not have the impact it did in France. Thus, the objective fact of the infection of innocent victims does not mechanically trigger a "scandal." The latter emerges from the combination of mobilizations (of the victims, the media), as well as a set of institutions (the statist character of the French blood system implicating politicians), the profile of the victims (a large share of Spanish hemophiliacs belonging to the stigmatized Gypsy population), etc.[2] Our approach also permits us to examine the contaminated blood scandal's broad societal effects, that is, how it both reflected and served as an agent of a wide-ranging transformation in the relationship of the journalistic field with the medical field, and ultimately with the whole spectrum of relatively autonomously social spaces.

If the press played an important role in the social response to this epidemic, it is because the very newness of this illness, the means by which it is transmitted and its extreme gravity left the field open to stereotypes that the media could either amplify or, on the contrary, combat. It is also because, once its means of transmission were known, the struggle against the epidemic was fought in key ways through the mass media inasmuch as, in the absence of any effective treatment, information concerning the means of contamination was an essential element in prevention. In short, like it or not, a veritable public health mission had been thrust upon the journalistic field.

When one considers the history of AIDS from the point of view of its media coverage in France, what is surprising is the contrast between the early years of the epidemic and the period after 1985. Whereas one might have expected to see an initial phase marked by media coverage that played up the fears and fantasies of society as a whole and a second phase characterized by the progressive mastering of the epidemic and increasingly restrained coverage, one actually observes nearly the opposite. During the early years, the mainstream press practiced almost astonishing restraint, notably resisting efforts by the extreme right to politicize the disease and stigmatize or exclude those suffering from it. Beginning in 1985, all that would begin to change.

On the one hand, actual research seemed to be marking time, since the scientific community was riven by internal struggles. On the other hand, sensationalistic stories proliferated with the media's systematic search for scandals around the epidemic. Gradually, AIDS became a topic of journalistic interest just like any other, that is, one that did not require special treatment, nor any particular seriousness, nor any greater responsibility for the accuracy of the news that journalists reported. In the name of "freedom of the press," any opinion, or nearly any, was considered acceptable thus allowing one to say and publish anything, with the sole proviso that a "right to rebut" or discretely rectify incorrect information also be respected. Many doctors and researchers deplored the climate this created around AIDS. Specialized medical reporters saw the coverage of the epidemic fall into the hands of political reporters or other reporters with no medical or scientific expertise, those, in other words who were only interested in uncovering the latest scoop.

Political and Scientific News

If scientists, like political officials, have always attempted to control the news that concerned them, it has generally been for diametrically opposed reasons. For politicians, the media is effectively one of the tools they use in their struggles. Thus, if political actors attempt to control journalists, it is less in order to keep them away from their games than it is to use them more effectively. The specifically political means of domination and the struggle to get elected rely to a great extent upon the use of symbols designed to impose a political vision of the world through the mainstream news media.

What varies, according to the political and media systems in question, is the type of rapport which is created between the agents of the political and media fields, the control that the political leaders can exert upon the press, which run from overtaking its very means of production, to the indirect and therefore always uncertain control exerted today through public relations experts who, at the behest of their clients, put together press packets and even events for the use of journalists. Politicians and journalists are in an instrumental relationship, an almost structural situation of mutual dependence; they are destined to collaborate on the production of news. This is an ambiguous relationship which often oscillates between admiration and contempt, friendship and animosity, submission and revolt. In France, the border which separates politics from political journalism is unclear and forever being crossed: journalists may legitimately serve a given politician or party, and politicians become journalists. The respective interests of the agents of these two social universes often converge, both benefiting from the production of news. One can see this in particular in the increase in exposés, scoops, interviews, or "exclusives" whose political benefit pushes politicians to increase the number of statements they make following the Mertonian logic of the self-fulfilling prophecy or that of the "official discourse" and its performative effects.[3]

In contrast, for the agents of the scientific field and, more generally, of the intellectual field, the press is not an adequate forum for debate, the preferred spaces being those of peer-reviewed journals and volumes edited by respected figures which serve the dual purpose of filtering out and consecrating research. The scholarly community attempts to retain its autonomy by keeping journalists away from its internal battles. The scientific field only recognizes its own internal standards and controls its members' careers by maintaining a monopoly on their consecration. It expects journalists to limit themselves to issuing official information, that is, information which is guaranteed by a scholarly institution. Additionally, scientific news is not suitable for scoops and journalistic sensationalism because it takes time for discoveries in this domain to be confirmed, understood, and recognized by the scientific community. The scientific community limits itself, most of the time, to policing the accuracy of the information that appears in the mainstream press. Any interest that the media may occasionally take in the most recognized members of the scientific community often makes a certain amount of publicity necessary (interviews, articles, photo shoots), which is in direct opposition to scientific activity and even detrimental to it. As the French Nobel prize winner Georges Charpak, who since his nomination had been lured from his laboratory by "the call of society," recently declared in a humorous outburst: "I am tired of living Madonna's life for the past year!"

The suspicion that scientists display with regard to the media, often denouncing the titles of articles that they judge to be sensationalistic and the oversimplifications they contain, is thus of a structural nature: it expresses the autonomy of this field, of its theories and methods, and displays a desire to retain and reinforce the border which separates the scientific community from the press and from the public at large.

What is more, discoveries which the scientific community considers important are not necessarily of interest to the media in so far as they do not always have direct consequences or applications that can be immediately recognized by the public. Journalists can lend disproportionate importance to certain discoveries or figures by the simple fact that they are more "newsworthy" than others. It is to escape this tendency toward distortion that scientific information usually remains under the control of experts, that is, either the scientists themselves or journalists with some scientific competence who at least respect the scientific community. Scientists' direct access to the mass media is itself relatively controlled by the scientific community, which punishes those who make use of it without respecting the internal hierarchies of this field, namely, the official scientific authorities.

Journalistic activity is in many ways opposed to the rules which regulate the functioning of the scientific field. The competition between journalists is subject to little regulation; the race for news often encourages premature or inaccurate statements. Errors are rarely subject to spontaneous or highly visible rectifications because these would damage the credibility of the journalists as well as the economic interests of the newspapers for which they write. In contrast, in their professional capacity, scientists entertain many different hypotheses, that is, often false but potentially fecund ideas. Publication is, however, closely controlled because the scientific field must clearly mark the limit that separates untested ideas from those that are scientifically established. If the tentative, unverified hypotheses of ongoing research are both indispensable and legitimate within the space of the laboratory, they seem much less so in the mass-mediated public space. By conferring such external notoriety upon research-in-progress, the media risk upsetting the normal functioning of the scientific field.

Institutional News

Scientific institutional monopolization of the production and public diffusion of scientific information has been further reinforced in the sectors of medicine and medical research where a professional order exists as well as a rigidly hierarchical internal power structure. What is more, the uncertainty that inevitably hangs over medical discoveries generally incites prudence. This is why the medical community, which is very hostile to self-medication, has never quite been happy with the publication of medical information in the mainstream press. This is why it asks the press to "be responsible" in order not to generate "false hope" or, inversely, to foster panic.

In the 1970s, medical journalism represented an opportunity, which, though limited, became somewhat more attractive to politicized young doctors (in the wake of the demonstrations of May 1968) or to students who, having given up the study of medicine, wanted to benefit as much as possible from their professional training. But these candidates for work as medical reporters quickly found that the growing specialized medical press was not in fact "real" journalism. The specialized publications produced for the various media specializations are not autonomous. Rare are the journals that can survive through subscriptions; most are highly dependent on the financing of the pharmaceutical industry. Journal editors were thus often reduced to touting the work of their sponsoring laboratories. In France some young medical reporters tried to develop a medical press independent of pharmaceutical lobbies, but readership never attained a level sufficient to keep them in circulation.

On the other hand, the mainstream press did not offer many opportunities for specialized medical reporting. Health sections were rare in general interest and political publications. Few journalists were willing or able to attain the necessary specialized training. Medical information thus remained largely immune to the influence of journalism. Few in number, little known to editors, and often closely associated with medical authorities, medical reporters had little prestige within the field. Scoops were rare and risky and the search for sensationalistic news was little appreciated by a medical community that was prudent in its public statements and that felt that journalists ought to be equally prudent.

The health section of *Le Monde*, one of the most prestigious French dailies, was an exception. Created in 1956 and then expanded in the 1970s, it was run from the start by Dr Claudine Escoffier-Lambiotte and generally included reportage by three regular journalists. Thanks to the depth and accuracy of its articles (on drugs, abortion, biological research, etc.), *Le Monde*'s health section dominated the mainstream press as well as the specialized medical press. It gained great prestige even among doctors, and those with a journalistic bent took internships at the paper. Escoffier-Lambiotte exerted what some called a "masterful" authority, imposing on medical reporters at other news outlets (of whom a certain number were not doctors) her relatively "unjournalistic" conception of medical news. In fact, she did not define herself as a journalist, but rather as a doctor lost in the world of journalism. Her close ties to the medical community – she sat on the board of directors of the Institut Pasteur, had created a foundation for medical research, knew all the most important figures in medicine, signed her articles using the title "doctor" –

brought her closer to the world of medicine than that of journalism. In sum, Dr Escoffier-Lambiotte's shaping contribution was to impose upon a great political daily such as *Le Monde*, and beyond on to the mainstream press as a whole, the concept that medical news should be treated with an extra measure of reserve and respect.

Dr Escoffier-Lambiotte's indisputable success in medical reporting is also explained by the fact that she had some of the qualities of a good journalist: a clear talent for writing, an ability to react quickly to events, and an unparalleled network of contacts in the medical world. If her section presented certain characteristics consistent with the conception of news held by Hubert Beuve-Méry, the founder of *Le Monde* (austere reporting, distance from the most immediate events, refusal of sensationalism), it also occupied in this essentially political newspaper a position somewhat apart, which contributed to its autonomy inside *Le Monde*. To the extent that medical news was seen as highly specialized and technical, the editor-in-chief rarely intervened in the selection or treatment of news topics. In short, the section was protected from the ordinary agitations of journalism.

Internal and External Transformations

At the beginning of the 1980s, medical reporting still bore the clear imprint of *Le Monde*'s dominance. But a certain number of transformations, both in the journalistic field and beyond it, progressively modified the way that medical reporting was defined.

The transformations external to journalism were first those that affected medicine itself. The period was marked by a constant increase in health costs. The share of the gross domestic product represented by the consumption of medical goods and services was 8.8 percent in 2001 as opposed to 5 percent in 1970 and 3.5 percent in 1950.[4] This process had the effect of turning part of the biological sciences beat to economic affairs and thus politics. During the early 1970s, in order to treat this new and increasingly important aspect of medicine, Escoffier-Lambiotte hired a young graduate of Sciences-Po, one of France's most prestigious grandes écoles (elite specialized institutions of higher education). To the extent that the health sector was becoming increasingly politicized, it became the object of more and more common political jockeying. Beyond this new politico-economic dimension of medicine, progress in genetic engineering posed political problems of other kinds, notably ethics. Moral and political authorities who were called upon to set limits upon science thus began to compete for medical news attention. The health section was therefore forced to cover an ever increasing number of topics that fell outside of the category of medicine in the strictest sense.

Parallel to these transformations caused by both the overall development of medical techniques as well as groundbreaking research, there were profound changes in the general population's expectations of the healthcare system. Under the effect in particular of increased educational levels and the corresponding expansion of the middle classes, individuals' relationships to their bodies and illness, and therefore to doctors, began to change: consumption of medicines increased steadily while the demand for medical information, not only on great medical breakthroughs, but on ordinary illnesses and treatments, increased. A growing proportion of the population expected that medical advances would provide a higher quality of life. One heard more and more often about "comfort medicines," plastic surgery, and thermal cures. The healthcare profession slowly lost the exceptional status that had been conferred upon it, which translated legally into a de facto very restrictive concept of medical responsibility. The confidence and hopes which had been generated by more than 40 years of spectacular and constant advances in medicine progressively gave way to more critical and demanding attitudes. Moreover, the development of "alternative medicine" revealed, on the part of certain sections of the population, a certain wariness with respect to official medicine. Finally, consumerism invaded the health sector via a large increase in the number of healthcare workers from the late 1960s onward,[5] and a corresponding intensification of the competition between practitioners and an increasing willingness to be open about the economic factors that affect the profession ("patients" becoming "clients").

The journalistic field translated these transformations and these new demands into its own terms. Throughout the 1970s, commercial pressures and competition for readers among the national press had intensified. *Le Monde* progressively lost its monopoly on "serious" news. In 1981, a relaunched *Libération* began taking readers away from *Le Monde* with a more visually spectacular and stylistically avant-garde style of journalism.[6] Over time, while retaining their distinct characters, the two major differences between the papers diminished: as its readership grew, *Libération* slid politically to the right and, going beyond its original activist orientation, became a business like any other, while *Le Monde* gradually renounced its trademark austere editorial style. By the mid-1990s these two dailies were relatively close in style, apart from certain specific details that were the products of their separate histories and those of their readers. Journalists at the two papers, like their readers, often switched from one to the other.

In the second place, and probably more importantly, the 1980s were marked by a profound restructuring of the media field due to the increasing importance of magazines and television news. In the mid-1980s a new weekly newsmagazine called "Thursday's Big News" (*L'Evénement du jeudi*) was launched. With its provocative or lurid covers especially designed to attract readers, the magazine imposed a new, more aggressive tone upon the weekly political press of the time (*Le Point*, *L'Express*, *Le Nouvel Observateur*). But probably the most important transformation was produced by the growth of private television stations – before 1984 all of France's then-existing three channels were public. With the privatization of TF1 (the most-watched public channel) and the creation of two new privately owned general interest channels (Channel 5 and M6), competition within the journalistic field, both television and print press, intensified. In France, print journalists had long deliberately ignored television news programs, which they judged to be too close to the government's point of view to be taken seriously. They were contemptuous of news that was fabricated by mere "talking heads" under government control (Gaullist France had a "minister of information") rather than emanating from "real" news professionals. During the 1990s, however, such dismissive contempt could no longer be maintained.

Fairly quickly, televised news programs, now free of direct political tutelage, became subject to the laws of commercial television, where ratings demand that one fulfill the public's expectations, be they real or perceived, intuitively felt or technically measured, by favoring striking or moving images over political or historical analysis, and often unimportant yet popular topics instead of objectively important but complex, non media-friendly ones. Television then progressively imposed this vision of news upon the printed press, including to some extent *Le Monde*. The most prestigious outlets of the written press thus developed "after-sales service" strategies and an emphasis on story pick-up, especially in the business pages, in order to benefit by free advertising in the other national media, especially the wire service Agence France Presse (AFP) and the television stations. The amplifying power of radio and television leads print journalists to pursue these pick-ups, which are important for journalists because they improve the standing at once of their stories, their outlets, and themselves.[7]

The effects of television's importance in the selection of subjects deemed worthy of making the news in papers situated at the "intellectual" pole of the journalistic field appears particularly clearly in their contents, for instance in the growing space devoted to sports and capsule news and the declining importance of local as against international news. As a television medical journalist explained with regard to *Le Monde* in a 1995 interview: "They are coming closer to doing what everyone else does. . . . They do everything everybody else does, they cover things they never would have covered before. . . . What do we do that's so different from what they do? You add invasions of jellyfish, sun creams, and flu epidemics, and they do too." In a decade, the entire economy and hierarchy of news production was transformed by television. Television news became, according to the expression of an executive of a private station, "less institutional," that is, separate from the state, and "closer to the concerns of the average person," which is to say, in fact, more dependent on what ratings say about public expectations. In order to understand the written press's mimicry of the audiovisual media, it is necessary to add the dire financial situation of many national papers (*France soir*, *Le Monde*, *Libération*, *L'Humanité*). This competition intensifies the feverish search for an audience.

A Monopoly Threatened

If, for a time, medical reporting managed to resist this major transformation in the treatment of news, it could not escape it totally, nor for very long. But the mediatization of medical news was progressive and came about according to the relatively autonomous logic of the journalistic field, after internal struggles which led to the imposition of a new definition of medical reporting and a redefinition of the relationship between the journalistic field and other social fields, especially the scientific and political fields. The beginning of the 1980s was indeed marked, due notably to the public's increasing demand for news and the expansion of the medical sector, by an increase in the number of medical reporters in the specialized as well as the mainstream press.

Because of its multiple dimensions (scientific, social, political, moral), the AIDS epidemic was immediately viewed by a certain number of young doctor-journalists as an exceptional opportunity to confer upon medical reporting the importance it deserved and give it its own place in the mainstream press: "I became immediately interested in AIDS because I felt that it was a very 'media-friendly' illness" one such journalist said. AIDS indeed furnished the opportunity for certain journalists to turn the health section into a journalistic section "like any other," with its scoops, its revelations and its exclusive interviews. Medical reporters, after internecine struggles among themselves, their editors, and the medical community, brought health news off the inside pages where it was buried with its essentially technical topics and put it on the front page. These battles effectively set the journalistic field against other social spaces. Indeed, the contaminated blood scandal shows that, beyond the struggle of a few doctor-journalists who were more or less supported by editors, who fought to redefine health news, what was really at stake was the reaffirmation of the position that the journalistic field occupied in the field of power, and in particular its power to act upon the scientific, political and legal fields.

Convincing the press: the mobilization of hemophiliacs

In France, despite the massive number of infections – which was long underestimated – the majority of hemophiliacs did not initially speak to journalists. This attitude owed much to their dependence on the physicians who treated them, who constituted their "second family." The silence of hemophiliacs also drew on complex feelings of guilt they experienced: guilt at the high cost of their treatment, which was borne by society; guilt felt by the parents of hemophiliacs, who for the most part were not unaware of the risk they were taking before conception. Finally, strongly handicapped in their integration in school and the workplace and trying to forget their illness, they had difficulty announcing this second stigmata, which tended to be associated with homosexuals and drug addicts.

Before the contaminated blood scandal, hemophiliacs certainly made up the least known of the "at-risk" groups. Few in numbers, they were represented by the Association française des hémophiles (AFH). In opposition to this "official" association, the Association des polytransfusés was created by Jean Péron-Garvanoff in 1987, with the goal of obtaining reparations through the courts. A jazz pianist in his 50s, infected along with other members of his family with the AIDS virus, Péron-Garvanoff was sometimes presented as "the hemophiliac who broke the scandal." Anne-Marie Casteret, then a specialized journalist at the newsmagazine *L'Express*, was one of the few to lend him an attentive ear. In December 1987 she published an article entitled "AIDS:

The Hemophiliacs' Tragedy" ("Sida: la tragédie des hémophiles"). In it, Péron-Garvanoff accused the blood transfusion centers of "having delivered contaminated products until the end of 1985 even though foreign firms had marketed heated batches without any risk of AIDS since 1983." In an interview some months later in *Libération* and a report broadcast on the TF1 midday television news (January 21, 1988), he reiterated his accusations against "a certain number of people still in office" and demanded "compensation." However, these reports were scarcely picked up by other outlets, no doubt among other reasons because of the lack of conclusive evidence, the political conjuncture, the doctors' silence, and the technical nature of the topic.

Faced with this limited response, Péron-Garvanoff pursued a new strategy. "Péron [had] approached all the mainstream news outlets – in vain! So at the end of 1988 he contacted the [far-right scandal] weekly *Minute*. The first article appeared fifteen days later, and was followed by ten or so others," wrote two journalists who worked for far-right publications and edited a book on the scandal (Louis-Armand de Riedmatten and Jean Roberto, *L'Affaire du sang contaminé*, Editions du Rocher, Monaco, 1992). On January 25, 1989 the weekly ran a story headlined "Non-Assistance to Hemophiliacs in Danger," and observed that "we have not finished discovering new scandals connected to AIDS."

The scandal thesis reappeared in the mainstream press when hemophiliacs feared that past indemnification agreements with the French state would "annul" the responsibility of the national center for blood transfusions. After the car of Michel Garretta, director of the CNTS, was burned, many articles were published on "the forgotten AIDS victims," most notably in *Le Monde* (November 3, 1989) and *L'Express* (December 22, 1989).

It was not until 1991 however that the tragedy of post-transfusion infections gradually became the full-blown "contaminated blood scandal." In the first stage, articles appeared on the subject but were confined to *France soir*, which put them on the first page (March 19 and 20). The leading television station, TF1, then devoted a report on the lunchtime news to "hemophiliacs . . . who continue to await justice" without the rest of the national press paying any attention. On April 25, Anne-Marie Casteret, now a medical journalist at *L'Evénement du jeudi*, published a three-page article with the title: "The Report that Accuses the National Center for Blood Transfusions." ("Le rapport qui accuse le centre national de transfusion sanguine"). It was accompanied by extracts from a report from the May 29, 1985 meeting of the doctors of the CNTS, in the course of which director Michel Garretta explained: "All our lots are contaminated. . . . It is up to supervisory authorities to assume responsibility for this serious problem [whether or not to withdraw the lots] and possibly to forbid us to give away these products, with the financial consequences this would represent." However, it was probably less the article itself than how it was picked up by specialized journalists that triggered the first wave of articles and reports. The *Evénement du jeudi* story was carried in an AFP dispatch. Many other outlets then picked up the story on April 25 and 26: *Le Monde* published a story on the back page, the public channel Antenne 2 devoted a report on its evening news, and the private TF1 gave a brief news item on its noon broadcast.

Between 1991 and 1993, few stories spent as much time on the covers and front pages of the national press as the contaminated blood scandal, which aroused immense indignation, to the point of being presented as one of the scandals of the century. Implicating the doctors who occupied responsible positions, one of whom received the stiffest penalties ever incurred, the scandal gave rise to three trials. It also had considerable political effects. Three former ministers including a former Socialist prime minister, Laurent Fabius, were judged by the national court. Edmond Hervé, secretary of state for health, was given a suspended sentence. The scandal also brought about the creation of two inquiry commissions, in the Senate and then in the National Assembly, the compensation of those affected, as well as a reorganization of the French blood transfusion system.

At first, the competition between medical reporters centered on jockeying for positions in the press without calling into question the existing structure or hierarchies of the subfield. Particularly for young journalists just starting out, most of whom dreamed of working at *Le Monde*, the very definition of "good health news" was seen as being embodied and controlled by the paper and its long-time medical news editor. With the retirement of Claudine Escoffier-Lambiotte in 1985, the competition among medical reporters progressively intensified. For all these journalists who met and were trained while covering AIDS, and who belonged to the same generation, some of whom had studied together and who now had their own regular columns in the mainstream press, it was no longer a question of struggling for a position at *Le Monde* (the positions were limited and above all already occupied, and probably for a long time), but more radically, to challenge the very dominance of the paper. Indeed, the young journalists who followed in Escoffier-Lambiotte's wake showed that they were in fact her "natural heirs." They distinguished themselves from other medical reporters by not belonging to any medical journalists' associations, rarely attending press conferences, and working exclusively with each other, often obtaining documents or information before everyone else.

Yet, unlike Escoffier-Lambiotte, this new generation of *Le Monde* reporters was no longer able to impose its definition of medical information upon the rest of the journalistic field. If they were often doctors, so were their competitors at competing media outlets, which had not been the case before. And all of them alike were buffeted by new power relationships within the broad journalistic field that simply had not existed during the 1960s and 1970s. The transformation of the problems surrounding the contamination of some blood supplies into a generalized scandal was probably the most decisive moment in the process of imposing a new definition of medical reporting. This definition was to be more "aggressive" with respect to authorities (in accordance with the dominant social image of the journalist who shows his independence by denouncing those in power and by investigating the hidden corridors of power). It was also to become more political in that the health news section, and the content of its articles, tended to become like any other section, which was more and more important for a certain number of social agents, be they scientists who wanted to be known to the public in order to gain their peers' rapid recognition, or politicians who used medical journalists for political payback or to advance their own careers.

The Two Systems

The contaminated blood scandal, which set *Le Monde* against most of the other national newspapers, brought into broad daylight this previously hidden journalistic battle. Media coverage of AIDS functioned according to two different systems of news production. At first, the news on AIDS followed an exceptional system which traditionally characterized medical information, that is, the system of news reported by specialized journalists in collaboration with medical authorities, with their censure and control process designed to avoid gross errors. Later, AIDS news was reported according to the system of "ordinary information." In other words, it was placed at the heart of a space in which news and views of all kinds are set against one another "democratically." In this system, what counts is not knowledge or insight, but the capacity to elicit emotion.

At first, coverage of AIDS was monopolized by a small group of science journalists, for the most part trained as medical doctors, who were fascinated by this new and journalistically promising topic. These young doctor-journalists quickly became friendly with the small team of young doctors and researchers working on AIDS. This network had been formed in 1982 on the basis of personal affinities and outside official structures to work on what was then a marginal and strange illness lacking in prestige from a medical point of view. They all shared more or less the same "left wing," "critical," anti "medical establishment" ideology which grew out of the May 1968 protests. They were all conscious of the risks of stigmatization and were practically obsessed by the risk of errors in media coverage. They maintained a rigorous control over the news and each term that was used. This prudence did not exclude the existence of reciprocal professional benefits shared among the specialist journalists and doctors. Very quickly, each understood the benefits of such a close collaboration: the young journalists, in direct contact with high level researchers, could gain access to first-hand information in order to write their articles on a topic that was becoming journalistically important, while the young researchers could rely upon the media to make their work known and bring recognition to their group by the established medical authorities who had not yet taken full measure of the gravity of the epidemic. This fairly exceptional collaboration had, among others, two major effects.

On the one hand, one observed an increasing mediatization of the young researchers which allowed them to accumulate public recognition that some would convert, in particular starting with the discovery of the virus by the Montagnier team at the Institut Pasteur, then by Robert Gallo in the United States, into professional consecration, thus accelerating their careers as well as providing them with funds to pursue their research. On the other hand, the information reported at the time was very precise because of the technical competency of the journalists covering it. Since they worked in collaboration with the researchers to write their articles, they enjoyed a de facto monopoly on AIDS coverage. It was in the interest of this small world which sprang up around the AIDS epidemic that its reporting be "rigorous"; amateurs were quickly ferreted out and denounced and errors were carefully rectified. Until 1985, the different parties perceived the relations between scientists and the press as very good and characterized by a desire for an intelligent collaboration.

Disinterested collaboration to facilitate the early accumulation of scientific knowledge and public awareness about AIDS slowly gave way to individual triumphs, fragmenting the research community both professionally and personally. Researchers were riven by conflicts linked to the sharing of the profits generated by the discovery of the virus, by the ever greater spread of the epidemic, by the media notoriety, sometimes considered excessive, of certain members, and by the increasing importance of the Institut Pasteur in this group, which some felt was too great (the "Gallo–Montagnier schism" over who first discovered the virus only aggravating the divisions further). At the same time, an intensified challenge to *Le Monde*'s former dominance of medical reporting broke up the happy community of journalists covering AIDS, a breakup all the more violent to the extent that the colleagues had also become close friends. These two relatively autonomous processes combined, each clan or figure of the scientific sector counting a supporter among the medical reporters. AIDS reporting, which had been "journalistically neutralized" for a time, became a news story like any other, with its struggles and its competitions, and especially, its battles for scoops.

As with the journalistic field as a whole, medical reporting tended to be characterized by a tension between two poles with contradictory imperatives, an intellectual, scientific specialized pole still best embodied by *Le Monde* and a pole dominated by economic and/or political considerations, by ratings, the subjection to public opinion and the demands of the public, represented by television news reporting. The treatment of news was profoundly affected by these cleavages, at first, in a discrete, coded fashion, perceptible in fact only to those small groups competing with one another, but later, more openly. Beginning in 1985, a new "medical journalism," governed by the real or perceived expectations of the public, replaced the old, specialized regime of medical information.

Today the economic imperatives which regulate the choice of programs and which have replaced the original educational imperatives can be seen in the very organization of health related news programs. The first health programs on television, in the 1960s and 1970s, revealed both in their direction and in the topics they dealt with a certain relationship with the medical community which excluded the journalist, that critical middle person between the public and the authorities, to the benefit of a respectful host. These programs dealt mostly with surgery, medicine's noble and prestigious discipline. Typically on these shows, a top medical official would receive in his clinic the producers of the news show who, outfitted in white smocks, discretely watched the necessarily successful surgical interventions. Then,

Battles for scoops

> "The T [an organization that had given information to journalists] documents, as I remember, came out much later. This was simply because I'd had enough of seeing S [a competing journalist] making scoops with info that we'd all had for a long time [laughter]. So I went back to my old files and said: 'This has never been published, I'll give them T.' [burst of laughter] But I had T at the beginning of the scandal. . . . When C [a competitor] started up the scandal again, everyone took it up again. So it was a bit like we were confronted with a spiral. We who had broken the scandal but now were forgotten, we had to be there." (Journalist with a national weekly, 1992 interview)

A journalist with a big national daily (1992 interview) tells how, in order to be first, he wrote an article on a inquiry report which was to be released to the public the next day but which he had not yet seen. A few minutes before the paper was put to bed, an informant read him a few extracts from the report. He recalls: "I wrote the article in advance, the framework, by explaining what one would no doubt find in the report. If you reread the article and the document, they are nevertheless rather far apart. The pages were read to me at 10:00 and the press deadline was 10:30."

with deference, the journalists asked questions which allowed the surgeon to demonstrate his perfect mastery of the topic at hand. The viewer was therefore implicitly reminded of the preeminence of science, and supposed to receive knowledge much as one would in school.

Today, medical news programs display, in both choice of topics and their treatment, a reversal of this relationship. The program now takes place on television studio soundstages where a professional journalist "host" moderates between an audience that asks questions and practitioners who, one by one, respond, along with famous actors or singers who may be invited on the show to improve ratings. The topics address the most common concerns, or those which bring the best ratings such as: backaches, sexual problems, diets, etc. The irrefutable words of the medical official are thus replaced by conversations, affirmations and challenges between the audience and the doctors, the journalist playing the role of referee channeling the demands from "below."

The transition between the two modes of treating medical news analyzed here should not be understood as a normative opposition between a golden age of deferential journalism and the vulgar conduct of more investigative or reader-friendly reporting. The sociological interest is first of all to account for the social mechanisms governing this change.

Conclusion

Beyond the basic problems it poses, the contaminated blood scandal is in the end a good indicator of the increasing power of the mainstream media in the production of "social problems." In the space of a few years, AIDS went from the science pages of *Le Monde* to the headlines of the popular press. During the 1990s, the special programs on AIDS produced for television with didactic objectives under the control of experts were likewise largely replaced by accusatory investigative newsmagazines and debate programs in which health officials accused of illegal or unethical acts were invited, indeed summoned, by journalists to come and justify themselves.

The scandal represents in fact a kind of quasi-experimental process allowing one to measure the successive distortions that, by the very logic of its functioning, the journalistic field imposes upon a reality that it takes possession of as its targeted public expands. One can follow the story as it moves from the health pages to the front pages of the newspapers, until it finally emerges on television and in the popular press. A similar process was at work in recent French coverage of urban youth violence, in which case "live" television coverage of spectacular and thus media-friendly events (confrontations with the police, burning cars or supermarkets, etc.) produced a "screen effect." In other words, media often select the most spectacular aspects of a complex social reality in order to attract the maximum audience. Depending on the media for their knowledge of the world, many people come to regard this distorted media reality as reality itself.[8]

In the case of the contaminated blood affair, one can see the setting in place of this screen effect and the resultant blurring as it is reported on by less specialized journalists (or those specialized in domains other than medicine), and as the weight of nonscientific (in particular economic and political) considerations tended to increase in news production. Journalistic treatment of AIDS thus came to be more

Human interest and emotion: the shift in medical news framing

The terrible tragedy of hemophiliac children infected by HIV was one of the main angles chosen by journalists covering the scandal's first trial.

Extract from the program "7 heures" on the national public radio station France Inter (June 22, 1992). Ludovic is a hemophiliac child infected with the AIDS virus.

> PRESENTER Ludovic is 16 years old, an age at which one has one's whole life before one, but Ludovic does not look at the future like other teenagers. He is one of 1,200 hemophiliacs who needs to regularly change his blood. And today, at age 16, Ludovic is HIV positive. This morning we will try to understand his thirst for justice if not for vengeance.
> LUDOVIC I hope that those accused are severely punished because, if you look at what they did, it's horrible because in some cases they've decimated the families that were infected. And, again, I don't think all the people [responsible] have been accused.
> JOURNALIST You were infected. What does it mean to you now to see the people who infected you in the defendant's box, going to trial?
> LUDOVIC On the one hand it is a small pleasure . . . but what's more interesting is that for each infected person, M. Garretta [the director of CNTS] would get 25 years. So, if you look at the number of people infected and dead, that would already make centuries in prison.

A young journalist with a private television station, head of investigations for a news program (from 1992 interview):

> I said to myself: we will only really reach people with the testimony of those who have children like we do, who experienced this tragedy, who are experiencing it, who are living it in their everyday lives. So we very quickly struck upon the idea that we would have to privilege testimony and that this chronology [that of selected facts] would have to be accompanied by families' calendars, that each family has its calendar, what I call the calendar of horror. . . . For those listening to us [the viewers], there has to be a human aspect and it's the families who express it, and then, once we've captured their attention, we show the responsibilities, we pose questions . . . It's true that when you listen to the testimony of families talking about the life or death of their children, you absolutely cannot fail to be touched by it beyond any journalistic interest, or even, at the limit, a sort of satisfaction – which is a bit sick – in . . . shooting down those who thought they were invulnerable.

sensitive to audience demands, and most significantly, more vulnerable to manipulation.

Notes

1 See, notably, Dorothy Nelkin, *Selling Science: How the Press covers Science and Technology* (W.H. Freeman and Co., New York, 1987); Anne Karpf, *Doctoring the Media: The Reporting of Health and Medicine* (Routledge, London, 1988); Mike Moore, ed., *Health Risks and the Press: Perspectives on Media Coverage of Risk Assessment and Health* (The Media Institute, Washington, DC, 1989); and Sharon M. Friedman, Sharon Dunwoody, and Carol L. Rogers, eds., *Communicating Uncertainty: Media Coverage of New and Controversial Science* (Erlbaum, London, 1999).

2 Even if it suffers from certain inexactitudes concerning the role of the press in France and Spain, Véronique Pujas's analysis illuminates the ways in which different national situations can help turn an objective tragedy into a media scandal. See V. Pujas, "Explaining the Wave of Scandal: The Exposure of Corruption in Italy, France and Spain," in *Political Journalism: New Challenges, New Practices*, eds. Raymond Kuhn and Erik Neveu (Routledge, London, 2002), esp pp. 151–4. See also E.A. Feldman and R. Bayer, eds., *Blood Feuds: AIDS, Blood, and the Politics of Medical Disaster* (Oxford University Press, New York, 1999) and Douglas Starr, *Blood: An Epic History of Medicine and Commerce* (Knopf, New York, 1998).

3 Politicians often hope to bring about a desired future through their reported statements, as, for instance, by saying during an economic crisis that "the end of the crisis is near." On the "performative effects" of official discourse, see J.-L. Austin, *How to do things with Words* (Harvard University Press, Cambridge, MA, 1962) and Pierre Bourdieu, *Language and Symbolic Power* (Polity, Cambridge, 1991, and Harvard University Press, Cambridge, MA, 1991).

4 Source: Laurent Caussat, Annie Fenina, and Yves Geffroy, "Les Comptes de la santé de 1960 à 2001," *Série statistiques*, 54 (June 2003), Direction de la recherche, des études, de l'évaluation et des statistiques (DREES).

5 This period was equally marked by a strong growth in the number of doctors: 59,000 in 1967 versus 194,000 on January 1, 2000. Source: *L'Annuaire des statistiques sanitaires et sociales* (La Documentation française, Paris, 2000), p. 163.

6 *Libération* was founded in 1973 by Jean-Paul Sartre and Simone de Beauvoir as a politically engaged but formally unaffiliated daily newspaper. In its early years, it refused all advertising and attained a steady circulation of only 30,000. – ED.

7 "At the paper, they really like it . . . the directors are always happy when they see N [a national daily] on television," explained a journalist with a national daily (1993 interview). Announcing certain scoops to one's colleagues by fax or a phone call has become a reflex at many outlets. This is especially the case with *Le Monde*, sometimes drawing ironic comments from their colleagues at other outlets: "One gets sick of doing *Le Monde*'s after-sales service," explained a journalist with an all-news radio station (1998 interview).

8 See Patrick Champagne, "The View from the Media," in *The Weight of the World*, ed. Pierre Bourdieu (Polity, Cambridge, 1999, and Stanford University Press, Stanford, CA, 2000).

7

Economic Journalism in France

Julien Duval

In France, relations between journalism and the economy were a classic subject of political reflection from the end of the nineteenth century to the Liberation in 1945. They became current again at the end of the 1990s, when it appeared that, following privatization of television and the buying-up of newspapers, a growing number of media outlets were controlled, and sometimes owned, by large industrial or financial groups. While some thought these capitalist transformations would not have editorial repercussions, others argued that journalists could find it difficult to report "freely" on the big groups dominating the media sector. Some even judged that the French media now almost unanimously repeated an ideology, sometimes called *la pensée unique* or "market journalism," that suited the interests of financial markets and business circles.

This article brings a sociological method and problematic to these questions. Although posed here in a highly particular framework – the specialized journalistic subspace of economics news in France in the 1990s – they reflect the general issue of journalism's independence vis-à-vis the economic world. When it has some relative autonomy, economic journalism can at least partially realize the ambition of informing citizens about the world they live in and satisfying agents' political interests in news concerning a field that weighs on the whole of society. But this study shows that the journalistic subspace specializing in the economy had little autonomy from the economic field at the end of the 1990s. While in relatively autonomous fields, economic capital and capital specific to the field tend to be concentrated in distinct agents or firms, the most influential media outlets in this subdomain were tightly integrated into the economic order. For this reason, and according to the mediations specified in this article, their economic pages tended to represent the economic world in a way that contributed much more to its conservation and legitimation than to its critique and transformation.

This analysis also offers a demonstration of a methodological approach – correspondence analysis – closely linked to field theory, but which has not previously been used for research on the news media.[1] In contrast to statistical methods that aim to isolate the "independent" effects of certain properties, correspondence analysis allows us to study the mutual influence of attributes that, in reality, neither exist nor act in a state of isolation. In this respect, it has an affinity with a sociological theory attentive to the diversity of types of capital in the social world as well as the mechanisms for converting them.[2] Correspondence analysis thus grasps individuals (or organizations) in terms of what distinguishes them from one another, of how they deviate from the average. Finally, it allows us to produce graphics, which, somewhat like maps of cities or regions, permit the spatial representation of fields, "space[s] of relations . . . just as real as geographical space[s]."[3]

Applied to the case of economic journalism, this method avoids, for example, focusing on a few isolated characteristics (in particular, the identity of media owners) and takes into account the ensemble of mutually interacting properties (outlets' reputations, their place in the advertising market, etc.). Correspondence analysis also encourages us to think about the "independence" of the media relationally, since the structure it exposes demonstrates that no media outlet is entirely independent. The flipside of independence with respect to political forces is almost always dependence on economic forces, while the economic independence boasted of by some marginal media organizations – which call themselves free, for example, because they refuse all advertising – appears, as always, highly relative.

This article first of all proposes an initial analysis of French economic journalism that allows us to understand the hypotheses used to select and construct statistical variables. After this methodologically crucial step, results of statistical analysis are used to propose a new, empirically based description of the space of economic journalism in France at the end of the 1990s. This space is organized around three poles, and it can be shown that each of these poles tends to be associated with a specific way of covering economic affairs. Finally, we see that the current configuration of French economic journalism owes much to broad transformations of the journalistic field since the 1980s: the media outlets with the most influence on the profession in effect became much more dependent on the economic world during this period.

Between the Economy and Journalism

First of all, we need to characterize the relevant individuals and institutions in the space of "all the relevant relations" that unite or divide them. The construction of statistical variables, like the definition of a statistical population, rests on an initial sociological analysis of the field under examination. Irreducible to a pure relation of economic forces, economic journalism constitutes a subspace at the heart of the journalistic field, a subspace traversed by two logics. On the one hand, journalistic production is subject to economic interests, more precisely to the interests and ends pursued by agents or institutions involved in the economic field. The calls to order of certain media investors, the blackmail of advertisers, the discipline sometimes imposed on journalists by marketing methods, the public relations manipulations of business sources – all are manifestations, to be sure very different, of the subordination of journalistic production to economic interests. It is possible to construct simple indicators to grasp an outlet's exposure to economic logics: the composition of the firm's capital; its dependence on advertisers, measured by the share of advertising in turnover; the concentration of its advertisers; and each outlet's "rating" in the advertising market (see part 2A of the appendix to this chapter).

On the other hand, journalistic production also is shaped by forces connected to journalists themselves, defined by the primacy of the "duty to inform" and provide accurate information over the censorship and "canned news" potentially borne by the economic field. The construction of indicators measuring the hold of journalistic logics on an outlet is indirect and requires reference to the conditions in which they are affirmed. In France, economic sections have long functioned as an advertising medium for investors or owners, as illustrated not only by Emile Zola's 1891 novel, *L'Argent* (Money) but also by the financial scandals involving newspapers at the end of the nineteenth century and between the two world wars. Beginning in the 1920s, forces arose that tended to counteract the influence of business circles on economic reporting. Political formations, often connected to the left, as well as representatives of the journalistic profession, which experienced a decisive phase in its development during this period, denounced the venality of a press that served the business world before "democracy." Starting in the 1930s, the state seemed to make the imperative of a press relatively free from the influence of "money" its own. It granted journalists new rights and undertook a reform of press ownership in 1945. The state and the journalistic profession thus appear as the bearers of a "moral" conception of journalism, represented since the 1950s by the *Association des journalistes économiques et financiers* (AJEF). Although it lacks real power on the market, the association fosters contacts among practitioners and plays a symbolic role by promoting the values of independence and morality among economic journalists and their partners, as well as the practices on which the journalistic profession has built itself. The association celebrates journalistic "independence," a radical break between news and "public relations," and the virtues of "specialization" and "competence." It thus constitutes one of the forces that help encourage disinterested practices – heeding only "the duty to inform" and resisting external pressures from the business world – into a universe always at risk of falling into exclusive dependence on economic logics.

It is possible to construct indicators of the degree to which the media function according to a "journalistic logic," giving this apparently abstract and subjective idea a more concrete content: the attractiveness of each outlet to former journalism school students[4] (in other words, to the agents best placed to defend the constitutive values of the profession) or the big business schools[5] (often the milieu of competent "specialists"); representation via one of an outlet's economic journalists in the offices of the AJEF; and producing economic news that is picked up by other outlets (see part 2B of the appendix to this chapter).

In practice, economic and journalistic logics are not always at odds. Editorial independence is frequently a selling point. As the managers of a periodical for investors explain this in a subscription drive: "We work all the more freely because we do not depend on any financial group." A satirical weekly highly regarded in France for its "independence" from the powers that be, *Le Canard enchaîné*, is also highly profitable. Conversely, editors of company newsletters have little credibility within the profession; their stories, regarded as advertising, are almost never picked up by the mainstream press. All in all, firms and practices directed exclusively by either economic or journalistic logics appear doomed to fail. The ambiguity common to all spaces that function according to a law other than that of the economic field seems to be more pronounced in the case of economic journalism,[6] where field-specific logics seem to be asserted much less by the refusal of economic compromises than, for example, in the literary field. The celebration of the economic journalistic subfield's own values, above all "independence," is euphemistic rather than being an outright denial of economic influence. Professional ethics thus oscillates between forces which, within autonomous universes, tend to counteract economic pressures, and those which, within the commercial professions, put the satisfaction of the client in the most immediately economic sense first – not to deny them but, on the contrary, the better attain to them.

The Space of Economic Journalism

Correspondence analysis allows us to construct a space of 44 media outlets which participated in the production and diffusion of economic news in France in the nineties (see part 1 of the appendix to this chapter). It avoids studying isolated indicators (whose significance can be ambiguous) and permits us to focus on the interrelations between variables, while at the same time bringing out the combinations of economic and specific capital (the recognition of outlets within the journalistic milieu itself) at work at a particular time. It simultaneously allows us to see if professional norms, which can be ambiguous, tend more to legitimize or to counteract the influence of external powers from the economic field on the journalistic space.[7]

Among the outlets covering the economy some combine considerable specific capital with diverse links to the economic field while others are independent enough in this respect, but lack internal capital (see figure 7.1). The horizontal axis is the result of this opposition. The axis opposes, on the one hand, the most important business news dailies (*Les Echos*), the oldest center-right political daily (*Le Figaro*), and a new, relatively mass-market economic news monthly (*Capital*); and, on the other hand, two relatively small circulation, left-wing weeklies (*Politis* and *Charlie Hebdo*). This opposition is moreover inseparably economic and journalistic (neither of the two main groups of variables is more significant in terms of its contribution to the axis).

It shows first of all the different autonomy of outlets vis-à-vis the economic field. Reading the first axis from left to right, one sees an increase in overall advertising dependence (with the dominant advertisers more likely to be profit-oriented businesses rather than humanitarian organizations or cultural organizations), the percentage of audience composed of executives, and the likelihood of belonging to a

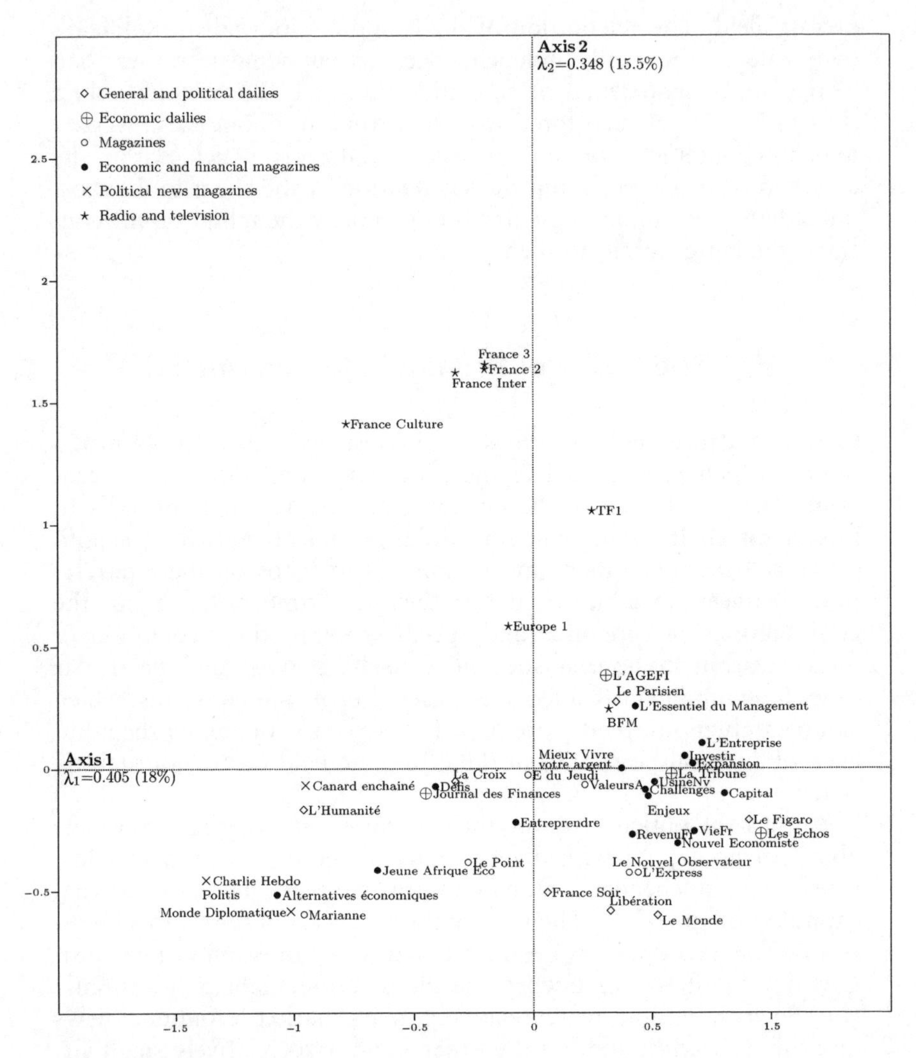

Figure 7.1 The media space
Distribution of outlets in the first factorial plan.

media chain. Economic autonomy also divides public enterprises and those under cooperative control (often managed by journalists) from outlets controlled by a family or private group (where managerial functions almost always escape journalists). Graphical representation brings out this opposition. Within the audiovisual media, there is an opposition between the private sector (TF1, Europe 1, and BFM) and public enterprises (France 2 and 3, France Culture, France Inter, consigned to the left part of the diagram). In the written press, it opposes well-financed papers (e.g., *Le Figaro*) that are part of a larger chain to the two old Christian and Communist dailies (*La Croix* and *L'Humanité*), both of which benefit from public subsidies and whose capital is mainly held by employees, editors, readers, or "friends" of the paper. The former are distinguished from the latter, notably, by the number of employees and the size and composition of their revenues.

The opposition also includes degree of professionalization. Professional excellence, at least in its more objectifiable forms, tends to go along with dependence on the economic field. The diagram is thus characterized by a concentration on the left of higher proportions of graduates, high pick-up rates by other papers, and symbolic capital expressed by editorial offices in Paris's historical press and business district. Obviously, not all the newspapers on the right possess all these marks of distinction; on the other hand, almost none of those on the left boasts any of them (except perhaps *La Croix*).

A second cleavage structuring the space of economic journalism finds statistical expression on the vertical axis, which to a very large extent reflects the audiovisual media and characteristics like state ownership or audience that radically distinguish it from the written press. Given the scope of the audiovisual media's diffusion, the stakes involved for the state and, increasingly, big business, are perceived to be of an entirely different magnitude.

The Executive Effect

As the triangular distribution in figure 7.1 indicates, economic journalism is organized around three poles. The first (right) is made up essentially of the daily and weekly press, and characterized by a combination of internal legitimacy and restricted economic autonomy. The second pole (top) corresponds to the audiovisual media: commercially dominant, it produces very little economic news and, as a result, its stories are almost never picked up. "We can't be seen as following television," explains an economic print journalist, "but . . . if we do, it's only because a minister or the head of a firm comes on prime-time to make an announcement."[8] The third pole (bottom left) is dominated in all respects; its paradigm is the "alternative" press.

Within this space, "the economic and financial press" is situated at the first pole. It is characterized not only by intensive coverage of the economy, but also by the professionalization of its journalists and its proximity to Anglo-American journalism, on which it often styles itself: *Forbes*, *The Economist*, and *Business Week* are models for the "executive" economic magazines (*L'Expansion* et *Le Nouvel Economiste*), while *Le Point*, a general-interest weekly, regularly publishes translations of their articles. What these French periodicals have in common is above all the same submarket of readers: heads of firms, executives, and investors.

As the distribution of the four advertising-based variables shows (see figure 7.2), the subspace rests on strictly social oppositions. The modalities associated with financial advice, business services, and luxury advertisements – aimed at groups such as heads of firms, executives, or investors with economic capital and/or the power to make purchasing decisions at work – tend toward the first pole (right). In the audiovisual media (top), we find advertisers tied to the food sector, the only one characterized by the highly heterogeneous publics of the national channels. The modality associated with advertisements for literary products, corresponding to the fractions with the most cultural capital, is found in the bottom left.

The analysis shows that, in terms of our variables, *Le Monde*, usually characterized as center-left, and *Le Nouvel Observateur*, a general-interest weekly which owes it reputation to its involvement in certain great leftist struggles of the 1960s and 1970s, are positioned much closer to the major business news daily *Les Echos* than to leftist periodicals like *Politis* or *Le Canard enchaîné* (figure 7.1). One thing the big political papers (including *Le Monde* and *Libération*) and the specialized press have in common is combining strong internal legitimacy with dependence on the economic field. This combination is possible because economic dependence occurs through these outlets' ties to their readers – heads of firms, executives, or investors. It thus takes a form that is scarcely, if at all, sanctioned by professional norms, as opposed to pressure from investors or advertisers, which often limits discussion and debate within economics journalism. Developing and maintaining connections with readers tightly integrated into the economic field is at the heart of a dynamic characteristic of this dominant pole. Thus provided with readers who either by profession or inheritance are naturally inclined to want economic news, journalists for these outlets can develop sections that would be much next to impossible for outlets with working-class or nonprofessional readerships to set up and cultivate. Since this elite readership is also a highly prized target market, outlets like *Le Monde* and *Le Nouvel Observateur* can simultaneously maintain their economic and their field-specific capital: the former allows them to invest resources in business reporting and thus

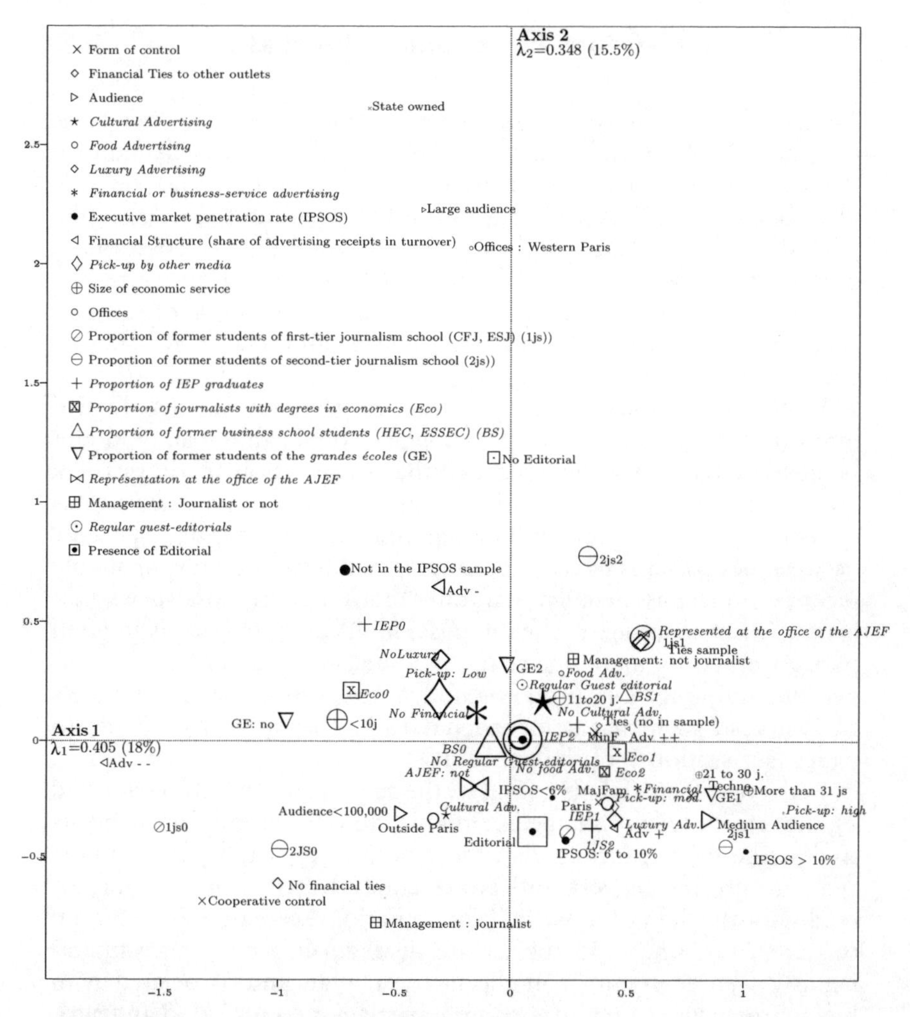

Figure 7.2 The space of media characteristics
Distribution of modalities in the first factorial plan.
Note: Supplementary elements in italics.
Size of indicators is proportional to frequency.

to produce economic news. It is thereby converted into specific capital, maintaining the paper's reputation (through, for example, citations and pick-ups from other press organizations) and attracting readers and advertisers, and is thus in turn reconverted into economic capital.

Definitions of Economic Journalism

The structure of the space (constructed, we must recall, on the basis of factors liable to influence journalistic production) sheds light on the way outlets cover the economic world. Although no variable directly related to political orientation has been introduced into the analysis, all the "left" outlets that did not rally to laissez-faire capitalism in the 1990s are collected at the bottom left of figure 7.1. The three poles thus in effect bring out three definitions of journalism, three ways for outlets to talk about a universe on which, one way or another, they depend.

Economic sections of press outlets are generally further divided into subspecialties or "rubrics." Though seldom examined, no doubt because of their false obviousness, the organization of rubrics is a good indicator of a media outlet's approach to economic news. This system of division plays a filtering role, discriminating especially between news that is likely to be investigated by a journalist or simply picked up (because it falls "naturally" into a rubric) and news that is not. A rubric, at least when it exists in different outlets, is in good part governed by a routine that, combined with the effects of competition and imitation, produces obligatory events, centers of collective interest, such that content tends to be the same from paper to paper (see section 3 of the appendix).

In the first factorial plan (that is, the space produced by axes 1 and 2), the terms used within media organizations' economic departments to describe rubrics form a distribution that is especially dense on the right, where the biggest outlets are concentrated (this can only be read with the help of a partial representation; see figure 7.3). Within this area, just under 30 rubrics are distinguished by being simultaneously well represented in the factorial plan and associated with high frequencies. Often devoted to a particular sector (food and agriculture, banking and insurance, chemicals, distribution, computers . . .) or financial in nature (finances, investments, estates . . .), these rubrics are found in a great many papers with very limited economic autonomy. Conversely, they are absent from the audiovisual media and "alternative" papers. In other words, these are the rubrics that appear most frequently in the most economically specialized outlets but which others lack, thus allowing us to see that economic "specialization" often consists in covering news of practical interest to economic managers, executives, or investors.

The rubrics concentrated on the left outline a sort of model economic department among the outlets, with the economic pages

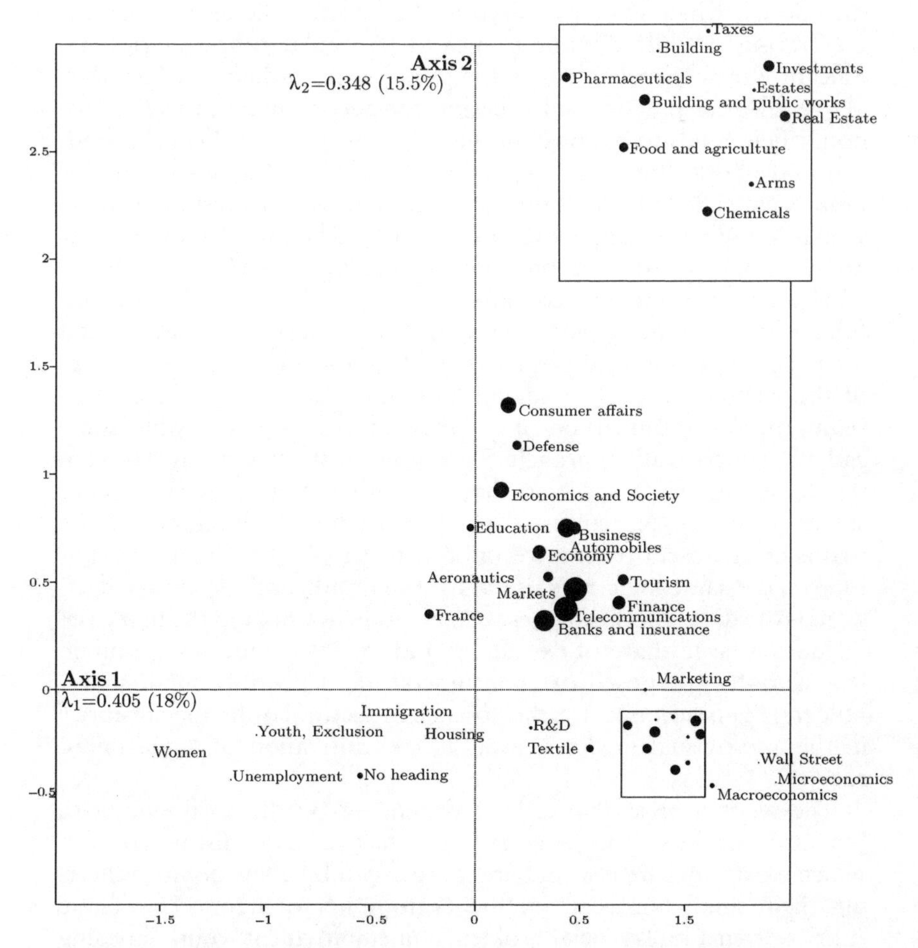

Figure 7.3 The space of rubrics
Economic rubrics (supplementary elements) in the first factorial plan.
Note: Only modalities with rubrics appear, and, among them, only those scoring over 0.3. Size of indicators is proportional to frequency.

serving above all to provide readers with practical information, be it for personal investment decisions, professional decisions, or career strategies. They consist of the juxtaposition of sectoral rubrics, financial rubrics, rubrics devoted to different functions within firms (management, marketing . . .), and, finally and more marginally, some news on politics, "macroeconomics," or society. All the economic departments of media outlets situated in this area are organized along this model, which is best realized in the business dailies (*Les Echos*, *La Tribune*). While the importance of particular rubrics varies significantly from paper to paper, the principle according to which they above all offer practical information for agents involved in the economic field tends to be constant. In this respect, what Michael Schudson said about "business" reporting in the United States is true for France as well: "On the business page, journalists presume readers who ask, 'What is happening in the world today that I should know about as an investor to protect or advance my financial interests.' "[9]

The organization of economic services on radio and television follows different principles. The economic services of the audiovisual media are, with minor divergences, replications in miniature of those of the written press. The adaptation sometimes consists in emphasizing the social dimension of events, and more often in what some call a "pedagogical" approach. Some journalists pick up stories from the dominant written press as they are. Others use rubrics like "consumer affairs," "agriculture," or "automobiles," developing news that is often absent from the economic pages of the written press but follows the same logic: it is useful for their audience's economic decisions – the difference being between an audience that, in the first case, includes a large share of executives and managers and, in the other, is essentially composed of "consumers" (and possibly small shareholders). This accounts for the absence of sectoral or financial rubrics in the audiovisual media as well as the cultivation of "consumer" rubrics.

The written press that is least dependent on the economic field, but also the least "professionalized," has its own distinct rubrics which exist nowhere else and are represented by a few points, reflecting their small numbers, on the bottom left of figure 7.3. These rubrics often address social problems (unemployment, youth, housing . . .) seldom covered in the business press; they appear more often in the political press, but usually in noneconomic sections ("France" or "Society"). Whereas they are covered in the dominant media outlets by distinct services, economic, social, and political questions are often mixed together in the alternative press. Less specialized, at risk of appearing less professional, and abstaining from the dominant outlets' struggle to produce scoops, these journalists have a different way of talking about the economic world than that of the dominant media. For this they can rely on the characteristics of their readership and their ties to institutions (the Catholic Church for *La Croix*, the French Communist Party for *L'Humanité*), researchers or teachers (*Le Monde diplomatique* and *Alternatives économiques* in particular), or illustrators (*Charlie Hebdo*). They thus address topics that receive little or no coverage elsewhere (no doubt because they seem to lack practical interest for executives and managers) such as the economies of developing countries, "critical" theory and research in economics, the distribution of income and inheritances, or the underground economy.

Transformations of the Space Since the 1980s

Rather than simply conclude that economic journalism, in France as elsewhere, is ever and always condemned to a meager autonomy in capitalist societies, it is important to acknowledge how much its current condition owes to transformations since the 1980s. Over 20 years, the major national newspapers usually regarded as being on the left have in effect completely embraced what was termed above "the executive effect." At the same time, their economic coverage has been largely aligned with that of the specialized press aimed at executives and decision-makers. Thus, these papers have, by their transformation, contributed to a homogenization of media coverage of the economy and legitimized economic journalism trapped within the beliefs and problematics of the economic field. Since they represent journalistic "institutions," changes at papers like *Le Monde*, *Libération*, *Le Nouvel Observateur*, and even *L'Expansion* can have repercussions for the whole space. We can imagine that if the stories they publish tend to be picked up, those they do not (anymore), and which they alone would be able to publish, have almost no chance of appearing elsewhere, especially on radio and television, which do little economic reporting of their own.

Libération, a newspaper born of the "ultra-leftism" of the 1970s and founded on principles such as equal salaries, has been transformed since the beginning of the 1980s. Paid advertising appeared; "friendly" industrial groups invested, their stake rising to almost 50 percent over the years.[10] Its circulation quadrupled within five years. The launch, and especially the failure, of a new format in 1995 resulted in the newspaper being effectively bought up by the Chargeurs investment group, which, if its manager is to be believed, respects "journalistic independence" but has imposed strict management imperatives in return for its involvement. The great political daily *Le Monde* also has an anticapitalist tradition, in this case inherited from the postwar period. Yet it has evolved in the same direction: starting in 1985, major industrial and financial groups made significant investments and advertising expanded. Today, *Le Monde* is still majority-owned by internal investors, including journalists and other employees, but the grip of market logic has increased perceptibly, as evinced, notably, by an increasingly sensationalized front page designed to increase street sales (see also Champagne in this volume, p. 59).

Under the sway of this marketing logic, these newspapers have refocused on the segments of their readership most sought by advertisers. The share of managers and executives among *Libération* readers, for example, rose from 22 to 39 percent between 1984 and 1987.[11] At *Le Monde*, winning back executives and decision makers, especially through a redesign of the economic pages, was one dimension of a new format launched in 1995. At both papers, an increase in market pressures and the transformation of economic coverage were synchronous.

At *Le Monde*, economic reporting began to change in the mid-1980s and reached a decisive stage with the new format in 1995, when the "Economy and Society" heading was replaced by "Business and Finance." In the paper as a whole, pages devoted to macroeconomics coverage, union news, and academic studies declined. Economic-related editorials are increasingly written by journalists who specialize in microeconomics and finance. Beyond this, the paper cultivated advertising-rich supplements dispensing estate-planning advice or investment opportunities in developing countries (where it had previously devoted supplements to their economies or cultures). "We could not keep on going just focusing on the State . . . [T]he strategies of big business and the play of financial markets are much more important for our daily life . . . So we had to adapt, and put a lot more emphasis on business," explained editor-in-chief Jean-Marie Colombani.[12] He was echoed by a mass mailing on the occasion of the new formula: "Business. Because business decisions are just as important as those of the State."

The evolution of *Libération* was less spectacular, but of the same type. *Libération* created an economic section at the beginning of the 1980s, then "Markets" and "Investments" pages. By the end of the 1990s, the section was tightly focused on business and finance. The journalists continued to exhibit a "social" sensibility, but only from time to time and with a slightly ironic tone.

In sum, these two historically "left" dailies have come closer to the traditional business press, from which they now even sometimes recruit economic journalists. They seek out interviews with managers and economic officials in direct competition with this same business press. Whereas in the 1970s the economic journalists of *Le Monde* wrote popularizing studies of capitalism for university presses, in the 1990s they published profiles of French captains of industry. Today *Le Monde* and *Libération* participate in a more or less homogeneous job market in which specialized business journalists circulate between both business news and general news publications.

Business school graduates are still in the minority, but they often quickly reach senior positions in the economic services and are better represented among the younger generation. Many are graduates of the IEP-Paris, and especially of the new *Eco–fi* (economics–finance) department. Of the economic journalists working in the 1990s, the share of IEP graduates ranged from 23 percent among 55–65-year-olds to 37.5 percent among those aged 25 to 35; the share of economics university graduates from 13.9 to 34.3 percent (a good part of the increase coming from management or finance graduates); and that of former business school students from almost none in the senior age brackets to almost 10 percent among the youngest.[13]

The characteristics of economic journalists who, thanks to the appearance of new publications and the development of economic sections in the generalist media, entered the profession in the 1980s confirms the impression of some within the business world. One public relations executive with more than 20 years experience explained the discrepancy between dealing with French and British journalists: while the former "didn't look at the file," "weren't up to date," and "understood nothing," the latter "caught on right away" and "asked good questions." More recently, the gap seemed to have decreased: "I think they [French media] are not hiring badly at the HEC now," this person reported, referring to a major French business school. Expressing a view widespread in the business world (where French journalism is frequently criticized in comparison to the British or US press), this testimony shows how changes in recruitment appear as professionalization from the perspective of the economic field.

In sum, increased professionalization (and specialization) of economic journalists does not only represent a potential bulwark against the usual editorial interference. Insofar as it expresses the rising influence of journalists formed by an education designed for business practitioners, the professionalization process actually decreases the autonomy of the subspace of economic journalism vis-à-vis the economic field.

Conclusion

By the end of the 1990s the autonomy of the most influential French producers of economic news in relation to the economic field had weakened considerably. Not only were their investors often large industrial or financial groups, they were highly dependent on the advertising market and drew a large share of their readers from social groups tightly integrated into the economic world. Strongly subordinated to the economic field, the space analyzed here tends to inform economic agents rather than citizens; it contributes to the smooth operation of the economy much more often than it offers political analyses of it. The analysis proposed here has not only established these two observations; it has shown that they are connected. Thus, it suggests that media outlets strongly integrated into the economic world tend, by their discursive production, to legitimate the existing economic order.

These conclusions have implications well beyond French economic journalism in the 1990s. The mechanisms described, even if they are no doubt particularly visible in economic news sections, are likely at work in a large part of journalistic production – for example, in the domain of political news. Beyond this, the analysis shows how field theory allows us to fruitfully pose the question of journalistic independence in relation to the economy, which is almost always reduced to just that independence that allows them to report on the investors and advertisers who finance them. Finally, statistical analysis has revealed a tripolar structure that is undoubtedly not specific to the space of French economic journalism. It would certainly be worth while to apply the methods employed here to other journalistic specializations and other national contexts. These methods, linked to field theory, can be highly valuable within a comparativist optic. They constitute a powerful tool for understanding the variations and invariants which, according to country and specialization, affect the structure of journalistic spaces, and with them the whole of journalism.

Appendix: multiple correspondence analysis

1 **Population.** A population of outlets (newspapers, magazines, radio and television stations) was constructed, not as a representative sample of all outlets with economic coverage, but by collecting the most "important" – those with the greatest influence within the space, which are picked up in business or government press reviews, frequently cited, and/or listed in journalistic "Who's Who" directories. In total, 44 were examined, listed according to genre (figure abbreviations in parentheses). General and political dailies: *La Croix*, *Le Figaro*, *France Soir*, *L'Humanité*, *Libération*, *Le Monde*, *Le Parisien*; general business dailies: *Agefi*, *Les Echos*, *Journal des Finances*, *La Tribune*; general interest magazines: *Evénement du jeudi* (E du jeudi), *L'Express*, *Marianne*, *Le Nouvel Observateur*, *Le Point*, *Valeurs*

Actuelles (ValeursA); economics and financial press: *Alternatives économiques*, *Capital*, *Challenges*, *Défis*, *Enjeux*, *Entreprendre*, *L'Entreprise*, *Expansion*, *L'Essentiel du management*, *Jeune Afrique Economie*, *Investir*, *Mieux vivre votre argent*, *Nouvel economiste*, *Revenu français* (Revenu fr), *Usine Nouvelle* (UsineNv), *Vie Française* (VieFrç); Political news magazines: *Canard enchaîné*, *Charlie Hebdo*, *Le Monde diplomatique*, *Politis*; Radio and television: BFM, Europe 1, France 2, France 3, France Culture, France Inter, TF1.

2 **Twenty-two variables.** Twenty-two variables were used. In the final analysis, 12 (with 39 modalities) were kept 'active', i.e., used to construct the space. The other ten variables served only as supplementary elements, either because they were made redundant by active questions, or because of the unreliability of the data. (The supplementary elements were then statistically projected onto the space initially constructed with just the active questions.) These variables may be divided into two general categories (A and B).

A **Economic characteristics** of the business on which the outlet depends (9 variables: 5 active, 4 supplementary)

(a) **Legal and financial characteristics**
- (i) Form of control of the company or group owning the outlet (active, 5 modalities: state; majority family control; minority family control; internal or foreign; cooperative).
- (ii) Financial links with other outlets possessing an independent editorial structure (active, 3 modalities: no links to other media; links with other outlets within the present population; links with other outlets not in the present population).

(b) **Outlet's weight** in the media and advertising markets:
- (iii) Audience (active, 3 modalities: large audiovisual audience; circulation above 100,000; circulation below 100,000).
- (iv) Advertising market "rating" among business decision makers. The criterion is the 1998 penetration rate among "working French employers and executives," relying on the authoritative French source of this information (IPSOS) (active, 4 modalities: above 10%; 6 to 10%; below 6%; rate not calculated because the outlet is audiovisual or [almost] absent from this market).
- (v) Dependence on advertising revenues (active). Since the percentage of advertising revenue in turnover is unknown for all of the written press, it was estimated

based on the ratio of advertising to number of pages. The population was divided into 4 ordinal modalities, from outlets that are entirely or almost entirely reader financed (Adv−−) to those that rely most on advertising (Adv++).

(vi–ix) Outlet's economic position in the advertising market (largely made redundant by the social composition of its audience). For want of a better source, this aspect was operationalized as "type of advertiser." Four cases were distinguished (4 supplementary binary (yes–no) variables): financial advisers or business services; cultural (universities, excluding business and management schools, or literary publishers) or humanitarian organizations; airlines (not travel agencies) and luxury goods (jewelry, name-brand perfume, high fashion); food distribution and marketing.

B **Journalistic Characteristics** (13 variables, 7 active and 6 supplementary)

(a) **News production capacity**

(i) Size of economic service (active, 4 modalities): 1 to 10 economic journalists; 11 to 20; 21 to 30; 31 or more.

(ii) Story pick-up (supplementary). A synthetic index was constructed based on counts in three dailies (*L'Humanité*, *La Tribune*, and *Le Monde*) in 1998 and 1999. To standardize the results the pick-up had to mention the outlet of origin and involve an economic rubric. On the basis of these three variables, a fourth was constructed with three ordinal modes: high pick-up rate (by the three dailies); moderate; low (or none).

(b) **Symbolic capital within the journalistic field as a whole**

(iii) Since it takes time to accumulate symbolic capital, age is a relevant indicator, but is hard to report uniformly. Date of establishment was therefore made supplementary and replaced by the geographical location (active) of the editorial offices, which is strongly correlated with the former and can be more accurately reported. 3 modalities: central Paris, including the nineteenth-century press district; western Paris; elsewhere (northern Paris or outside the city).

(iv–vi) Attractiveness for graduates of the Institute for Political Studies (Institut d'Etudes Politiques, or Sciences-Po) of

Paris (supplementary, 3 ordinal modalities); of the two most prestigious and oldest journalism schools, the CFJ (Paris) and the ESJ (Lille) (active, 3 ordinal modalities); and of less prestigious journalism schools and specialized higher education (active, 3 ordinal modalities).

(vii) Use of guest editorials (supplementary binary variable) by well-known authors outside the organization.

(viii) Faithfulness to the French "political/literary" journalistic tradition, one sign of which is the existence of an editorial (often appearing on the front page) taking a political position, signed by a member of the editorial committee (active, binary variable).

(c) **Symbolic capital specific to economic journalism**

(ix–xi) Proportion of economic journalists having studied economics in the dominant institutions of higher education (supplementary, 3 ordinal modalities); proportion of graduates from the most prestigious business schools, the HEC, l'ESSEC, and l'ESC Paris (supplementary, 2 ordinal modalities); proportion of graduates of the *grandes écoles* (active, 3 ordinal modalities).

(xii) Whether the outlet was represented in the 1990s in the office of the AJEF (economic journalists' professional association) (supplementary binary variable)

(d) **Journalists and Management**

(xiii) Journalistic control of management function. An imperfect but relatively uniform indicator of this is the characteristics of the publisher in the written press or the general director in radio and television. A binary variable (active) isolates cases where the manager is a former journalist.

3 **Section headings.** Section headings were collected from outlets' organization charts and analyzed using a technique inspired by textual statistics. For each outlet, all of the words used to designate rubrics were collected. Conjunctions were eliminated, and different forms of the same term were standardized. Each word (or group of words, in the case of expressions like "economy and society" or "international business") was associated with a binary variable, allowing the isolation of outlets with at least one rubric including the word. The diagrams display only those associated with a rubric. A variable was created for outlets that do not use sections. All theses variables were then projected as supplementary elements on the previously constructed space.

Notes

1 The French statistician Jean-Pierre Benzécri is generally credited for developing this method. See his *Correspondence Analysis Handbook* (Dekker, New York, 1994). See also Henry Rouanet and Brigitte Le Roux, *Analyse des données multidimensionnelles* (Dunod, Paris, 1993), esp. pp. 205–300; Michael J. Greenacre, *Theory and Applications of Correspondence Analysis* (Academic Press, London, 1984); and Wouter de Nooy, "Fields and Networks: Correspondence Analysis and Social Network Analysis in the Framework of Field Theory," *Poetics*, 31 (2003), pp. 305–27.

2 As Bourdieu explains in *Homo Academicus* (Polity, Cambridge, 1988 and Stanford University Press, Stanford, CA, 1988), pp. 69–70:

> The basis of the method is the table of deviations (in the case of a two-by-two table) between the result observed and the result which would be obtained in the hypothetical case of random distribution, where all the statistical units behaved according to the general average, the rows and columns of the table being reciprocally proportional. The analysis of correspondences represents these deviations visually in factorial plans which weight them according to their distance from chi-square: positive deviations (where the results observed are more frequent than the results expected), negative deviations (where they are less frequent) or zero deviations (where they are equal) . . . Each statistical unit does or does not possess a certain number of attributes (coded as presence/absence 0–1), and we take into consideration both the deviations between individuals [media organizations, Ed.] and those between variables . . . [A]n attraction between two [variables] is represented in spatial terms as a conjunction . . . A negative deviation, or repulsion, between two [variables] is translated as a spatial opposition.

Bourdieu also emphasizes that with correspondence analysis the "redundancy of the categories of analysis (frequent in sociology, where we often use indicators which are highly correlated with each other . . .) does not not entail any fatal statistical error." See also Pierre Bourdieu and Monique de Saint-Martin, "Le patronat," *Actes de la recherche en sciences sociales*, 20–1 (March 1978), pp. 3–82.

3 Pierre Bourdieu, "Social Space and the Genesis of 'Classes'," in *Language and Symbolic Power*, ed. J.B. Thompson (Harvard, Cambridge, MA, 1991 and Polity, Cambridge, 1991), p. 232.

4 Graduates of the most prestigious journalism schools may of course perceive media outlets as prestigious and take jobs with them in part because of the higher salaries and benefits offered, in which case any distinction between economic and cultural capital is elided. While such economic factors help account for the lesser prevalence of journalism school graduates at "alternative publications," it does not entirely explain why they tend to avoid (and not be appreciated) by many of the most commercially oriented media outlets.

5 In general, journalistic prestige is notably more difficult to measure than economic characteristics, not least because the latter are much more likely to be already statistically objectified in a number of ways. The construction of adequate variables and accompanying data sets to measure journalistic cultural capital, in all its manifestations, remains one of the greatest challenges for field analysis. For the case of economic journalism, the analysis of an autonomous pole is further complicated by the fact that many measures of prestige in this specialized subdomain – such as higher education in business schools and economics departments – are also closely correlated with economic logics. This close interrelationship, however, is not a statistical problem, but a reflection of the field's very constitution. After proceeding on the assumption that as in other autonomous subfields, specific and economic logics would be opposed, interviews with journalists themselves revealed the high internal prestige accorded these (heteronomous) diplomas. Removal of the professional variable most closely linked to heteronomous logics – a degree from a business school – does not in any case substantially modify the findings.

6 Pierre Bourdieu, *The Rules of Art* (Stanford University Press, Stanford, CA, 1995 and Polity, Cambridge, 1996), esp. pp. 141–73; Pierre Bourdieu, "Une révolution conservatrice dans l'édition," *Actes de la recherche en sciences sociales*, 126–7 (March 1999), pp. 3–28.

7 Figures 7.1 and 7.2 represent the distribution of points along the two axes which accounted for the greatest proportion of total variation (18 and 15.5 percent respectively or, if one uses the "modified rates" that some mathematicians consider the most relevant, 41 and 28 percent respectively). I do not discuss here the other axes, which were analyzed but are of much less sociological and statistical interest. The Greek lambda signs in the diagram refer to the raw values (0.405 for axis 1 and 0.348 for axis 2).

8 All quotations from Paris-based journalists are derived from interviews conducted by the author between 1996 and 1999.

9 This is opposed to the front page, where "journalists write in anticipation of readers who ask, 'What is happening in the world today that I should know about as a citizen of my community, nation, and world?' " See Michael Schudson, *The Power of News* (Harvard University Press, Cambridge, MA, 1996), p. 14.

10 Jean-Claude Perrier, *Le Roman vrai de "Libération"* (Julliard, Paris, 1994).

11 Pierre Bourdieu, "*Libé*, vingt ans après," *Actes de la recherche en sciences sociales*, 101–2 (March 1994), p. 39.

12 From interview with Jean-Marie Colombani, *Le Cercle de minuit*, France 2 (television), January 19, 1995.

13 Based on author's analysis of *Guide des journalistes économiques* (Editions Jean-François Doumic, Paris, 1991, 1995 and 1997).

8

Media Consecration of the Political Order

Eric Darras

If "democratic" competition aims, directly or indirectly, at provisionally naming agents to particular positions of assigned state power for the duration of an electoral term, according to Pierre Bourdieu there always at the same time remains a struggle over the right to say *what is*, and therefore what is not, political. The ongoing redefinition of the field is the central stake of relations of forces and accommodations, on the one hand, between people and institutions and, on the other, among people. The range of possibilities, however, is always constrained by rules and roles fixed by *institutions* (constitutions, parties, idioms), inasmuch as they are objectivations of the tangled work of the people of the past long before they pass to those of the present.

Consequently, the French and US political fields (frontiers, structures, rules of the game, fields of possibilities) are different because they inherit different social histories and highly dissimilar relations of forces. In the United States, for example, money is a more decisive resource in political life than in France; owing to the political importance of interest groups, political professionals' monopoly over political representation is less secure than in France; and the (re)defined powers of American judges, their status as independent prosecutors, have considerable and specific political effects no French judge could imagine.

It nonetheless remains that these two political fields can be compared, provided that we avoid exporting an ethnocentric perspective that attributes mechanisms and representations specific to the French political field to that of the United States. It is thus necessary to recall that the conceptual model of a political field only becomes meaningful by being put to an empirical test. Bourdieu specifies that "comparison is possible only from system to system, and that the search for direct equivalences between features grasped in isolation . . . risks unduly identifying structurally identical properties or wrongly distinguishing structurally identical properties."[1] To take a simple example, the title "senator," nominally identical in France and the United States, refers to completely dissimilar political positions; conversely, the position of French ministers is structurally comparable to those of certain US federal administrative officers.

In sociology, the explanatory primacy of relation, theorized by Bourdieu against substantialisms of all kinds, allows us to rank political positions within the field by the *relative* disposal over certain amounts and types of resources (economic, cultural, and social capital) that each of the *interdependent* positions has at a particular time. But these resources change with the evolution of structures for allocating value. In France, one's chance of reaching a ministerial position increases with one's social and professional background, the prestigious degrees one can bring to bear, etc. For about 20 years a female politician has had a reasonable chance of obtaining a ministerial portfolio, just as the hierarchy of the great state bureaucracy has changed somewhat, with finance inspectors (*inspecteurs de finances*) having the inside track to the core of the government over members of the state council (Conseil d'état). Similarly, many regard the commercial logic of television as exerting an ever greater influence on the political field, and thus on the recruitment of political professionals. We will see that this hypothesis is amenable to empirical confirmation: the similarities between France and the United States in the choice of political invitees on television demonstrates that, if television has contributed to the transformation of political discourse, it plays at best a marginal role in the most important element – the selection of people and dominant political institutions.

For Bourdieu, the journalistic field is, as it were, absorbed into the political space.[2] Statistical objectivation of those invited on *Meet the Press* from 1949 to 1995 and its French equivalents (the long-running *L'Heure de vérité* or "Hour of Truth" and its most significant predecessors) from 1966 to 1995 allows us to give empirical flesh to these accounts.[3] Analysis shows that, despite the profound differences between the two media fields (and especially the greater dependence of US networks on commercial forces), the logic of invitations on political television proves to be remarkably similar: in France as in the United States, access to television remains almost exclusively reserved for the political elite. The frontiers (1) and hierarchies (2) of the political field impose themselves on journalists in charge of political programs in France and the United States, and a comparative approach reveals that the specificities of the two political systems have been transferred to television throughout the history of invitations: namely, the decisive roles of interest groups, federal administrative agencies, states, and senators in the United States, as opposed especially to the preeminence of the executive in France. The most traditional explanations are necessary but insufficient (3), and comparative analysis in terms of field theory demonstrates, against all expectations, the structural subordination of the journalistic field to the political field (4).

The crude ethnocentrism of early works of American political science, in the line of Almond and Verba,[4] long discredited the use of comparative method in France. Nevertheless, revised by field theory – which offers an alternative to sterile oppositions between the primacy of the actor or the system (American rational choice theory being exported via comparativism) – international comparison can offer decisive methodological advantages. Not only does it allow us to increase the available data and provide an antidote to ethnocentric explanations; above all, as Durkheim understood, only comparison enables us to discriminate among the various explanatory factors of a social phenomenon which need to be taken into account. The ambition is not to compare these programs *among themselves* with a view to establishing a sort of winner's circle; it is to understand their specificities, their respective interactions with the political spaces in which they are situated. It is precisely these differences that help us account for the relations of interdependence between journalists and political invitees on television.

The Imposition of the Frontiers of the Political Field

First observation: the longest lasting political programs invite politicians almost exclusively (table 8.1). A truism? No. This is moreover truer in France than in the United States, where the frontiers of the political field are more porous. Top tier politicians occasionally appear on nonpolitical programs, especially during election years. To the extent that political shows "of reference" become less and less common, because of the growing importance of audience ratings (politics being virtually "unsellable" on television), an oligarchical phenomenon – the monopolization of political shows by high political dignitaries – would seem to logically accentuate itself. For this reason, the televisual-political space is increasingly protected from

Table 8.1 Guest lists of French and US political interview shows

	French Political TV Shows 1966–95 (n = 503)		Meet The Press 1949–79/1984–5/1994–5 (n = 1,855)	
General	(%)	(n)	(%)	(n)
National political field (government, parties)	80	(402)	66	(1,228)
Foreigners	6	(28)	10	(187)
Civil service/bureaucrats	0.5	(2)	9	(172)
Interest groups	4	(19)	6	(115)
Intellectuals/experts	5	(24)	6	(107)
Industrial leaders	2	(10)	1	(17)
Clergy	2	(10)	0.3	(6)
Sports/show business	0.5	(2)	0.3	(5)
Others or insufficient information	1	(6)	1	(18)

what is usually called "genre mixing." Furthermore, comparison reveals differences between national definitions of politics: in the United States, the shows are more likely to include foreign political figures, interest groups, and "bureaucrats," especially those from federal administrative agencies.

For the most part and following an ethnocentric logic recognized by journalists themselves, invitations of foreign personalities on US political magazines coincide, as in France, with certain of the military, political and economic interests assumed by the government of the United States (Israel, Great Britain, Germany, South America . . .).

In the United States, political parties and unions do not have much control over the representatives of issue-oriented and other independent political groups. Interest groups participate in political debates, decisions, and functions (such as financing candidacies) on a scale and following procedures unknown in France. As a result, the groups in the media are at once more various and more numerous than in France. But in fact, interest group leaders such as the feminists of NOW largely appear on television to the extent that the federal government is already interested in them, for the most varied reasons. Herbert Gans offers the caricatural example of the Socialist Workers' party, which appeared on *Meet the Press* only after it was revealed that it had been infiltrated by the FBI.[5] All in all, age, representativeness, proximity to or imbrication within Washington's political and administrative fields, and other indirect modalities of governmental investiture explain the visibility of the most important interest groups on television.

In France, members of the highest courts, the Conseil d'état and the Conseil constitutionnel, do not appear on political television. On the whole, it is the same in the United States. The disproportionately modest participation of captains of industry, like that of generals, on the television programs reserved for the political elite (1 and 2 percent of invitations on *Meet the Press*, respectively) recalls that holders of economic and military power have little interest in publicly demonstrating their proximity to political power. Nevertheless, the televisual visibility of these US officials proves to be quite superior to those of their French counterparts for the most part invisible on television, due to the lesser interpenetration in France of the political world with that of the high bureaucracy, military, and judiciary.

Thus, the absences from these programs teach as much as the presences, and the theory of *reflection*, according to which the structure of invitations would merely mechanically reproduce the structure of power, appears somewhat naïve. There can be an "interest" in avoiding, or seeming disinterested in, media attention.[6] On the other hand, as opposed to high court judges or heads of multinational firms, the main political leaders have to appear on television in order to believe, and make others believe, in the reality of their power, and thus appropriate (and expropriate from other decision makers) responsibility for the course of events. National television undoubtedly plays an essential role in this interested imputation of responsibility by maintaining the common sense whereby politicians wield real power. Here, field theory allows us to get beyond excessively structuralist or determinist models by recalling that the interests in mediatization are plural and evolving.

In France, the government (roughly, the executive in the United States) seems to be clearly privileged by television, while other major institutions – the National Assembly and the Senate, the European Parliament, regional and local elected officials (big city mayors, presidents of general or regional councils) – are almost completely absent. This televisual hegemony of the national political level is not found in the United States, but that does not make the statistical distribution of political invitations more democratic.

The Imposition of Political Hierarchies

On *L'Heure de vérité*, the longest-running program in the history of French television, just 16 people shared more than half the invitations over 13 years (1982–94). This phenomenon is neither new nor specific to this program: we find the same oligarchic recruitment to earlier programs such as *Face à face* in 1966. Nor is it specifically French. In the United States, less than 50 people, most of them high federal officials, regularly constitute the news.[7]

Naming the names of invitees could be misleading: the temporary occupants of positions are less revealing of political television's logic of recruitment than the positions themselves. The political-televisual space seems to be reserved not for individuals, but for the political positions they hold – precisely the most prestigious in the political field. In France, it can be shown that the principal trophies of the political arena are concentrated in the hands of these 16 political professionals: presidents of the Republic, prime ministers, heads of the main political formations, and principal government ministers (cabinet secretaries).

We would not expect to find the monopolization of invitations seen on *L'Heure de vérité* on *Meet the Press*, which extends over a much longer period and, *a fortiori*, is situated within a federal system. Nevertheless, the structure of invitations is similar, as a detailed inventory of invitees and invitations shows. Six political invitees (1.4 percent of the total) share one-tenth of all political invitations. Among the 25 politicians who appear most often (6 percent of all invitees), we find 18 candidates for the Democratic or Republican presidential or vice-presidential nomination, 13 senators, and 8 governors, against only 2 representatives – all in all, 12 Democrats and 13 Republicans.

In effect, membership in the first circle of invitees to political shows can be explained by reference to the highest position of the US political field: the presidency. Nevertheless, in France as in the United States, the head of state, once in office, does not frequent political programs. The reason is simple: though absent from the political shows, the president is on television all year long through news programs, televised addresses, swearing-in ceremonies, press conferences, and programs specifically reserved for the head of state, as well as appearing on political shows through the mediation of spokespersons.

Journalists know that top-ranking politicians participate on the premise that he or she will only be confronted by a rival of (at least) the same "symbolic weight" in the political field. By recognizing (that is to say, accrediting) the ritual of the program, political invitees first of all recognize their equals. The televisual-political forum becomes the pretext for a consecration by contagion,[8] and appearance on television therefore operates like a symbolic *skeptron* distributed among political peers.[9] If political shows are indeed "rites of institution" (more than "rites of passage"), it is above all because they express preexisting positions and relations of force more than they produce them.[10] The privileged grantees to these political–media rituals are

Table 8.2 Political capital of guests on French political TV shows (within national political field)

Titles	French political TV shows 1966–95 (n = 402) (%)	(n)
President and prime minister	21	(83)
Top ten ministers of state (cabinet secretaries)	28	(109)
Other government ministers	14	(54)
Subministers (ministres délégués, secrétaires d'état)	7	(27)
Leaders of the principal political parties and candidates for President	15	(58)
Other political professionals ("second rank")	14	(56)

thus clearly distinguished from the politicians that never reach them: the rite renders visible and accredits the gaps between positions in the political field.

Top-ranking political personnel (former members of government, top officials of the five main political parties, and former presidential candidates) take up 82 percent of invitations on the main French political shows since 1966 (see table 8.2). The national executive in effect monopolizes political television at the expense of the legislature. All the same, it does not suffice to be a minister to appear on the most prestigious programs: one's chances of appearing on television rise with one's accumulated political capital.

In France as in the United States, the visibility of politicians on television is that much greater if they occupy an elevated position in the political field. Invitees to political shows have thus been preselected by the political field and not by journalists, as famous as the latter may be. We therefore cannot blame journalists for the notable absence of female invitees: if there were only 11 female politicians in the whole history of *L'Heure de vérité* (1982–1994), this is above all due to their exclusion from the political battlefield.

How is this broad process of political discrimination to be explained?

Necessary but Insufficient Explanations

Let us consider the first set of explanations, internal ones, to begin with. We need not deny the justification journalists themselves advance: they invite "those who count," whom they have a (democratic) duty to question. Priority is given to presidential candidates and senior ministers because they are the "real decision makers," or, better, because responsibility for political decisions is attributed to them. The televisual hegemony of ministers helps accredit the doxic belief that only the government possesses political power, and more broadly celebrates representations of political power as real power. This first type of explanation leads to a second: in France as in the United States, television's national audience requires that priority be given to people, themes, and parties that are "isomorphic" with the media, and thus national. In the United States, the networks (i.e. "coast-to-coast television") are inseparably products and media of a process of nationalization (of stakes, people, problems, and solutions, which are thus redefined as political and relevant to the jurisdiction of national politicians and Washington). It remains that in France as in the United States, deputies or members of Congress – "representatives of the nation" – seldom if ever make it on the most prestigious political fora. Moreover, many themes and politicians of national significance never appear on a national forum, and we have seen that certain business leaders who steer society, to take up Weber, have absolutely no interest in being made visible via the media. It is therefore better or worse founded journalistic beliefs concerning the definition of "real" political power that are at work. Here, journalistic objectivity as the internalization of official values plays a central role.[11]

Next we come to a series of economic explanations, and thus to organizational constraints and geographical biases.[12] In the United States, in order to minimize the cost of news, journalists privilege themes and political elites in Washington, who are near at hand and always available. This geographical bias is explained in particular by the fact that in the United States (as in France), national news is mostly political news, and thus comes from the political centers of Washington (or Paris). We should not underestimate this tautological explanation: news is created where its (co)creators are, and this means the correspondents of the *national* press. In addition, celebrities, including political celebrities, are in a sense "pre-sold products,"[13] and thus minimize the risk of failure in terms of audience size or impact in the print press. Field observations of editorial rooms made by numerous American researchers reliably insist on the importance of organizational constraints. In television, journalistic work is essentially collective; the division of labor requires routines that advantage sources that are easy to access, available, and able to anticipate the exigencies of journalistic work.[14]

Finally, the third explanatory register: relations between journalistic and political elites. The easy explanation via collusion and contacts seems simplistic, even if it is not always absurd, especially in France. At the moment, the most important political show is on at the least economically penalizing time for the grid, Sunday morning. This is not only because it satisfies the minimal democratic requirements of the FCC or the CSA,[15] but also because it improves the image (especially in terms of impact in the print press, where Sunday remains a slow news day) of the main general interest stations, which cannot risk displeasing the country's most important political decision makers. All the more so since television, in the United States as increasingly in France, has become the emerging sector of powerful firms that depend on public markets, and thus on good relations with political decision makers. In France, ethnographic observation reveals that it is almost always the station's president–CEO who welcomes political invitees and accompanies them to the makeup room, confirming the essential lobbying role of the weekly political program.[16] In contrast, the most prominent journalists do not *necessarily* maintain friendly relations with politicians.

The collusions appear subtler at a higher level of sociological clarity. Politicians also control journalists through a variety of positive sanctions (warm handshakes, addressing them in an informal manner, invitations to lunch or even dinner, encouragement, confidences, off-the-record remarks, exclusives, deliberate leaks, etc.). Otherwise, despite

> intra- or intergroup competition, regular access to the media is generally reserved to people with extreme wealth or other, institutionally-based power resources. This power is in effect at once a result and a durable cause of regular access. Routinized access to the media is one of the major sources, and one of the main resources, of existing power relations.[17]

Numerous case studies confirm that the professional ideology of objectivity ensures the preponderant visibility of dominant political sources, even when this contradicts journalists' personal political preferences.

Field Theory in Perspective

Field analysis, which allows the position-taking (in the "choice" of invitees), positions, and dispositions of the inviters as well as the invitees to be studied simultaneously, integrates the preceding explanations while pushing them further. It allows us to specify other types of relations, all the more effective in being less visible, which occur through affinities of habitus (and thus relatively similar social trajectories) and/or mechanisms of structural homology between politicians and journalists.

We thus need to understand in each case the specific relation of domination between the journalist and his or her source – here, his or her political interlocutor. While Max Weber defines domination as "the probability that a command [or order] . . . will be obeyed,"[18] orders here carry less the sense of injunctions (for instance in the manner of Alain Peyrefitte, General de Gaulle's information minister, who gave direct "orders" to television news) than of Order – the harmonious organization or durable arrangement of relations between agents and institutions (in the sense of a "return to Order" or "rank"). The journalistic Order is inserted within the political Order, and thus is Ordered without any need for orders. In France, moreover, the former is certainly the historical product of the latter; a true sociogenesis of the journalistic field, showing in what ways it has progressively but insufficiently become autonomous from the political universe, remains to be undertaken.

But, once again, field theory allows us to escape excessively mechanistic or structuralist explanations. If most of the time only a political elite makes it on television, exceptional configurations of the field are nevertheless possible. To take an extreme example, the hypothesis of the omnipotent journalist, who can "launch" a political personality, is not entirely unfounded. The exceptions confirm the rule: it is because this ritual is reserved for the political elite that an unauthorized grantee (the invitation of a second-rank politician remains exceptional) confers a veritable consecration. Appearance on a key political program can prove extremely fruitful in propelling the career of a second-tier politician: the program's symbolic efficacy can turn out to be quite real if the grantee lives up to his *pretension*. Here, the properly magical force of a political program rests on the belief in the media at the heart of political and media circles. If, for sociologists, the political omnipotence of television remains more hypothetical than real, the *belief* in this omnipotence, shared by politicians, has real effects. But the journalist's margin of maneuver remains limited: he can only invite "rising youth" in "homeopathic doses,"[19] since he invests the program's accumulated symbolic capital and risks diluting top-tier politicians, and possibly diminishing the status of his program.

The Internalization of Political Institutions: The Professional Habitus of Journalists

By analyzing the frames (in Bateson's sense, taken up by Goffman) of journalistic understanding, we see that television professionals internalize the representations by which the actors and institutions of the Political Order dominate them. The structural subordination of the journalistic field is made possible by journalistic self-censorship via the more or less confused absorption of the relative importance of political *institutions* (the constitution, the government, the Congress,[20] the dominant parties, and especially in France, the National School for Administration/Ecole Nationale d'Administration or ENA[21]). Through a journalistic habitus constituted in this way, the political affairs that appear as problems for journalists – the major themes of the day, the important figures – are those whose importance is institutionally recognized as such: those that *constitute authority* in the minds of journalists.

Subjectively and objectively adapted to their position, the most prominent political journalists are hired, paid, and rewarded to reproduce the political common sense with which they are imbued and in part distinguishes them from their less successful competitors. The most productive journalists are those who have best assimilated the theodicies that support representative government and the social system as a whole (the real power of politicians; the political participation of the "people"; the "separation of powers"; etc.). The professional habitus of French journalists is part of a primary socialization that includes dispositions toward academic docility, reinforced and rewarded through a doxic education at the Institut d'études politiques (IEP, or Sciences-Po) in Paris, a veritable factory of the dominant ideology,[22] and eventually completed, for the youngest, by an apprenticeship through a journalism school. The limited autonomy of journalists is thus explained by a higher education that is completely independent of the universities, the critical spirit of political journalists today being more often forged by the reading of technical manuals than of Nietzsche, Marx, or Schumpeter.

Within this relation of domination, journalists and politicians remain partner–rivals: they share the same values, but are not situated on the same level. This largely misrecognized self-censorship, the submission of journalists to official structures, is achieved especially through the repressed social distance that separates them from their political sources. The journalist's position *in his face-to-face relation* with the elected representative of the people, who benefits not only from the anointment of universal suffrage but also, most often, from considerable social and educational resources remains inevitably problematic. In other words, while there may be broad affinities of habitus between some journalists and politicians, it is important to remember that going to Sciences-Po is often an end in itself for journalists, while it is only the starting point of higher education for many of their political interlocutors, who subsequently go on to ENA. Aside from the prestige of his office, then, the top-tier French politician remains, with exceptions, much better credentialed, more admired and appreciated – although these days not better paid – than the star political journalist.

But the harmony of interests between journalists and politicians goes much further. The professional recognition of a journalist remains a direct function of his or her proximity to power, address book, and the "big interviews" that can be flourished against peers as well as bosses. It is as if the "little world" of politics always functioned according to etiquette and the logic of prestige.[23] To extend the analogy with the feudal court, which Elias regarded as the laboratory of modern political life, we must note the intersecting relations of domination, which at once unite and divide political and media agents, that evolve at the summit of the state. Political and journalistic elites are caught up in a particularly dense and complex net of reciprocal dependencies. The "top" politicians produce the authority and legitimacy of the "top" interviewers, and vice versa.

Similarities within Differences

Comparative analysis in terms of field theory can allow us to evaluate the relevance of these playing fields. The political order is similarly but differently reflected in the United States by *Meet The Press* and in France by *L'Heure de verité* (see tables 8.2 and 8.3).

Reported by political job (50 who work with the president,[24] 50 governors, 100 senators, 435 representatives), chances of appearing on *Meet the Press* rank as follows: (1) senators, (2) members of the federal government, (3) governors, (4) members of the House of Representatives. The peculiarities of the American political system are thus found on US political programs, tending to confirm the hypothesis of a structural subordination of the journalistic field to the political field.

While in France members and former members of the government (executive) are hegemonic on political programs, this is not the case in the United States, although they are clearly primary.

Table 8.3 Political capital of guests on *Meet the Press* (within national political field)

Titles	Meet The Press (1949–79/1984–5/1994–5) (n = 1,228) (%)	(n)
US senators	36	(438)
Members of the US presidency (president, vice president, cabinet, executive office, presidential advisors)	24	(291)
State governors	17	(196)
US representatives	12	(149)
Mayors	6	(68)
Chairpersons of the Republican or Democratic national committees	2	(32)
Other political professionals	4	(54)

French television, however, remains markedly more "Jacobin" (centralized) than US television. Although there are nearly twice as many French as American elected officials,[25] American political shows, unlike their French equivalents, give real visibility to legislative power. The specific hierarchies of the American political field allow other types of political professionals access to television, in particular, US senators and representatives, and governors from the various states. Thus, the American political system is traditionally distinguished from the French on two levels: on the one hand, parliamentarians have political prerogatives that cannot be compared to those of legislators in the Fifth Republic; on the other hand, the United States operates as a federal system. But television reflects the order of political hierarchies more subtly by privileging the most powerful ministers or cabinet secretaries (interior, treasury, defense, education and welfare, justice) and certain governors and senators – those, essentially, of national significance (and, for the most part, with potential presidential ambitions). By contrast, the French Senate is for the most part composed of politicians at the end of their careers and, for that reason, nonexistent for television. The probability of a governor, senator, or representative appearing on NBC's feature political program seems to depend above all on the political importance of the state he or she represents: the three states most represented on *Meet The Press* are among the most powerful of the union, i.e. those with the most seats in the House of Representatives (New York, California, and Illinois).

This more or less crude internalization of the relative importance of political institutions by journalists is confirmed by the de facto exclusion of "small" parties: in the United States as in France, membership in a dominant party is a condition sine qua non of access not only to positions of political power, but also to the most prestigious political fora. Even in France, where the political spectrum is clearly more open than in the United States, taking all programs together, the "parties of government" (RPR, UDF, PS) take up more than 80 percent of the televisual space outside elections.

The Exceptions Justify the Rule

All the same, the structural subordination of the journalistic field to the political field (the imposition of political frontiers, hierarchies, nominations, and moods on the media) can be more or less effectively frustrated – but not for the reasons usually advanced. Thus, notably, private financing does not seem to disrupt the political oligarchy of political shows in any way. The privatization of TF1 in 1986 did not lead to any significant change in the political invitees on the famous program *7 sur 7*.[26] If the structure of invitations remains on the whole homogeneous, this is not only due to the long-standing submission of public service channels to the logics of competition and audience maximization, but above all to political factors.

Unarguably, politicians and political parties anticipate the imperatives of television. As summarized by Neveu, the political trade has been enriched by a new form of expertise "constituted by the mastery of media, the ability to anticipate reception and media imperatives."[27] But monocausal explanation, according to which the television journalist can select a politician who "looks good on television," who has "a good potential image," etc., is clearly inadequate. It creates the impression that new profiles of political recruitment have emerged which privilege self-presentation. In France, at least, the firm implantation of television viewing habits by the end of the 1960s (much later than in the United States), and then the advent of commercial television in the 1980s, played at best a marginal role in changing political career paths. On this point, comparison with the powerful causal role played by the ENA since 1950, for instance, or the successive transformations of the RPR (the party of de Gaulle and Chirac) in the mutations of the political field since 1974, certainly calls into question the most spectacular claims of unbridled media power. In the United States, one thinks in particular of the recent evolutions of the Republican party or the effect of neoconservative think-tanks as elements that could usefully complicate lazy explanations that depend on television's audience-seeking mise-en-scène of the president's sex life, or, worse, culturalist explanations pointing to Puritanism. Such accounts obscure precisely the knot of social relations at work at a particular time, the complex interactions that alone can account for the media coverage of Clinton's erotic encounters while Kennedy never had to worry on this count.[28]

If journalists really possessed powers of selection, we would expect them to co-opt politicians equipped with the social properties valorized by the journalistic field – especially at the level of age, cultural capital, and physical capital (self-presentation, bearing, bodily *hexis*). Thus, it is not for nothing that the political elite that monopolizes the televisual space logically wields the most prestigious resources of the political field: in France, they are older, better credentialed, have more exclusive educations, and are more often male than is the average political professional, including top-tier political personnel. If commercial television may have marginally contributed to the redefinition of professional excellence in politics, the purely "telegenic" factor only appears in exceptional cases.[29] Statistical objectification reveals the normal operation of the relation between high political officials and political journalists, and thereby authorizes a rupture with the professional common sense that postulates the omnipotence of television. In some cases, academic specialists on the journalistic field, lacking sufficient scholarly distance, often focus on the exceptions at the expense of the rule. In so doing, they are captured by their object of study and wind up adopting precisely that journalistic logic which (over)valorizes rarity. This telegenic factor is not only *not* entirely new (politicians have always been characterized by their ability to seize public discourse), it is neither necessarily durable nor even *naturally* favorable to the grantee (according to the configuration, being telegenic can be redefined as a stigma: "superficial," "inconsistent," etc). The telegenic factor is in any case not the only, nor even most decisive, factor in the current transformation of the political field.

Political leaders are not political leaders because they are telegenic; to the contrary, in nearly all cases, they are telegenic because they are already consecrated political leaders. A regular and predictable phenomenon, the invitation of politicians on political television arises neither from their "media talent" nor the "whims" of journalists. To the contrary, only the specifically political resources progressively acquired in the political field, capital objectified by titles (governmental, from positions within parties or unions, from standing in elections) and awarded to a large extent autonomously by the political field, allows access to political television.

Notes

1 Pierre Bourdieu, *Practical Reason: On the Theory of Action* (Stanford University Press, Stanford, 1998 and Polity, Cambridge, 1998), p. 6.
2 See *On Television* (The New Press, New York, 1998), p. 76, where Pierre Bourdieu writes: "in a certain way, the journalistic field is part of the political field on which it has such a powerful impact. Nevertheless, these two fields are both very directly and very tightly in the grip of the market and the referendum."
3 This paper is an updated version of an original comparative study that examined the entire universe of guest lists for *Meet the Press* from February 6, 1949 through January 28, 1979. *Meet the Press* transcripts and guest lists available via Lexis-Nexis were subsequently examined for 1984–5 and 1994–5. Since the only significant difference between the 1980s/1990s samples and the 1949–79 data was a slightly higher proportion of US Representatives and a slightly lower share of state governors (probably reflecting an increasing "nationalization" of American politics during the period), the US data is presented in aggregate form. For the French case, in addition to *L'Heure de vérité* which was broadcast from 1982–95, guest lists from all political interview shows lasting at least three years were included: *Face à . . .* (1966–9), *A armes égales* (1970–3), *Les trois vérités* (1973–6), *Cartes sur tables* (1977–81), and *Questions à domicile* (1986–9).
4 Gabriel Almond and Sidney Verba, *The Civic Culture: Political Attitudes and Democracy in Five Nations and Analytic Study* (Little, Brown, New York, 1965).
5 Herbert Gans, *Deciding What's News* (Vintage, New York, 1980), p. 13.
6 In the same sense, academics, artists, or religious leaders have, to a certain extent, an interest in economic disinterestedness. Bourdieu's pioneering studies on the housing market could be extended by recalling that, if the national ascent of the Bouygues construction firm was based on television advertising, well before the largest public channel TF1 was purchased by the firm, Francis Bouygues himself never appeared on television. See Pierre Bourdieu, *Les structures sociales de l'économie* (Seuil, Paris, 2000), pp. 72–9.
7 Gans, *Deciding What's News*, p. 12.
8 Pierre Bourdieu, "The Hit Parade of French Intellectuals, or Who is to Judge the Legitimacy of the Judges?" in *Homo Academicus* (Stanford University Press, Stanford, CA, 1988, and Polity, Cambridge, 1998), pp. 256–70.

9 Pierre Bourdieu, "Political Representation: Elements for a Theory of the Political Field," in *Language and Symbolic Power*, ed. J.B. Thompson (Harvard University Press, Cambridge, 1991, and Polity, Cambridge, 1991), pp. 171–202.
10 Pierre Bourdieu, "Rites of Institution," in *Language and Symbolic Power*, pp. 117–26.
11 Gaye Tuchman, "Objectivity as Strategic Ritual," *American Journal of Sociology*, 77 (1972), pp. 660–79; Timothy Cook, *Governing with the News* (University of Chicago Press, Chicago, 1998).
12 Edward J. Epstein, *News from Nowhere* (Random House, New York, 1973); Joseph R. Dominick, "Geographic Bias in National TV News," *Journal of Communication*, 27, 4 (1977), pp. 94–9.
13 Jay Rosen, "The Talk Show and the Terror of Conversation," *ETC.*, 47, 4 (winter 1990/91).
14 Patrick Champagne, *Faire l'opinion* (Minuit, Paris, 1990).
15 The Conseil supérieur de l'audiovisuel is the functional French equivalent of the the US Federal Communications Commission; the French regulatory organization is inspired at all levels by the FCC, even if its authority is restricted to radio and television (and not to telecommunications).
16 Comparison with the United States makes certain French peculiarities more visible: the careers of the most senior administrative officials in public radio and television, who are often former political journalists, remains tightly dependent on their proximity to various top-ranking politicians.
17 Harvey Molotch and Marilyn Lester, "News as Purposive Behavior: On the Strategic Use of Routine Events, Accidents, and Scandals," *American Sociological Review*, 39 (1974), p. 107.
18 Max Weber, *Economy and Society*, vol. I (University of California Press, Berkeley, CA, 1978), p. 53.
19 "Je m'efforce d'introduire à dose homéopathique des jeunes qui montent," F.-H. de Virieu (moderator of *L'Heure de vérité*), *Libération*, April 3, 1987.
20 For an emblematic illustration, Tom Brokaw, while serving as moderator of *Meet the Press* was asked about the silence of the American media in general and of NBC in particular during American-sponsored aerial bombardments of El Salvador in 1982 and responded: "Congress is supposed to represent the people, and when there is no opposition in Congress, there isn't much that we can report" (quoted in Lance Bennett, *News: The Politics of Illusion*, Longman, New York, 1988, p. 138).
21 ENA has become practically the only means of access to the top positions of state in France, not only in the high civil service, but ultimately ministerial (cabinet secretaries) and executive positions at the head of the largest French companies, private as well as public.

22 See Pierre Bourdieu and Luc Boltanski, "La production de l'idéologie dominante," *Actes de la recherches en sciences sociales*, 2–3 (1976), pp. 4–73; See also Alain Garrigou, *Les élites contre la République: Sciences Po et l'ENA* (La Découverte, Paris, 2001), p. 95.

23 Norbert Elias, *The Court Society* (Pantheon, New York, 1983).

24 Rather than limit the total population of "those who work with the President" to the 20 or so members of the cabinet (including the president and vice-president), it is preferable to artificially "inflate" their number to 50 in order to include other official and unofficial advisors.

25 If we add the 80 European deputies to senators and deputies, there are 978 French elected officials as opposed to 535 American national legislators.

26 Eric Darras, "Le pouvoir médiacratique?" *Politix*, 30 (1995), pp. 183–98.

27 Erik Neveu, *Une société de communication?* (Montchrestien, Paris, 1994), p. 94ff.

28 See Gans, *Deciding What's News*, p. 245.

29 In the United States, governors Jesse Ventura and Arnold Schwarzenegger obviously come to mind, as do former actors and entertainers in the House of Representatives such as Sony Bono and Fred Grandy (Gopher on the *Love Boat*). In most if not all of these cases, however, these celebrities had significant fundraising or other connections to the parties, and once nominated, had to work hard to establish their political seriousness. Often, their success, certainly to the extent that it has continued, has been dependent on sponsorship by party establishments, as with the crucial legitimacy and strategic advice provided Schwarzenegger by former California Governor Pete Wilson and his staff.

9

Channeling into the Journalistic Field: Youth Activism and the Media Justice Movement

Eric Klinenberg

In this chapter I explore the ways that Pierre Bourdieu's field theory explicates the conditions in which actors and organizations involved in struggles over the substance and structure of media production – including corporations, foundations, government agencies, educators, editors, journalists, and activists – operate. I argue that field theory is particularly useful for identifying the relational forces that establish the positions and dispositions of media producers, critics, and consumers, and therefore for mapping the range of challenges that youth media activists and other groups interested in effecting change within journalism face.[1] Bourdieu's related concepts of capital (cultural, economic, social, and symbolic) provide additional explanatory power, since the varying distributions of capital among different agents determine their capacity for effective action. Field theory also attunes us to the structural and conjunctural conflicts and affinities that unite or divide similarly disposed actors, and in this case helps to show how competitions for resources split potential allies. But field theory is vague on certain key questions. What, for example, are the criteria for determining whether activists have entered the journalistic field as participants? If they are outsiders, then do they belong to a field organized around dissent?

In his political work Bourdieu advocated for the autonomy and integrity of fields of cultural production, and he was concerned about the "intrusions" of the journalistic field into other fields (especially the scientific, cultural, and political fields), and of the intrusions of other fields (economics, power, etc.) into journalism.[2] The case of youth media organizations allows us to ask whether and how exogenous pressures from subjects who are objectified by the media can exert force on the journalistic field from below, and also to consider whether this form of heteronomy can help journalists to produce work that better meets their own criteria for excellence. Media activists insist that they are making necessary intrusions, because mainstream organizations have failed to live up to their own professional standards of fairness and accuracy. They claim that their political intervention is designed to help reporters and editors realize their own craft values – even though the activists themselves lack the cultural capital that is necessary to produce the journalism they desire.[3] Finally, the case of youth media organizations opens up one of the questions that Bourdieu and his collaborators posed during his later work in and on the journalistic field: whether it is possible to use media to critique and change media, or whether the field is too tightly controlled to allow for structural transformations from within.[4]

My inquiry is based on semistructured interviews and occasional visits to youth media organizations in Chicago and New York. I have also surveyed the ecology of youth media organizations for the United States as a whole, with particular emphasis on Chicago, New York City, and the Bay Area in California. In addition to the research in and on youth media organizations, I spent three years conducting ethnographic work inside news companies, and part of this study involves examining how reporters treat youths. This chapter traces the creation and circulation of images and texts about young people as they move from newsroom to youth media organization, and back again. It identifies some of the new forms of communication and confrontation that are entering the media field, and, in turn, opening up new possibilities for youths and their advocates as they fight for media and social justice.

Media at Street-Level

Street-Level Youth Media occupies two floors of an old storefront row house in Chicago's West Town neighborhood, but its interior office, community space, and political mission are unmistakably contemporary. On my first visit hip-hop blasts from speakers that hover atop the large open entry room. A goateed employee in his twenties comes over to shake my hand, then leaves to summon the directors. I turn to see two rows of large-screen television sets that are assembled sculpturally on the south wall. When they are not displaying multimedia work, the screens make an installation on their own. There are posters everywhere, with in-your-face political messages about youth power, diversity, free expression, and cyberculture. A bank of computer terminals lines the east wall, and each machine is open to local youths and members. In the center of the room are two beaten-up conference tables; behind are the back rooms, where the real work – media education classes, video production, digital photography, online content creation – happens.

What is now Street-Level began modestly in 1993, when Andres Hernandez, a local artist and community activist, assembled a group of residents and friends who were concerned about gang activity, street violence, and other youth problems. Along with two other artists, Hernandez organized a public art project that involved participation from members of competing neighborhood gangs. They helped broker a period of relative peace in West Town, and stepped up their art projects so that the youths would produce highly visible, block level installations and represent themselves publicly. By 1995 there was enough local interest in the project that Hernandez formalized the group, creating Street-Level Youth Media with a mission to help young people express themselves and learn how to attract attention and respect nonviolently. Soon other neighborhood teenagers joined the gang members already working on Street-Level, and the directors branched out into new media forms, such as video poetry (particularly on the themes of identity and self-presentation), candid videos of street life, and local history. According to a Street-Level director, "The overarching idea was to tell stories about the people here, and about the neighborhood, so that residents and the community at large could see what's behind the criminal images of our youths and learn who they really are."

The organization's mission expanded as more local young people expressed interest in participating. The neighborhood public schools, which had little funding for arts education, wanted to bring their programs into the classrooms. City government officials grew interested in the uses of Street-Level as an after-school and summer employment program. With the help of the Illinois Institute of Technology it built an elaborate website. In 2003 its annual budget was around $1 million, and among the dozens of big-name supporters it thanks on its website are Microsoft, IBM, Apple, 3Com, Lotus, Adobe, The Tribune Company, Marshall Fields, PricewaterhouseCoopers, and Kraft, as well as the University of Chicago, the MacArthur Foundation, The National Endowment for the Arts, and the Illinois Arts Council.

Funded by grants and government contracts, Street-Level thus built the largest free-standing youth media and arts organization in the United States. In addition to a dozen full-time staffers, between 800 and 1,600 youth volunteers work with the organization annually. Street-Level now offers courses in digital photography, photo shop, multidimensional digital imaging, audio production, video production, animation, web-production, and multimedia work such as graphics and interactive programming. Drawing entirely on youth camera operators, youth performers, and youth artists, Street-Level began disseminating its work beyond the neighborhood. In 2003, for example, they were organizing one Street-Level art installation at the internationally renowned Field Museum and another at the Chicago Historical Society (entitled "Neighborhood Voices: Out of the Loop"), an elaborate web installation with support of the library, and a series of television programs, called Live Wire, on cable access channels.

Elementary media literacy instruction is also a fundamental part of the program. According to one instructor, "We start out most workshops with critical media analysis, trying to break down the big television programs. We ask 'What do you see?' 'Why do the media represent you that way?' 'How can you confront this?' "

During the 1990s dozens of organizations in American cities and online emerged to ask young people similar questions about the ways they were being represented by major media, and, in turn, to teach youths how to use and produce media to better represent themselves. Several of these groups developed a larger political project as well: they wanted to change the content of coverage, the routine work practices through which professional journalists produced public (mis)information about young people, the composition of editorial staffs which covered their demographic, and the large media structures that shaped the way cultural producers treated youths in their programming and publications.

The leaders and participants were politically savvy, so they understood how challenging it would be to transform even the substantive content of journalistic coverage, let alone the structural composition of the major media. Yet they discovered a series of obstacles as they developed their projects. Since media companies, either directly or through foundations, were often major contributors of money or volunteer staff, the youth organizations often felt inhibited in criticizing these sponsors. Likewise, government agency contracts to provide artistic and technical instruction for schools also constrained the youth organization's mission, even as they provided needed support. Intense competition for limited funds at the local level created contentious relations between groups that were otherwise positioned to be natural allies, splintering activists with similar dispositions. Youth producers wanted to make serious public contributions to knowledge and politics, but found that when they used platforms (such as video) dominated by the major media their work was treated as amateur and dismissed as "cute."

The Emergence of Youth Media Organizations

There is great variation in the organizational forms and media platforms that these activists developed. Some, such as Street-Level, joined into partnerships with city government services or school systems and developed deep ties to elite corporate and foundation funding agencies. This move to the mainstream elevates the level of economic and social capital in the group, but runs the risk of compromising its cultural and symbolic capital, since patrons perceive the organizations as training centers or partners rather than as critical cultural producers. Moreover, youth organizations which work closely with governments and nonprofit groups risk shifting the locus of their activities into the educational field, where their mission transforms to meet the pedagogical demands of officials and foundation officers rather than the political objectives of founders and members.

Other groups, such as Wiretap, are low-budget operations that exist primarily as portals for circulating critical media reports and art work on the web. Groups like this are typically administered by a small number of professionals and staffed by networks of young teenage and twenty-something activists, artists, and journalists who are intent on effecting social change. They do less skill-based pedagogy and use the web to produce new forms of political connections and social movements. Some of these organizations trace their deep roots to community television, radio, newspaper, and guerilla arts projects of the 1960s, when small groups tried to provide alternative media products to people frustrated with the mainstream offerings. But they all emerged during the 1990s in the context of an internet-driven information revolution, and – although there are some prominent youth radio programs that get airtime on large public stations – most youth media projects emphasize video, digital media, and web-based work. Their economic and social capital is relatively limited; but their cultural and symbolic capital, particularly in the new media fields, can be formidable.

Youth media organizations emerged from historically specific social and political conditions. First, what Manuel Castells calls "the power of identity," and identity-based social projects, established self-representation as fundamental to youth media programs, particularly for young people of color and lesbian, gay, or bisexual youth.[5] Second, the barrage of news reports and media programs depicting young people as dangerous, uncontrollable, and criminal predators (a process that many critics call the criminalization of youth), coupled with sweeping local legislative and juridical projects to gut juvenile justice programs and treat youths as adults in criminal cases, led youth media organizations to focus on representing youths as decent human beings or, in some cases, victims rather than victimizers. Third, the governmental, corporate, philanthropic, and cultural interest in teaching urban youth technical, computer-based skills helped generate public and private sector support for media literacy programs, even while other education and recreation programs were losing funds. Fourth, a technologically savvy and media-saturated generation of young people has expressed strong and consistent interest in developing media literacy and producing their own material – oftentimes these youths feel more comfortable learning in educational environments such as the one at Street-Level than they do in the school classroom, which relies on older media forms.

Though they have no shortage of interested members, these organizations face daunting political and pedagogical challenges. It is difficult enough to teach young people to become media literate, conduct media criticism, and produce multimedia presentations that command public (or even familial) attention. But many groups also want to directly confront major media outlets and push them to change the way they cover or construct youths and youth issues. They are, in effect, trying to open up a new sphere of political activism, one that operates both in and through the media field. They are establishing a social movement that does not merely use media as a tool for effecting change in another sphere of action, the kind of project that is so well analyzed by Todd Gitlin or Charlotte Ryan.[6] Their aim is to criticize, create, and repackage media forms and content with the double objective of, first, transforming the ways that journalists and media companies represent youth issues, and second, using the new media products to effect change in other fields – particularly criminal justice. At the first level, then, these youth media organizations are fighting for media justice and fair representation.[7] The administrators and young participants believe that they are misrepresented – in the case of young people of color, even criminalized – by the media.[8] They demand better treatment. The larger reason they fight for media justice, though, is that they believe social justice is impossible without it, since in their view (a strong, practical version of the "media effects" model) media representations set the terms and conditions for a larger set of social issues.[9]

Youth organizations face another set of strategic questions involving their own use of media in their activism. Can the major media outlets that they are contesting be opened to public self-criticism, or even to public recognition of the problems with criminalized youth representations? In other words, can they enter the field and effect change within it? This is a particular challenge for critics of what many activists and experts consider the most influential media form, television. Youth media organizations want to transform the mainstream media, and they demand the respect and recognition of big media players. But, outside of cable-access channels, television has little time for them, or for the confrontational video projects they produce. So, whether as outside critics or, potentially, contributing producers, how can they engage with television insiders and reform the way television depicts them? Given their limited economic, social, and cultural capital (they lack resources for production, access to big stations, and content that meets standards in the large news and entertainment market), what expectations do they have for their own media products and social justice projects? What are the core objectives of these new organizations and who are the key institutional actors? Since these organizations are often focused on new media, it is important to ask what are the possibilities for media activism and criticism that emerge from web-based production and distribution systems?

It is also important to identify the possibilities and constraints that affect youth media organizations inside their own field of activism – a field structured around its own set of struggles for resources and influence. In major cities, for example, there are usually several youth media groups, each with its own specialized agenda and a unique set of relationships. They generally share overarching projects, and occasionally staff members circulate between groups. But they also compete for funding and public attention, and in practice they have difficulty coordinating. Several scholars of globalization and social movements believe that new media projects create an infrastructure for coalition building at the international level. Many media scholars are excited about the capacities for integrated international production and distribution channels, too.[10] In theory, youth media organizations are ideal for building these kinds of projects, since their main issues – media justice, misrepresentation, self-expression, and criminalization – are nearly universal in contemporary societies. But do they have the capital or the ambitions to create these kinds of global ties? How, if at all, do global media provide new outlets for young people to speak back?

Criminalization and the Fight for Fairness

In 2002, the Youth Media Council (YMC) and its parent organization, We Interrupt this Message, published *Speaking for Ourselves: A Youth Assessment of Local News Coverage*. The report, which was researched by a team of 17 youths between the ages of 14 and 17, documents the rise of local news coverage linking young people to crime at the very moment that youth crime rates dropped precipitously. Using a simple content analysis of how the San Francisco Bay Area's leading local television news program (which a Columbia University study also deemed the leading newscast in the United States) represented youth issues, the YMC found that about two-thirds of the station's stories focused on youths and crime, with 11 youth crime stories for every report on youth poverty. Of the roughly 500 quotes in the stories, 70 percent were from adults, mostly from police, prosecutors, and politicians. Youths, in other words, were usually spoken for or spoken about, rather than given voice in news reports – exactly the kind of domination through the exercise of symbolic power that Bourdieu explored in *Distinction*, *Language and Symbolic Power*, and *The Weight of the World*.

Young people and their protectors were rarely given access to the microphone. The stories typically reported on crime or violence without providing viewers with information about the social context. Even stories about education – in a region notorious for its low quality public schools – focused on deviance; and there were few stories about public policies for youths or about cuts in the social programs that helped improve young peoples' lives. When reporters looked for experts to explain what should be done, they usually chose people who suggested harsh legal measures. According to the Youth Media Council, during the 1990s this kind of news coverage played a major role not only in criminalizing young people of color, but also in generating public support for more punitive social policies. Indeed, since 1992, 42 states have loosened criteria for charging children as adults in criminal cases, and California began spending more money on jails and prisons than on its public universities. This sweeping legal challenge to the rights of childhood is one of the major concerns of youth advocates in the United States today.

A national media training and strategy center with offices in New York City and San Francisco, We Interrupt this Message created the Youth Media Council in 2001 as "a youth organizing, leadership development, media capacity-building, and watchdog project dedicated to amplifying the public voice of marginalized youth and their communities."[11] Its funding comes from a more narrow and less wealthy group of donors than Street-Level, and its sponsors include a number of small progressive community organizations. Speaking for Ourselves, YMC's first major public project, is an unusually powerful document rich in cultural capital, since its young authors level their criticism about criminalization by television news programs with the support of an empirically driven content analysis. It is also a politically sophisticated report. The YMC is not interested in simply documenting the extent to which young people are misrepresented, nor in merely castigating the journalists and news agencies who portray youths as criminal. Instead, they offer their report as an invitation to news organizations to take them up as partners in conversation and, perhaps, as cocreators of a more just form of youth coverage. In their words:

> We can transform media bias into media justice by building strong relationships between news outlets and youth organizations, and increasing the dialogue between journalists and youth community members. . . . We continue to live and die on the word of experts and reporters. It is therefore critical to our survival that journalists and communities work in partnership to report on public policy issues that frame the contours of our conditions and draw the boundaries that define our lives.[12]

These are big hopes. In practice, city journalists do little work to establish relationships with young people, and there are few forums in which the two groups interact. The weak social capital of more critical youth media groups makes it difficult for members to gain access to the newsroom or to news managers, and therefore they struggle to enter the field as players. During my time in different city newsrooms I never heard reporters or editors speaking about, let alone with, youth media organizations and their representatives.

Chicago from Street-Level and Beyond

When major local media outlets pay attention to young people, it is usually because the kids are in trouble. As consumers of local television news and newspapers, Chicagoans and their suburban neighbors gain strong impressions about the social problems that are reputedly concentrated in places like West Town (and anomalous when they appear in elite, white suburbs). The problems are predictable, because news media address them so often, yet they are still scary and serious:

Youths are joining gangs and committing treacherous acts of violence against each other and their community; they are jeopardizing their future by dropping out of school; they are performing poorly on standardized tests; they are having babies even though they are children themselves; they are loitering and endangering street life for the public; they are circulating in and out of juvenile justice facilities; they drink and do drugs; they listen to hateful music and take pleasure in violent movies and video games; they own guns; they behave like adult criminals; they disrespect authority; they are out of control. Stories with these motifs are a staple of local news in every US city; and in recent years national publications have published profiles such as "Kids Without A Conscience" (*People Magazine*), "Teenage Wolf Packs" (*US News and World Report*), and "Wild in the Streets" (*Newsweek*), while in some regions stories about youth and crime outnumber stories about youth and poverty by a ratio of ten to one.[13]

Most young people in West Town do not recognize themselves in these stories; they view mainstream journalistic depictions as demeaning caricatures, based on stereotypes and motivated by the ill will of elite reporters. Even local adults, whose own experiences as parents, aunts, uncles, and cousins have made them concerned about the issues of youth deviance – and, equally, of the ways local officials, including teachers and police officers, treat local teens – believe that the major media misunderstand and misrepresent the city's youths. Although Street-Level is in the neighborhood, residents of West Town who want to represent themselves in their own terms, and with their own voices, have few resources to do it. In Bourdieu's terms, they are victims of symbolic violence, whereby the journalistic and political institutions with the most capacity to shape public discourse about a group do so with little regard for the group's own self-conceptions. They also believe that this symbolic violence translates into the social violence of prejudice, heightened inequality, and punitive treatment by police officers, school officials, and neighbors who learn to fear their community. But what can they do to directly confront local reporters and the large news companies for which they work? What happens when communities work with institutions such as Street-Level to mount a challenge to their city's media system?

First, they get frustrated. It is nearly impossible for any single organization to effect change in the major media landscape, and breaking the conventional media practices at the local level – particularly in large American cities – is also difficult. The executive director of Street-Level explains that "we're up against a giant here, and it's overwhelming sometimes. There's always a challenge to get our message out – even to the community, let alone the city. But even then it's hard to compete – in message and content – with reality TV, MTV, and the media monsters that dominate the public." Street-Level, after all, is the largest youth media organization in the United States, and its public art projects and museum installations are products of a diligent, well-connected administration, as well as a successful education program for youths. Yet administrators fear that both the public and the corporations and foundations that fund them do not take seriously their critical political message. The public and their sponsors are pleased to see that young people are learning media literacy skills and staying out of trouble, and sometimes they treat the organization as if it is a social service agency. Another Street-Level administrator reports that "some people respond to our art or media projects by saying, 'Oh, that's so cute' – like it's a high school play. It's patronizing. We're dealing with tough issues, and the message is at a high level. We shouldn't be dismissed. But how can we get them to take us more seriously?"

Some administrators at Street-Level worry that they may be politically constrained because of the organization's close relationships with government agencies and powerful philanthropic groups. Would they continue to receive support if they were to address structural inequities in the media field, or if they leveled criticisms at their sponsors for the mistreatment and misrepresentation that the administrators and students notice? The economic and social capital that Street-Level accepts from government and large cultural foundations come at a high price, effectively converting the organization into a training ground and a state-sanctioned program. Street-Level leaders whom I interviewed were upset about the position they occupied, and while they worried that their projects had been defanged, they had become too dependent on support from large foundations and the state to make major changes.

Some youth media organizations adapt to their position by changing their understanding of how they are making a difference – "making virtue of necessity," as Bourdieu often said. They typically focus their efforts on the immediate communities surrounding them, just as Street-Level initially did with its original public art projects for West Town gangsters, and look for occasions when the city's news intersects with their issues. Street-Level members produced a public art project in an effort to contest Chicago's controversial anti-gang loitering initiative (a police policy that, in many critics' view, would have resulted in punitive police crackdowns on law-abiding black and Latino youths when they hung out in their own neighborhoods); and they confronted officials in the city's Graffiti-Busters campaign, capturing on video a debate about the meaning of tagging for different communities in the city. Youth media groups also turn to other platforms, particularly the web, where their art and media projects can circulate widely and their design skills help legitimate the content in ways that are difficult with more expensive media, such as video or film.

Perhaps most importantly, they take seriously their role as critical educators, taking pride in their ability to help young people express themselves, develop technical and artistic skills, navigate a media-saturated society, and learn how to speak up for themselves when they witness or experience injustice. As Steven Goodman, founder and director of the Educational Video Center in New York, writes:

> A critical literacy empowers low-income, urban teenagers to understand how media is made to convey particular messages and how they can use electronic and print technologies themselves to document and publicly voice their ideas and concerns regarding the most important issues in their lives. . . . This approach to critical literacy links media analysis to production; learning about the world is directly linked to the possibility of changing it.[14]

Many youth media organizations, particularly those that work with African-Americans and Latinos, boast about the number of graduates who become professional journalists, bringing their perspectives into the mainstream media and thereby slowly changing journalism from within. Bourdieu's theory regards this as one mechanism for generating change in the field: new entrants, particularly from marginalized or excluded groups or classes, can alter the compositional structure of the journalistic field. Yet, as the introduction to this volume explains, the most successful new entrants are likely to be those who have been professionalized to accept the "rules of the game," rather than radicals who want to effect major change. The American journalistic field has been slow to open its doors to marginalized groups, especially at the higher, administrative levels. Every one of the news organizations I have studied was significantly less diverse than the city in which it was located. None had a minority editor, publisher, or managing editor.

At Beyondmedia, a Chicago-based media activist organization in the North Side Rogers Park neighborhood, administrators and staff have rejected the strategy of changing the field by producing either new entrants or mainstream products. Following the model of 1960s alternative media outlets, Street-Level activists are less interested in directly confronting the city's major media outlets than they are in creating a new space for people disillusioned by the media market. Created in 1990 by an activist/educator, Beyondmedia set out to teach media literacy and community organizing skills to teens and young women concerned about women's issues in general, but especially homophobia and criminal injustices for women. The staff works primarily with young women, and they specialize in video production and media literacy courses. According to the executive director:

> We have a different idea of what works. For us, it's face-to-face contact, a strong experience, an emotional context. So we set up screenings and have public discussions with people who make the projects and with communities . . . But we don't have an infrastructure for doing public relations and getting stuff into [the major media] outlets . . . It's good to get coverage, and it's especially good for funders. But it's not the most effective thing for us. We're trying to create a different model. Getting into the [Chicago] *Tribune* is not our ultimate goal.

Instead, Beyondmedia tries to instill critical skills in their constituency and members by getting them to experience media more intimately, whether as producers or as engaged consumers. "Critical analysis of the power of media grows as you do different parts of our projects – critical, creative, and distribution," the director adds. "Kids here see the power of their work, and the power of media, because they see the big media system that they're engaging."

Between the Journalistic and Activist Fields

Beyondmedia, Street-Level Youth Media, and the other Chicago youth media organizations have strikingly similar criticisms of the major media, and their overarching projects are complementary and compatible. Each has carved out a special niche in the city's media and political ecology, and, in principle, they are well positioned to join forces to publicize their collective missions and even to collaborate on large projects. Yet in the first decade of their existence these collaborations did not happen. According to the staff at the different organizations, they are more likely to establish coalitions with social justice groups that work on issues such as criminalization, homophobia, or schools, than they are to work with each other. Indeed, as Bourdieu emphasizes, "to exist within a social space, is to differ, to be different";[15] as a result, the most intense competition often pits those who are closest to one another in their viewpoints and practices. This intrafield competition takes shape in the context of a struggle for recognition vis-à-vis outside funders. Although there are some media activists who have circulated through different media organizations, the struggle for resources pits them against one another, thereby undermining possibilities for a unified media justice project. As one Beyondmedia administrator explains, "The fear of collaborating is that funders can just write one of us off – they have to know how each of us is different."

Currently, then, the youth media activist network in Chicago is dynamic but contentious, productive but fragmented. While each group has a strong interest in directly or indirectly challenging the major media outlets that have established symbolic power within the field, there is no coordinated or coherent strategy for doing this work. The Chicago groups also had few connections to national youth media organizations. None of them had seen or heard about the Youth Media Council report on the Bay Area's leading television news station coverage of youths and crime, for example; and none had planned to do a similar project in Chicago.

Several of the large youth media education programs in Chicago are sponsored directly by the large media companies themselves, and staff members from major newspapers or television stations often volunteer to teach in the youth programs. On the one hand, this may mean that the conditions in the field are not set up to produce the kind of critical work that the Youth Media Council and other national media critics advocate. The youth media organizations are dependent on their sponsors, and they would be foolish to turn against them. On the other hand, the close relationship between sponsoring media companies and the youth organizations means that there may be more possibilities for establishing the kind of media/youth dialogue that the YMC report demands. Yet the contemporary news marketplace values explosive social problems and crime stories about youths more than it does the kinds of street-level, civic journalism projects that the youth groups want to produce and consume. In 2003, for example, both major Chicago newspaper companies began publishing new tabloid dailies designed to reach the youth and young professional market (ages 18–34). Neither consulted local youth media organizations in their planning process, relying instead on their own focus groups and market research.

Youth media organizations struggle to enter and alter the journalistic field. But, ironically, the active intervention of big media companies in youth media programs and media literacy campaigns exerts a powerful force inside the activist field. Carrie McLaren, the founder and editor of *Stayfree* magazine, has shown how Channel One, a for-profit school company in the United States, paid media literacy movement leaders to develop curricular programs devoid of the project's key messages about media inequities, yet full of marketing material.

"Some of the practices advocated by media literacy teachers are in fact well-worn advertising strategies," she argues.[16] The Cable in the Classroom project, which is backed by the Cable Television Association, used media literacy instructors to develop a "Spice Girls Curriculum" that asks students to compare the different kinds of Girl Power communicated by pop performers. According to McLaren, these programs have turned politically charged media literacy projects into exercises in "media appreciation" that both legitimate and deepen the commercialization of education.

Conclusion: Field Constraints, New Terrains

Field theory helps us understand the relationships between the various actors at work in this dynamic, and the relative positions they occupy in contests over the state of the industry. Youth media organizations act as allies and, because of their structural position with respect to dominant funding agencies, as competitors; large news companies and their journalistic staffs support youth media projects in the classroom but have not integrated their insights into the work of the newsroom; and government agencies provide funds for media organizations that perform educational services, so long as they do not raise major objections to the inequities generated or ignored by government policies. The activist organizations face particularly strong challenges because they are trying to effect change not merely within any single news company, but within a much larger journalistic field that contains numerous outlets and actors. Occasionally youth media organizations succeed in individual projects, getting their voices into mainstream media reports or producing their own material for distribution in newspapers, radio broadcasts, or public television stations. Yet even these successes are easily drowned out by the flood of stories and images about young people that violate the principles of media justice they are trying to advance. Moreover, the major television networks that reach the largest audiences are virtually impenetrable to small activist groups, and the news outlets that are most influenced by market demands are least interested in media justice issues.

Youth media and media justice activists have thus developed other strategies to effect change within the journalistic field. First, their pedagogical programs aim to repopulate the field with new entrants, particularly urban African-Americans and Latinos, who remain underrepresented in major news companies. According to youth media administrators and activists, reporters trained in their classes will broaden the perspectives of mainstream journalistic organizations and help bring currently neglected issues into the news.[17] But it is unlikely that there will be enough new entrants to help transform the composition of the field, as was the case in the French university system in the 1960s analyzed by Bourdieu in *Homo Academicus*, so the youth media graduates are more likely to advance more minor reforms.[18] Second, youth media organizations help to call attention to local issues that do not otherwise register as public matters. They try to connect what might first appear as parochial concerns to broader patterns in their city or region, and to push journalists to recognize the significance of problems they might not otherwise understand. Yet again, these practices do little to alter the overall structure of the field. Third, they express interest in building coalitions with other media activist organizations and generating political energy around larger projects. Several youth media organizations participated in the first National Conference on Media Reform in the fall of 2003, and they are beginning to develop broad networks to promote new campaigns. As the case of Chicago shows, the structure of the field produces competition between activist organizations and undermines possibilities for unified projects at the local level. But these conflicts could diminish as the fledgling groups develop stronger ties with funding agencies and secure their positions.

Field theory also helps explain why media activist groups typically wage their campaigns by using the language and forms of journalism – such as the Youth Media Council report – rather than through the conventional techniques of social movements, such as public demonstrations. Media activists mimic the techniques of journalists and train young people to develop media literacy skills so that they can gain legitimacy inside the journalistic field. Although they occasionally break into minor media outlets, such as public radio and television, they rarely obtain the levels of cultural capital that are necessary to place work in or earn the respect of the most powerful organizational actors in the field. This is especially true for television, where production costs are high and programs that do not meet the elite craft standards are dismissed as amateur.

Unable to surmount the obstacles that block access to the major commercial media, a new generation of media activists has thus invented a new forum for waging their campaigns: web-based, content-heavy internet portals that operate as a hub and clearinghouse for people interested in youth media, youth politics, and a wide variety of social justice issues. These projects do not involve the labor-intensive educational programming that remain the core of groups such as Street-Level and Beyondmedia, and they provide no face-to-face services for young people who want to develop media literacy skills. Yet they do provide information about community events, political demonstrations, and offline projects that would interest their audience; and they usually set up interactive spaces where young people can write to one another online. They also offer a strong set of critical voices, images, and artwork that directly challenge media which misrepresent youth and youth issues. Because they are online, they provide resources for a potentially limitless population of young people and advocates; and though I do not know of any online organization that currently addresses international media justice issues, they are well-positioned to do this kind of work.

Compared to more expensive and established media platforms, high-level production on the web requires less economic, social, and cultural capital, and it provides unlimited space for distribution. Major media companies have already staked out the space of the net with their brand names, leaving activists to search for openings on this new terrain. For now, the technological possibilities for connecting young critics and activists to other critics and activists, or critics to reporters and major media organizations, remain merely that: possibilities.

Notes

1 For a definition and discussion of the journalistic field, see Pierre Bourdieu, *On Television* (New York: The New Press, 1998), esp. pp. 70–3, and Rodney Benson, "Field Theory in Comparative Context: A New Paradigm for Media Studies," *Theory and Society*, 28 (1999), pp. 463–98. For a broader discussion of field theory, including versions by Bourdieu, Paul DiMaggio, and Woody Powell, see John Levi Martin, "What is Field Theory?" *American Journal of Sociology*, 109 (2003), pp. 1–49.

2 See Bourdieu, *On Television*, pp. 68–9, where he discusses the struggles over autonomy for journalists, and pp. 73–8, where he elaborates his argument about the effects of intrusion in different domains.

3 In *Impure Science: AIDS, Activism, and the Politics of Knowledge* (University of California Press, Berkeley, CA, 1998), Steve Epstein examines a similar case when objectified subjects of science challenge the expertise of specialists in a field of intellectual production – and ultimately improve the science. In fact, one could argue that Bourdieu's own "intrusions" into the journalistic field were motivated by the goal of helping defend journalists from the pressures of the market, and even of increasing the pressures of scientific reason.

4 Pierre Bourdieu discusses a similar problem in *On Television*, when he describes the difficulty of articulating a critique of television within the temporal constraints and production values of the platform. The French filmmaker Pierre Carles produced a film, *Pas vu, pas pris*, about his struggle to get a documentary film about the television business aired by his original sponsor, a major French television station.

5 There are hundreds of academic articles on the emergence of identity-based social projects; I cite Castells because he attempts to address the power of identity as a socially structuring force. See Manuel Castells, *The Power of Identity* (Blackwell, Oxford, 1997).

6 See Todd Gitlin, *The Whole World is Watching: Mass Media in the Making and Unmaking of the New Left* (University of California Press, Berkeley, CA, 1980), and Charlotte Ryan, *Prime Time Activism* (South End Press, Boston, 1991). These two texts address the challenge of using media to change the structure of other fields, whereas many youth media organizations are interested in changing the media field itself.

7 Some youth media organizations use the concept of "media justice" in the same way environmentalists use "environmental justice," explicitly referring to inequities based on class and race.

8 Here Gitlin's description of the crisis of public representation is apt: "Just as people as workers have no voice in what they make, how they make it, or how the product is distributed and used, so do people as producers of meaning have no voice in what the media make of what they say or do, or in the context within which the media frame their activity" (*The Whole World is Watching*, p. 3). Contemporary media activists set out to challenge this form of alienation.

9 See Shanto Iyengar and Donald R. Kinder, *News That Matters: Television and American Opinion* (University of Chicago Press, Chicago, 1987), for an account of how television coverage shapes public opinion. See Martin Gilens, *Why Americans Hate Welfare: Race, Media, and the Politics of Antipoverty Policy* (University of Chicago Press, Chicago, 1999), for a demonstration of how coverage of welfare issues through representations of African-Americans racialized welfare and reduced public support for social assistance programs in the United States. In *Speaking for Ourselves* (Youth Media Council, 2002), the Youth Media Council cites Gilens as a source for its media effects argument (p. 12).

10 On social movements and media, see Manuel Castells, *The Rise of the Network Society* (Blackwell, Oxford, 1996, ch. 5), and *The Power of Identity* (ch. 2); see also Meg McLagan, "Spectacles of Difference: Cultural Activism and the Mass Mediation of Tibet," pp. 90–111 in *Media Worlds: Anthropology on a New Terrain*, eds. Faye Ginsburg, Lila Abu-Lughod, and Brian Larkin (University of California Press, Berkeley, CA, 2002), and Jeff Juris, "The Cultural Logic of the Network: Transnational Activism and the Movement for Global Resistance in Barcelona," PhD dissertation, University of California, Berkeley, 2004. On the alter-

native transnational circulation of new media products and networks of production, see Arjun Appadurai, *Modernity at Large: Cultural Dimensions of Globalization* (University of Minnesota Press, Minneapolis, MN, 1996); Faye Ginsburg, Lila Abu-Lughod, and Brian Larkin, "Introduction," pp. 1–36 in *Media Worlds*; and "Alternatives to the Status Quo," in Edward Herman and Robert McChesney, *The Global Media* (Cassell, London, 1997).

11 *Speaking for Ourselves*, p. 1.

12 *Speaking for Ourselves*, p. 7.

13 See *Speaking for Ourselves* for a complete list of such stories.

14 Steven Goodman, *Teaching Youth Media: A Critical Guide to Literacy, Video Production, and Social Change* (Teachers College Press, New York, 2003).

15 See Pierre Bourdieu, "Social Space and Symbolic Space," in *Practical Reason* (Stanford University Press, Stanford, CA, 1998, and Polity, Cambridge, 1998), p. 9.

16 See Carrie McLaren, "Media Literacy Sells Out," *Stayfree*, 17 (2000).

17 Their position is a version of the "multiperspectival" news project advocated by Herbert Gans. See *Democracy and the News* (Oxford University Press, New York, 2003).

18 See Pierre Bourdieu, *Homo Academicus* (Stanford University Press, Stanford, CA, 1988 and Polity, Cambridge, 1988), esp. ch. 5.

Part III

Critical Reflections

10

Bourdieu, the Frankfurt School, and Cultural Studies: On Some Misunderstandings

Erik Neveu

The reception of a major body of work in the social sciences is inevitably accompanied by debates and misunderstandings. The sociology of Pierre Bourdieu, and especially his work on the media and journalism, has not escaped this law. At least three reasons can explain this. The first stems from the wealth and variety of production that has grown up since the first text devoted by Pierre Bourdieu and Jean-Claude Passeron to "mass culture" theorists was published in 1963.[1] This production also includes a great variety of work carried out by members of Bourdieu's research center or by others using his concepts.

The second, impressively theorized by Loïc Wacquant, arises from the effects of the international circulation of research.[2] This explanation gives pride of place to selective translation, which rarely follows the chronology of the original body of work. Thus, *On Television* has been translated into more than 25 languages,[3] while the essential text written in 1963 with Passeron has only been translated into Italian. These distortions combine with two others. One has been summed up by David Morley with the formula "theory travels better"[4]: while research brings out the theoretical conclusions of an empirical enquiry, the empirical material often appears obscure or exotic to foreign readers, whether it concerns a British television program like *Nationwide* in Morley's work, or the media interventions of the French "new philosophers" analyzed by Bourdieu or Louis Pinto.[5] The theoretical conclusions thus risk being rigidified, interpreted without an understanding of the terrain that makes sense of them. More generally, too few translations are accompanied by good introductions which reconstruct the singularity of the social (political, academic, cultural) spaces within which the work arose as well as its intellectual and sometimes political stakes. There is therefore an enormous risk of a work being interpreted into absurdity according to the logics of the social and university systems into which it is received: Seen from Brisbane or Toronto, isn't Paris very near Frankfurt? Isn't Bourdieu a cousin of Derrida or Barthes, as the existence of the epistemological monster "French Theory," which brings together authors whose only thing in common is often a French passport, would seem to suggest?

In the case of the sociology of the media, we can add a third element of misunderstanding which arises from the status of *On Television*. This short text, which inaugurated a book series aimed at a readership beyond that of scholarly journals, was explicitly presented by Bourdieu as a work of popularization, an "intervention" the limits of which he was sufficiently aware to conclude the volume with a text "in a more rigorous form" published two years earlier in his journal *Actes*. The goal of *On Television* was thus not to produce a worked-out sociological theory of television. It aimed to provoke a debate on the effects of the commercial media on the fields of cultural production (art, publishing) and current modes of news framing. Its huge impact in the French press and its sales of over 100,000 copies testify to the scale of its reception. This observation is not to prohibit critical discussion of its faults as a work of popularization,[6] nor to gloss over the fact that the book cites very few works on television, including those that would support its own conclusions. But it would rule out discussing the book as if it were of the same kind as *Distinction*, a confusion often made by foreign readers or French researchers who are all too happy finally to find a text that is vulnerable to their criticisms.

This chapter is intended as an intervention against precisely these kinds of mistakes. In particular, I aim to clarify an assimilation and an objection that contribute to misunderstanding of Bourdieu's work. The assimilation stems from a recent tendency to Germanize Bourdieu, to make him into a successor of the Frankfurt School, especially when this suggests that the media have an irresistible power over audiences who are condemned to passive, dominated reception. This unfounded criticism follows from an erroneous understanding of Bourdieu's critical attitude with regard to the French semiological current symbolized by Roland Barthes as well as the evolutions of

British-born cultural studies. The objection consists in suspecting field theory of being objectivist and mechanistic, of reducing media and cultural products to simple expressions of relations of force and the morphological structures of the field. In other words, sociologists close to Bourdieu supposedly regard texts (newspapers, books, televisions programs) as black boxes scarcely worth opening, since a sociology of the field of production largely suffices to make sense of them.

These two misunderstandings will be the subject of the first two sections of this chapter. The third section aims to inventory the analytical components of field theory's approach to the media. Identifying them allows us at once to avoid phony debates and to open a space of discussion on the strengths, lacunae, and contrasts of a body of work.

Er ist kein Frankfurter! On an Untimely Naturalization

In France and abroad, the appearance of *On Television* elicited a strange process of naturalization. The book has been criticized as making visible the supposed proximity of Bourdieu's analyses to those of the Frankfurt School, outbidding even its pessimistic vision of the power of the media.[7] What I will call the Frankfurt misunderstanding is moreover twofold. While the rapprochement was generally critical in tone, it sometimes took the form of an acquiescence, enrolling Bourdieu into a discourse denouncing a society ruled by media manipulation. This misunderstanding has multiple bases. In France in particular, it has fed on games of succession by those whose posture as heirs was further legitimated as they were able to assume more critical distance than those close to the sociologist, who were accused of hyperorthodoxy. It also drew on ignorance of the many texts published by Bourdieu since 1963 on the media and the reception of cultural goods, as well as on a misrecognition of the status of *On Television*. Finally, it was able to express a cultural *Zeitgeist* made up of contradictory elements: on the one hand, a professorial populism à la Fiske offering a naïve celebration of the virtues of commercial culture and of what de Certeau coined as the poaching skills of ordinary media consumers;[8] on the other, a form of campus radicalism which reduces contemporary forms of domination to discursive games and media influence.

A Case of bibliographical amnesia

Every survey of Bourdieu's work accords a large place to his initial involvement in the study of traditional peasant societies in Algeria and the Béarn region of France. A complete bibliography of his work[9] also reveals that the first text that went beyond these founding subjects was cowritten with Jean-Claude Passeron and published in *Les Temps modernes* in 1963 under the title "The Sociologists of Mythologies and the Mythologies of Sociologists." With great polemical verve, this text (three extracts of which are reproduced with permission in this chapter) attacked a number of essayists, foremost among them Edgar Morin, who were writing in France at that time on "mass culture" and its power. These criticisms can be readily transposed to the central analyses of the Frankfurt School.

The central axis of Bourdieu and Passeron's critique underlines the imposture of the vague concepts "mass" and "mass culture," which play on the confusion between the number of addressees (a mass of people) and the suggestion that this massification engenders a new substance in which social differences lose their significance. The discourse of mass culture is tautological. It evokes a principle of contamination whereby the possession of a television transforms a shipyard worker or a rural merchant into a "television viewer." This mantra obscures any sociological investigation that would start from a diversity of social groups in order to grasp their cultural practices and the influence the media and the often different programs they watch may (or may not) exert on them. It also displaces historical investigation of the precedents of this "mass" culture, such as that suggested by the broad circulation of the serialized novels of Victor Hugo or Eugène Sue in the nineteenth-century French press.

Bourdieu and Passeron's offensive also aimed to emphasize the deeply derogative image of the popular, regarded as passive and dazed, which gave rise to analyses of mass culture which claimed to rehabilitate the cultural consumption of the masses.

Is it necessary to point out how awkward this text is for those who would associate Bourdieu with Frankfurt? It is certainly possible, with a little bad faith, to emphasize that this text was cowritten with Jean-Claude Passeron – who later distanced himself from Bourdieu in the sociology of popular culture – in order to give Passeron sole credit for this lucidity.[10] The importance and originality of Passeron's sociological work and the extent of his subsequent disagreements with Bourdieu are not to be underestimated. But in his own texts as well as those he authored with others, Bourdieu regularly demon-

The founding tautology

> Distinctions loath a prophetic spirit. . . . From sacred rhetoric it borrows the strongest figure of its logomachia, vague and frightening naming: mass media, the "means of mass communication." Through the terrorist efficacy of the name, the "means of mass communication" condemn massified individuals without appeal to massive, passive, docile, credulous reception. The mass media may well convey the most diverse messages and encounter most unevenly receptive audiences, but the mass-mediologists, playing with a halo effect, content themselves with reviving the archetypal model of conditioning, that of the advertising image. Any sociology that seeks to reintroduce a modest evaluation of the phenomenon, with its nuances and its limits, is attacked in advance as bureaucratic science. . . . To spare itself the petty, insignificant task of distinguishing the power, content, and publics of each system of diffusion, at the risk of relativizing them, and to cut short impertinent investigations, it forges massive, obscure concepts that annihilate differences. For particular cultural vehicles, they substitute the abstract idea of mass efficacy, a perfect example of its genre. . . . The principle of such an amalgam, that of magic contagion, can be expressed as follows: everything that is part of a genre possesses all the properties of the genre, while to be part of a genre it suffices to have one of its properties.
>
> . . . Mass "culture" must therefore necessarily, on pain of heresy, be at the same time what happens to the masses culturally as a result of the mass media. . . . The masses are only masses as the massified addressees of a mass culture diffused on a massive scale. The very logic of his thesis immobilizes the mass-mediologist, preventing him from defining the three essential terms mass media, mass, and massification. Having three concepts and only two hands to handle them, he can only juggle. (Bourdieu and Passeron, "Sociologues des mythologies et mythologies de sociologues," pp. 1002–6)

strates close attention to the diversity of reception and to the variety of dispositions and perceptual schemes concerning media messages and cultural works.

A lasting focus

A number of things attest to Bourdieu's consistent sensitivity to the diversity of reception. From 1963 to 1970, he produced collective

The defenseless masses?

And why ignore the protections with which the masses arm themselves against surge of the media? A commonplace of popular and petty bourgeois conversation, the joke about the spell cast by television conjures up this spell differently than intellectual discourse, but no less effectively. Don't the most mass mediatic of the mass media desacralize an older medium? Daninos [a popular French comic of the 1960s – ed.] is not a bad sociologist when he notes that "people are talking more and more in the movie theaters, which is tiresome besides, and this, well it's television's fault. They've gotten so used to talking in front of their screen at home that they stop distinguishing between the small one and the big one."

. . . But intellectuals always have a hard time believing in defenses, i.e., in the freedom of others, since they freely claim a professional monopoly over intellectual freedom. . . . In order to prove the seriousness of their humanism, they believe they are bound to take seriously that which mandarin humanism takes to be futile, not seeing that to take the reading of magazines seriously – sometimes tragically – it is necessary to stop taking magazine readers seriously when these readers say they don't take magazines seriously. Why in effect ignore the fact that these readers no doubt believe much less in the mythologies dear to the sociologists of mythologies than the latter believe and, to be sure, much less than the intellectuals who always need to mystify in order to appear as demystifiers, only believing that the others believe in it? (Bourdieu and Passeron, "Sociologues des mythologies et mythologies de sociologues," pp. 1009–11)

works with numerous researchers (Passeron, but also Christian Baudelot, Luc Boltanski, Jean-Claude Chamboredon, Alain Darbel, and Monique de Saint Martin). The list of objects studied is just as varied (pedagogical relations, the use of libraries, museums, photography). Now, while these works appear above all as contributions to a sociology of education and culture,[11] they all share a coherent approach to the modes of reception and appropriation of cultural goods. This approach makes intelligible the way in which, according to their social characteristics (class, education, generation), social agents do not consume the same things and derive distinct meanings and experiences even from similar cultural practices. We could also note that in the most developed text in the second part of the hand-

Investigating or enchanting?

Studying the conscious or unconscious technical, aesthetic, or ethical choices of the authors of messages, their implicit or explicit intentions, and the real modalities of perception, fascination, or detachment of those who receive them, their expectations or attitudes – this would no doubt make good sense. But it would also reduce a providential pretext for prophetic predigitation to an ordinary object of science. The enchanters want to save themselves the disenchantment of discovering that the editors and photographers of Paris match, their colleagues, explicitly and methodically put into their message what would-be structural analysis, this magic wand, conjures out of it; they want to save themselves from the despair of observing that readers take up and understand this objectivated intention. It is thus the mass-mediologist who interposes a mythological cloud between two parties who themselves have no illusions. (Bourdieu and Passeron, "Sociologues des mythologies et mythologies de sociologues," p. 1020)

book, *Craft of Sociology*, there is a translation of Schatzman and Strauss' article from the 1955 *American Sociological Review*, "Social Class and Modes of Communication."[12] The central task of this work is to show the differences between different social groups' modes of reception, verbalization, and expression, and their methodological implications. As general editor of the Le sens pratique series at Editions de Minuit during the 1970s, Bourdieu showed great sensitivity to the question of differential reception of media messages, for the need to consider the audience's symbolic resources, in short, approaching communication sociologically, without a priori attributing overwhelming powers to messages or the semiological "codes" that convey them. In this capacity, Bourdieu's decision to publish a translation of Hoggart's *The Uses of Literacy* in 1970 put at the disposal of French readers an approach that broke as much with populist celebration as with hopeless expressions of pity toward the working class's supposedly impoverished relations to culture and the media.[13]

Turning finally to the period from 1975 to 1985, we find Bourdieu's first brief and already critical text focusing specifically on journalism, as well as the multiple expressions of a highly productive workshop in the sociology of culture which continually investigated the mechanisms of reception and transmission that now go under the heading "communications." Beyond journalism, *Language and Symbolic Power* synthesized a number of Bourdieu's central theses on questions of communication: the power of words does not reside in the words, and not just any message produces significant effects on just any linguistic market.[14] But this will to think the contradictory density of the modes of production, selection, and reception of cultural goods and media can also be seen in articles by members of his research group published in *Actes*, like those of Jean-Claude Chamboredon and Jean-Louis Fabiani on children's literature in 1977, by Louis Pinto on the weekly *Le Nouvel Observateur* in 1981, or the issue devoted to "Popular" images in 1985.[15]

Identifying Bourdieu with the Frankfurt School thus involves an enormous symbolic conjuring trick. At its most obvious and least scrupulous, it consists in obscuring hundreds of pages of books of articles. A craftier but, as we will see, not necessarily more convincing version consists in postulating, like Althusser reading Marx, one or more "epistemological breaks," attributing to Bourdieu a profoundly discontinuous development of contradictory problematics over the years.

Bourdieu, Semiology, and Cultural Studies

The difficulties of understanding Bourdieu's analyses of the media in the English-speaking world also arise from his position vis-à-vis cultural studies and French semiology (Barthes in particular), of which the Birmingham researchers were major importers. A first paradox: Bourdieu energetically fought semiological approaches, and nevertheless in practice constantly devoted close attention to the forms and materiality of media and cultural products. A second paradox: Bourdieu, with Passeron, was one of the very few French researchers who very early on paid attention to the founding texts of British Cultural Studies, publishing partial translations of them in *Actes*. Nevertheless, his work can be neatly distinguished from this "antidiscipline," which, reciprocally, long ignored the French sociologist's contribution.

Internal approaches, external approaches

The critique of "mythologies" formulated in 1963 was not directed only at Morin. The very reference to myth targeted Roland Barthes, the author of *Mythologies*.[16] Moreover, in 1970 Bourdieu published a work by the linguist Georges Mounin in his Le sens commun series which condemned structural semiologists without appeal (or much sensitivity to their contributions). For Bourdieu and research associates such as Patrick Champagne,[17] the opposition between internal analysis and external analysis constitutes a structuring schema in work on culture and the media. This is expressed with particular clarity in *Language and Symbolic Power*: "As soon as one treats language as an autonomous object . . . one is condemned to looking within words for the power of words, that is, looking for it where it is not to be found."[18]

This is a double refusal of theoreticism, and of the pontificating postures of the commentator and the hermeneutician, expressed by a person who was nevertheless a "major social theorist." Bourdieu's attitude expressed first of all what could be called a "practical" conception of theory. Concepts, theories, and abstractions are necessary in the social sciences. But they are above all there to solve puzzles, to be put to work on empirical facts and not to be the chewing-gum of intellectuals. This dispositional allergy to academic intellectualism is also the basis of an antisemiologism whose limits we must discern. This defiance simply signifies a refusal to subscribe to the idea that an understanding of the meaning and effects of media and cultural production can be had by dismantling their codes.

For Bourdieu, a science of "codes" drawing on linguistics and the tradition of literary studies (semiology) is not the royal road to an understanding of culture and the media. This privilege should be accorded to sociology (though not exclusively). Thinking socio-logically means investigating the diversity of receptions and understandings of messages, which semiology obscures by setting up the scholar's perceptual schemes as universal. Barthes seldom considered the different ways the mythologies he brilliantly dissected were received, whereas Bourdieu showed, based on research, how the definition of what can be photographed varies according to social group.[19]

A field approach thus invites us to think about media and cultural production as a *modus operandi* and not only as an end product (*opus operatum*). It reintroduces lines of questioning from the sociology of work into the analysis of culture (journalism, literature). It analyzes works – from Flaubert to a television program – as dependent on a network of interdependencies, competition, and relations between social worlds (politics, religion, the economy). In short, neither a newspaper nor a photograph nor a novel can be analyzed only by taking apart its codes, however brilliantly. It is necessary to question its reception and its social uses, the social condition of its existence and production.

Cultural studies in Paris?

At the risk of surprising Anglophone readers, it should be emphasized that even the term "cultural studies" is generally mysterious to French intellectuals,[20] and though French researchers have managed to produce important works on "culture," in France there is neither a discipline nor an "antidiscipline" organized around such a term. In the United Kingdom cultural studies developed in the fallows, in unoccupied spaces between a sociology that initially had little interest in culture and a literary studies that F.R. Leavis and the influential Cambridge journal *Scrutiny* had tried to expand without including the study of media culture. Despite the interdisciplinary initiative of the journal *Communications* in the 1960s, such a space did not exist in France, where beginning in the 1960s sociology and then history devoted sustained attention to culture. Like the Gaulish village in the Asterix comics, the last hold-out against the Romans, the French university is probably one of the last spaces immune to the planetary spread of cultural studies.

Nevertheless, Bourdieu (and Passeron) were among a very few French researchers to take an interest in the work of the founders of British cultural studies. In addition to helping publish in France Hoggart's *Uses of Literacy*, Bourdieu used his journal *Actes* to translate texts by E.P. Thompson, Raymond Williams, and Paul Willis.[21] Most of these authors were invited to France at the initiative of the Centre de sociologie européenne, directed by Bourdieu. This French interest grew out of convergences between the investigations of Bourdieu's center and those of the team Hoggart and Hall assembled at Birmingham during the 1960s. On both sides, we can identify an anti-legitimist reflex: a focus on the popular classes and the dignity of their cultures, and on objects neglected by the academy (the media, leisure, and popular literature, genres only then becoming legitimate like jazz or comics). We also find a common genealogical sensibility, a focus on the "making of" social groups and their cultures (the working class for Thompson, managers for Boltanski). Their shared commitments involved a way of looking at the social from below, starting from the most ordinary practices and being attentive to real-life relations to culture, and a common interest in ethnographic accounts, clearly visible in the decision to translate a text by Willis on the behavior of working-class youths in school. Finally, they recognized in one another a common rejection of a vision of culture that gives intellectuals a monopoly over reflexivity and the ability to resist the media.

The conclusion seems to impose itself. It is necessary to abandon quarrels over words and labels. Could we say that Bourdieu and the sociologists around him do cultural studies without claiming it? The reality is more complex, as two important facts show. On the one hand, neither Bourdieu nor the journal *Actes* followed the developments of British cultural studies from the 1980s on. On the other hand, what Thompson ironically called "the electrification of the Paris–London line" brought Barthes, Baudrillard, Foucault, Derrida, and de Certeau into British libraries, but introduced little Bourdieu, whose image was confined to that of the sociologist of education or the ethnologist of Algeria.

The reasons behind this seeming double embargo are clear, and similar to those that motivated Bourdieu's suspicion of French semiology. For Bourdieu, the ambiguity of cultural studies in the 1980s lay in its semiological orientation, the weak sociological basis of much of its production, and its gradual slide into postmodern relativism. This suspicion also arose from its insufficient sensitivity to the material conditions of production of cultural and media goods, illustrated by the increasingly evident divorce inside the United Kingdom between cultural studies specialists and adherents of political economy. We could add that the comprehensive view cultural studies researchers bring to their objects, particularly the popular classes, is not always exempt from populist celebration, whether it is discreet, as in Hebdige's discussion of mods, or frankly caricatural, as in Fiske's grandiloquent theorization of television viewers' capacities for resistance.

In a critical text on the orientations of cultural studies, Nicholas Garnham and Raymond Williams themselves locate the nature of their divergences and the intellectual price of English-speaking researchers' limited use of Bourdieu's contributions.[22]

Beyond binary choices

The extent of the differences between Bourdieu's sociology of culture and media on the one hand, and the accounts of semiology and cultural studies on the other, can now be brought out more clearly. Are the products of the media and culture the mechanical results of the relations of forces between fields and institutions? Answering this question in the affirmative would be a fundamental error and a misunderstanding of Bourdieu's sociology. Like that of Norbert Elias, its theoretical approach is based on moving beyond the scholastic oppositions that delight methods specialists and hinder sociological work: the individual v. society, structure v. agency, reflexivity v. the unconscious.

Field theory's interest in the conditions of production and reception of cultural and media products has never been accompanied by a refusal to pay close attention to the rhetoric of messages, to their "internal" properties. It is sufficient to read "La lecture de Marx" – where he dismantles the mechanisms of the theoretical emphasis of French academic Marxism – or *The Political Ontology of Martin Heidegger* to see Bourdieu's remarkable sensitivity to rhetoric and forms of speech.[23] There is not a sociological Bourdieu and a semiological Bourdieu, but a sociologist who interrogates how social structures and interdependencies extend into forms, how *parole*, in Saussure's sense, is penetrated and shaped by the social. He thus takes into account the ways in which these rhetorical forms can produce programs of perception, can find social support in common sense which give it its own efficacy. We find an illustration of this in Bourdieu's 1996 analysis in *Le Monde diplomatique* of the functioning of televised debates about the French social protests of December 1995, which shows how the ways of talking to various participants (experts, politicians, strikers) engenders relations of force, valorizing or undermining their discourses.[24]

This concern with moving beyond binary alternatives, with constructing theoretical tools to explore the contradictions of the social world, can be seen in the production and reception of media messages. Throughout his reflections on the journalistic field and its relations to other social fields, Bourdieu's sociology places the accent on relations of forces, on the ways in which the end product of the work of journalists within press organizations flows out of constraints. In so doing, the approach does not become mechanistic, nor does it make journalists mere automatons of a systematic machine. The sociological toolkit Bourdieu proposes is relational. It is relational at the "macro" level of the relations between fields and within the journalistic field. And it is relational at the "micro" level, by inviting us to take into account journalists' primary and secondary education, the daily details of their interdependencies, and how their dispositions fit their objective positions. In this way, it also allows us to conceptualize the margins available for intervention, resistance, and the renewal of journalistic practices.

The text by Chamboredon and Fabiani (see note 15) on children's literature illustrates this approach in the publishing world. It is based in large part on a central idea of sociological field theory: that of structural homologies between the structure of production of children's books and the space of reception. The article shows, for instance, that the more avant-gardist or intellectual publishers find their privileged clientele among families of the new petty bourgeoisie with strong cultural capital. But far from being a mechanistic work whose result is already present in its choice of theoretical framework, the text illustrates the suppleness and comprehensive power of Bourdieu's concepts. The article devotes considerable attention to the books' genres (documentary, fiction) and content, to their layout and illustrations. Far from presenting a monolithic system, it maps the role of a dense network of mediating institutions (critics, schools, bookstores) between supply and reception. By showing, for example, how a redefinition of childhood deriving from psychoanalysis shapes notions of "how books teach," or by observing how the styles of books, once the privilege of bourgeois families, have slid toward a popular readership, the research takes note of the complexity of the variables connecting the space of production to the space of reception. In this, it illustrates a saying Bourdieu often cites from Marx: "We must not confuse the things of logic for the logic of things." Far from being an objection meant only for the work of "others," this principle can be applied to those who use field theory, and is all the more applicable to their own approach insofar as it is based on inquiries that are more liable than metadiscourses to run up against the contours of the social.

The same remarks apply to questions of reception. In Bourdieu's work we find studies emphasizing the importance of phenomena of resistance and appropriation, the audience's ability to filter and select media messages. A central dimension of his work in the sociology of culture on photography and museums lies in the empirical investigation of differences of perception and judgment with respect to the same artworks.[25] Here field sociology explores at once the diversity of habitus as matrices of perception and understanding and – to borrow an expression from Andrea Press – how these dispositions constitute more or less "hegemonically vulnerable" groups.[26]

Other contributions (such as *On Television*) insist more on the media's power to define reality, to impose a problematic on its audience. The variable focus on the power of media messages on the diversity of receptions does not follow a linear logic, increasingly emphasizing the influence of the speaker. In a 1985 conversation with the historian Roger Chartier, Bourdieu insists on the differences in the reception of books.[27] The analysis of the "scholastic perspective" in *Pascalian Meditations* brings out the gaps and differences in perceptual schemes connected to different structures of cultural capital.[28] Interviews in *The Weight of the World*, published in France in 1993, illustrate the abilities of people of very different social statuses to speak critically about media images purporting to represent their lives.[29] Without excluding the tensions and the more contestable works of field theory on the media, what appears as an uneven emphasis on the addressees' autonomy and the media's power of imposition also reveals a theoretical position. The question of the power of the media and that of reception cannot be assessed a priori. It comes down to empirical questions. Field theory and its concepts offer a toolkit whose proper use is to reveal the changing structures of interdependencies, institutional mediations, and the concrete realization of dispositions, not to pose questions containing their own answers. Bourdieu points out, for instance, how the framing power of the media can be limited when the facts presented are part of the viewers' practical experience (unemployment, welfare), but greater when they concern facts far from their everyday experience (foreign policy for instance).[30]

A Three-Dimensional Approach

The reader may have concluded by now that this chapter, included as it is in a book entitled *Bourdieu and the Journalistic Field*, talks more about culture and his works on education than journalism strictly speaking. The reason is simple: the frameworks for problematizing what we now call media and communication are to be found in Bourdieu's sociology of culture, and secondarily in his sociology of education. They can be expressed by the image of a triangle or a three-dimensional approach which includes the study of the media.

Using Bourdieu for a sociology of media means first of all analyzing a space of production – a *field* – a structured system of institutions, organizations, and social roles (those of journalists) working to produce books, television programs, magazines, and newspapers. Analyzing this field thus involves thinking of it as a space of struggle, for example, the struggle to define good journalism. What is the mark of excellence: the largest audience? The precise and pugnacious questioning of a head of state? Using the social sciences to produce a deep understanding of an event? Analyzing a field also means investigating its relations to other fields (the political, the economic, but also the cultural or the religious). This is the first element of a research program on journalism and the media. We can add a simple observation. In addition to *On Television*, Bourdieu's relatively few writings on journalism are stimulating and generally highly accessible.[31] But none of them are based on an empirical investigation of the scale of those that underlie canonical studies like *Homo Academicus* or *The State Nobility*.[32] Bourdieu did not formalize a complete sociology of the "journalistic field" or its "structure and genesis." Always attentive to his use of words, he never used such a title. The fact that this sociology of journalism remained at the stage of working sketches rather than a treatise prevents no one from productively applying field theory to the media. The conception of sociology developed by Bourdieu consists in providing theoretical tools for productive work, not in annexing research objects to the master's property.

Undertaking a sociology of the media and journalism means in the second place taking an interest in the *materiality of images*, in their *grammar*, by asking how a television report is produced, edited, and presented, how an article is written for *Le Monde* or *USA Today*, and what they owe to their conditions of production and the anticipation of their reception. To invent a Bourdieu who regarded these forms as a black box one would have to overlook a whole shelf of his books and articles. Thus, his study on Heidegger explores the deployment of philosophical rhetoric in minute detail; his study on the television program *A Armes égales* neatly dismantles the ritual production of the position of journalistic objectivity and its effects.

Finally, the third dimension of the sociology of culture and media put forth by Bourdieu is that of *reception*, of the *social uses* of various cultural goods. This statement may be surprising. The most prominent works on reception in today's academic world are those in English connected to *cultural studies*, addressing the reception of television or literary fiction. The works by Bourdieu that push furthest in this analysis of reception, of the correspondences and homologies between the field of production and the declensions of reception, are to be found in his work on cultural institutions and practices. I would particularly suggest readings of *Photography: A Middle-brow Art*, *The Love of Art: European Art Museums and their Public*, and of course *Distinction* in this spirit.

The metaphor of a triangle can also be the basis for a critical rereading of the contributions of Bourdieu and sociologists using field theory. Everyone familiar with these works can confirm that the three spotlights (field, form, reception) are not always used at the same intensity. Do these variations follow certain regularities? Can they be explained by the questions addressed (investigating the "social uses" of photography leads more naturally toward reception than investigating the "hold" of journalism, which lends itself to the relations between fields)? Do we need to relate these variations in the hierarchy of accounts to objectivizable temporal changes within social structures? Are they first and foremost the result of the distinct analytical priorities demanded by the objects of study?

Here I will hazard a critical hypothesis. For a whole series of reasons relating to the political and intellectual situation in France, since the end of the 1980s Bourdieu put more emphasis on interventions in the public sphere. He was very sensitive to the rise of commercial logics in the world of culture and the media. He did not conceal his irritation at the operetta philosophers and fast thinkers in television studios and editorial rooms who promoted a steady stream of conservative doxa, sanctified by the media and part of the intellectual world, as an insurmountable horizon of thought. For a researcher concerned from the beginning to build bridges between the academic world and civic engagement, these positions were not a break. They may have led Bourdieu to overestimate the impact of the media on certain social fields, and to pay insufficient attention to what could be best spotlighted from the pole of reception – all the more so since the media field was not a social space for which he carried out the investigations that mark his major works. The awareness of these failings has certainly been heightened in France by appropriations of *On Television* that are stronger on critical good intentions than sociological rigor.

A famous saying by the philosopher Gaston Bachelard underlines that "every light casts shadows." No sociological theory can dispel every shadow, but the combination of these three theoretical spotlights, placed at the points of the analytical triangle evoked here, seems particularly powerful. For researchers, they offer an invitation to return critically to the appeal of field theory and, better still, to put it to the only proper use of a theory: to solve well-constructed problems.

Notes

1 Pierre Bourdieu and Jean-Claude Passeron, "Sociologues des mythologies et mythologies de sociologues," *Les Temps modernes*, 211 (1963), pp. 998–1021.

2 Loïc Wacquant, "Bourdieu in America," in *Bourdieu: Critical Perspectives*, eds. Craig Calhoun, Edward LiPuma, and Moishe Postone (University of Chicago Press, Chicago, 1993, and Polity, Cambridge, 1993), pp. 212–34.

3 Pierre Bourdieu, *Sur la télévision* (Liber, Paris, 1996).

4 David Morley, *Television, Audiences and Cultural Studies* (London, Routledge, 1992).
5 Louis Pinto, *Le "Nouvel Observateur," ou l'intelligence en action* (AM Métaillié, Paris, 1984).
6 This question was put to Bourdieu by Yvette Delsaut, eliciting the following response: "[The text] is meant to be accessible to readers who have so far been excluded, who bring their reading habits and consciously or unconsciously overlook its scientific construction . . . and dwell rather on anecdotes, on personal attacks . . ." in "Sur l'esprit de la recherche", pp. 234–5, in *Bibliographie des travaux de Pierre Bourdieu*, eds. Y. Delsaut and M.-C. Rivière (Le temps des cerises, Pantin, 2002).
7 See Cyrille Lemieux, "Une critique sans raison? L'approche bourdieusienne des médias et ses limites," in *Le Travail sociologique de Pierre Bourdieu: Dettes et critiques*, ed. Bernard Lahire (La découverte, Paris, 1999), pp. 205–30; Eric Maigret, "Pierre Bourdieu, la culture populaire et le long remords de la sociologie de la distinction culturelle," *Esprit* (March–April 2002), pp. 170–8.
8 Brigitte Le Grignou, "Les Périls du texte," *Réseaux*, 80 (1996), pp. 107–27.
9 Thanks to Yvette Delsaut and Marie-Christine Rivière (*Bibliographie des travaux de Pierre Bourdieu*), an inventory of all of Bourdieu's texts and translations is now available. See also Pierre Bourdieu and Loïc J.D. Wacquant, *An Invitation to Reflexive Sociology* (University of Chicago Press, Chicago, 1992, and Polity, Cambridge, 1992), esp. pp. 273–82.
10 Claude Grignon and Jean-Claude Passeron, *Le Savant et le populaire: Misérabilisme et populisme en sociologie et en littérature* (Seuil-Gallimard, Hautes Etudes, Paris, 1989).
11 At the same time, these works were also explicitly connected to the problematic of "communication," as the title of a collective volume from the period (1964) – *Rapport pédagogique et communication* – demonstrates.
12 Pierre Bourdieu, Jean-Claude Chamboredon, Jean-Claude Passeron, eds. *Craft of Sociology: Epistemological Preliminaries* (Walter de Gruyter, 1991); Leonard Schatzman and Anselm Strauss, "Social Class and Modes of Communication," *American Sociological Review*, XL, 4 (1955), pp. 329–38.
13 Richard Hoggart, *The Uses of Literacy* (Chatto and Windus, London, 1957); French translation with a foreword by J.-C. Passeron, *La Culture du pauvre* (Minuit, Paris, 1970).
14 Pierre Bourdieu, *Language and Symbolic Power*, ed. John B. Thompson (Polity, Cambridge, 1991, and Harvard University Press, Cambridge, MA, 1991) [*Ce que parler veut dire*, Fayard, Paris, 1982].
15 See Jean-Claude Chamboredon and Jean-Louis Fabiani, "Les Albums pour enfants" and "Le Champ de l'édition et les definitions sociales de

l'enfance", *Actes de la recherche en sciences sociales*, 13 (1977), pp. 60–79, and 14 (1977), pp. 55–74; Louis Pinto, "Les Affinités électives: Les amis du *Nouvel Observateur* comme 'groupe ouvert,'" *Actes de la recherche en sciences sociales*, 36–7 (1981), pp. 105–24; and the special isssue of *Actes*, 60 (1985) on "Images 'populaires.'"

16 Roland Barthes, *Mythologies* (The Noonday Press, New York, 1990 and Seuil, Paris, 1957).

17 See, e.g., Patrick Champagne, "Qui a gagné? Analyse interne et analyse externe des débats à la télévision", *Mots*, 20 (1989), pp. 5–23.

18 Bourdieu, *Language and Symbolic Power*, p. 107.

19 Pierre Bourdieu, *Photography* (Stanford University Press, Stanford, CA, 1990, and Polity, Cambridge, 1996), originally published as *Un art moyen* (Minuit, Paris, 1965). Also translated into French for Bourdieu's Le sens pratique series was *L'Invention d'un tableau* (1987) in which the Italian Salvatore Settis analyzed Giorgione's mysterious painting, *The Storm*. While highly semiological in its painstaking dissection of images and symbols, it is primarily a sociological work, insofar as it concentrates on making these images intelligible within the culture of sixteenth-century Venetian elites.

20 The first introductory book in France on cultural studies was only published in 2003! See Armand Mattelart and Erik Neveu, eds., *Introduction aux Cultural Studies* (La Découverte, Paris, 2003).

21 Respectively in issues 2–3 (1976), pp. 133–51; 17–18 (1977), pp. 29–36; and 24 (1978), pp. 50–61, of *Actes*.

22 See Nicholas Garnham and Raymond Williams, "Pierre Bourdieu and the Sociology of Culture: An Introduction," *Media, Culture and Society*, 2 (1980), pp. 209–23, esp. p. 210.

23 See Pierre Bourdieu, "La Lecture de Marx: Quelques remarques critiques à propos de 'Quelques remarques critiques à propos de *Lire le Capital*,'" *Actes de la recherche en sciences sociales*, 5–6 (1975), pp. 65–79; and Pierre Bourdieu, *The Political Ontology of Martin Heidegger* (Stanford University Press, Stanford, CA, 1996, and Polity, Cambridge, 1996).

24 Pierre Bourdieu, "Analyse d'un passage à l'antenne," *Le Monde diplomatique* (April 1996), p. 25.

25 This aspect is strongly visible in *Photography*, *Distinction* (Harvard University Press, Cambridge, MA, 1984) and *The Love of Art* (with Alain Darbel and Dominique Schnapper) (Polity, Cambridge, 1997).

26 Andrea L. Press, *Women Watching Television* (University of Pennsylvania Press, Philadelphia, 1991).

27 Pierre Bourdieu, "La Lecture: une pratique culturelle," in *Pratiques de la lecture*, ed. Roger Chartier (Payot, Paris, 1993), pp. 265–91.

28 Pierre Bourdieu, *Pascalian Meditations* (Stanford University Press, Stanford, CA, 2000, and Polity, Cambridge, 2000).

29 Pierre Bourdieu, ed., *The Weight of the World* (Stanford University Press, Stanford, CA, 2000, and Polity, Cambridge, 1999).
30 See, e.g., Pierre Bourdieu, "Public Opinion Does Not Exist," in *Communication and Class Struggle*, eds. A. Mattelart and S. Siegelaub (International General, New York, 1979), pp. 124–30.
31 See, e.g., by Bourdieu, "*A armes égales*: La parade de l'objectivité et l'imposition de problématique," *Actes de la recherche en sciences sociales*, 2–3 (1976), pp. 70–3; "*Libé*, vingt ans après," *Actes de la recherche en sciences sociales*, 101–2 (1994), p. 39; and "Questions aux vrais maîtres du monde," *Le Monde*, October 14, 1999, p. 18.
32 Pierre Bourdieu, *Homo Academicus* (Stanford University Press, Standford, CA, 1988, and Polity, Cambridge, 1988) and *The State Nobility* (Stanford University Press, CA, Stanford, 1996, and Polity, Cambridge, 1996).

11

Autonomy from What?

Michael Schudson

Many of the papers in this volume raise, in different ways, the fundamental question of how autonomous journalism is and, to the extent that it fails to be autonomous, whether it fails in the direction of subservience to the market or subservience to the state. The question of the autonomy of different cultural fields is both theoretically and empirically important. In terms of social theory, a number of initiatives have sought to cushion the harshness of an old-fashioned reductionism in which cultural and social phenomena become "nothing but" the emanations of underlying economic or political forces. For instance, British media studies has been distinguished by a move away from a rigid economic determinism (too far away, according to some) to a concept of the "relative autonomy" of the media or media industries. American sociologists, political scientists, and communication scholars whose links to Marxist thought have been weak or absent have long taken seriously the force of social institutions and social interaction in the construction of cultural products. Pierre Bourdieu's emphasis in the concept of "field" is another effort to put forward a vocabulary and framework for understanding how different realms of social life are related to one another but are also distinct from one another, each field having some measure of autonomy from the others and therefore needing to be understood to some degree in its own terms.[1] In his contribution to this volume, Bourdieu observes not only that social fields have their own logics but that some fields are more independent in their logics than others. Bourdieu cites poetry and mathematics as fields that are relatively more determined than many other fields by internal logics and structures than by relationships to external social, economic, and political phenomena. Different fields of human activity all – by virtue of being fields – have their own internal logic and some degree of insulation from the influence of other fields.

I myself have nothing invested for or against the notion of "field" for helping to understand journalism. But certainly one of the virtues of the concept is that it forces to attention the question, just as important to journalists themselves as it is to scholars of journalism, of how autonomous journalists really are and how autonomous the different elements and echelons of journalism are. The primary concern in these remarks, however, is a related question that Bourdieu's work does not address and that discussions of journalism rarely take on: how autonomous should journalism be? The assumption is strong inside journalism and in most academic discussions of journalism that the press should be fully autonomous, pursuing truth without constraint and without "fear or favor" as the founder of the modern *New York Times* wrote in 1896. But from the perspective of democratic theory, just how autonomous should journalism be?

In practice, journalistic autonomy is remarkably complex. One of the most compelling explorations of the kinds and degrees of journalistic autonomy is Daniel Hallin's 1986 study of American news coverage of the war in Vietnam. Hallin observes that press subservience to government officials and press acquiescence in an ideology of the Cold War muted criticism of the evolving Vietnam policy of the Kennedy and Johnson administrations. Criticism was muted – but not silenced. The television networks were more submissive than print. Print was more acquiescent in its headlines than in its news stories. Print news was more docile in front page stories than in stories on the inside pages. Front page stories were more cautious in their leads and opening paragraphs than in the closing paragraphs. As Hallin observes, at the top of the story, reporters led with the most recent and authoritative views of highly placed government officials. The further one went along into the story, the more the reporter included policy discussions and details that cut closer to the heart of where the policies were going and what they portended. As he wrote of one *New York Times* story, it "led with the statement least revealing of the actual course of the policy debate, and moved on, as coverage trailed off into the back pages, to information that progressively undermined the lead – and moved closer to the truth."[2]

For Hallin, the press was by no means autonomous from the state. Although Hallin acknowledges that, in the nineteenth and especially the early twentieth century, US journalism became increasingly professionalized and dominated by its own occupational routines and its own occupational ethic, he insists – as he does in his paper for this volume – that it is wrong to describe this as the differentiation of an autonomous sphere of journalism from an earlier incorporation inside the state. In the Vietnam study, Hallin put it this way:

> Far from sundering the connection between press and state, objective journalism *rationalized* that connection, in the Weberian sense of the term: it put that relation on a firm footing of a set of abstract principles embodied in the "professional" standards of news judgment. It was no longer possible for a party or politician to control any news medium as an official organ; and it was no longer necessary for high officials of government to do so. Their views were guaranteed access to all the major media – and protected against "irresponsible" attack – by virtue of the authority of their position, not their particular party or politics.[3]

For Hallin, the press did not live up to its ambition – or boast – of serving as a "watchdog" on government. The media were far too integrated into the political field or, more precisely in Hallin's terms, the media's relationship to politics had become rationalized in a way that privileged official government voices in the news. Even so, within a single news institution (the *New York Times*) and even within a single news story in that institution, variations in autonomy appear.

Press reports on politics, W. Lance Bennett has argued, are "indexed" to the views of high government officials.[4] Hallin's work, among many others, confirms this for the United States. In this volume, Eric Darras illustrates the same point for France, showing that French television news-interview shows select guests largely according to their ranking within the political elite. Other possibilities – that journalists choose guests who will broaden the political debate or guests whose personalities and rhetoric might entice a larger audience and so prove commercially more attractive – are nowhere to be found. The Darras case study runs directly counter to Bourdieu's claim in *On Television* that the journalistic field is engulfing the political field; for Darras, the political field has the upper hand. Of course, actual situations will vary, but one is inclined to give more credit to a solid empirical study than to the fairly crude generalizations of *On Television*.[5]

As Bourdieu suggests, journalists construct a sense of their own autonomy "against the commercial." In the American case, this is a matter of routine discussion among journalists: "How can we defend the autonomy of news against incursions from the business office?" There is a century-long tradition in the United States of journalistic fears of ceding territory and occupational freedom of action to directives from a profit-seeking publisher. Since the early 1990s, this issue has come up repeatedly: has national television news gutted its ability to cover news because of a profit-driven drive to cut costs? Did the *Los Angeles Times* violate every canon of journalistic integrity by running as "news" a supplement about the city's new convention and sports center that was actually a large paid advertisement?[6] Has the "wall of separation" between the business office and the news room been finally and fully broken down in a profit-driven quest for audiences?

In the minds of American journalists, autonomy is constructed as much against the political as against the commercial, and journalists police the possibility of acquiescence to political power with an even greater sense of moral indignation over violations. The First Amendment is the backbone of American journalism's understanding of itself, even though the First Amendment's prohibition on government laws abridging freedom of the press had essentially no significance in the courtroom until the 1920s. Moreover, the First Amendment has sometimes been read by the courts and used by news organizations in ways that identify press freedom or journalistic autonomy with the inviolable right of media owners to publish as they please. Consider the case of Pat Tornillo, who in 1972 ran for a seat in the Florida state legislature. The *Miami Herald* wrote a couple of scathing editorials about him. Tornillo asked for space in the paper to respond, citing a 1913 Florida "right-of-reply" statute that required newspapers to provide comparable space for reply, upon request, should a newspaper assail the personal character of any candidate for public office. When the *Miami Herald* refused to satisfy Tornillo's request, he sued. The Florida Supreme Court held that the right-of-reply statute served the "broad societal interest in the free flow of information to the public." Most democracies around the world would agree with the ruling. Right-of-reply statutes are commonplace. But the *Herald* appealed the Florida decision to the US Supreme Court, and the Supreme Court sided with the newspaper.

Why? On the face of it, a right-of-reply statute is a boon to public debate. Certainly in the 1970s and even more in the twenty-first century, when local television news largely ignores local politics and the only general news coverage of candidates for state and local office is provided by newspapers, the fact that most US cities boast only one daily newspaper would make a statute like Florida's desirable, even a necessary protection for democracy. But Supreme Court Justice Byron White saw in Florida's statute "the heavy hand of government intrusion" that "would make the government the censor of what people may read and know." For Justice White, this is impermissible. If the marketplace is to be the censor, that may be regrettable but it is fully in accord with the Constitution. It is only state censorship that the Constitution forbids.[7]

So American journalists have struggled for autonomy against both the state and the market, with mixed success. But suppose that journalism gained autonomy from the commercial field and also from the political field, would it then be autonomous? Bourdieu makes a shrewd observation that is relevant here: "Autonomy can lead to an 'egoistic' closing-in on the specific interests of the people engaged in the field" (p. 45). This is the point made over and over again in the United States by conservative critics of the news media. They object specifically to journalistic autonomy. They see journalists as a liberal elite that imposes its values on everybody else. Journalists, they say, are "politically correct" and are almost uniformly secular in a country with the strongest church-going tradition of any Western democracy. Journalists are feminists and pro-choice advocates when a very large and politically powerful segment of the population is deeply distressed by laws permitting abortion.

The conservative critics fail to see how wedded to the dominant political dialogue the news media are. They also fail to understand how seriously journalists take their flag of objectivity. Even so, there is a socially liberal, if not politically liberal, tone to the leading institutions of American journalism (although probably not to American journalism top to bottom). How much is journalism's autonomy, so far as it goes, an egoistic closing-in?

In the daily practice of journalism, autonomy is a prize that honest reporters and editors seek. They do not want to be overwhelmed by pressure from government officials, on the one hand, or from economic pressures from media owners or advertisers or market competition on the other. They want to be able to proceed according to their own best lights and in the service of their own best "news judgment." Of course, "news judgment" is not "their own" individually but their own as the collective construct of the journalistic field or the journalistic community. It is not codified. It is not fully coherent. In tough cases, it has to be debated among reporters and editors – "Is this a story? Is it a front page story? Is the tip or rumor that just came to us worth pursuing?" No formula covers every instance and no two news organizations operate in precisely the same way. Still, journalists all breathe the same air of their occupation and develop habits of judgment of great, sometimes stultifying, uniformity. In this respect, when journalists collectively gain autonomy from state and market, they do not individually gain free expression.

This raises the possibility that the "news judgment" of a corps of media professionals who are beyond the influence of state and market is not necessarily a prize one should want for the best interest of a democratic society. No doubt, journalists are right that commerce and government control are the corruptions they should most strenuously avoid, but the corruption of conformity to a climate of opinion in a group can be serious and damaging in its own right. Consider the conformity of opinion in a small quasi-religious cult that expects the end of the world on a predicted day and prepares to welcome the flying saucer that will save them from earth's destruction. When the saucer fails to land and the earth is not destroyed on the anticipated date, the group does not alter its faith in its millenarian vision but seeks to understand why it got the date wrong. Or consider the far more important case of scientific communities in Thomas Kuhn's powerful portrait of them. Kuhn shows that conformity to a reigning scientific framework continues even in the face of a growing array of puzzles that cannot be understood within it. Even when a new and more successful model appears, adherents of the old paradigm do not typically convert – they eventually die off while younger scientists champion the new view.[8]

If journalism is "autonomous" is it not subject to corruptions like this? Is it not even worse for journalism than for science? Journalism has no systematic means for policing its own intellectual narrowness. Journalists collectively do very little to challenge their own governing assumptions. What keeps journalism alive, changing, and growing is the public nature of journalists' work, the nonautonomous environment of their work, the fact that they are daily or weekly exposed to the disappointment and criticism of their sources (in the political field) and their public (whose disapproval may be demonstrated economically as readers cancel subscriptions or viewers change channels). Vulnerability to the audience (the market) keeps journalists nimble in one direction, vulnerability to sources (the government) in another. What can be good for journalism can also be disastrous – pandering in the one direction and propagandizing in the other. But absent these powerful outside pressures, journalism can wind up communicating only to itself and for itself.

What also keeps journalism alive, and what sociology typically and unaccountably forgets about it, is its dependence not on the state or the market but on the drama of events that neither state nor market nor journalists can fully or even approximately anticipate or control. Unanticipated events from assassinations to accidents lie at the center of journalistic passion but beyond the control (at least initially) of established power. The nuclear power plant accident at Three Mile

Island in 1979 forced American media attention to environmental issues and energy issues and the potential dangers of nuclear power generators as no protest movements or blue-ribbon commissions ever could. Unanticipated events on the scale of Three Mile Island or even more cataclysmic, September 11, are rare events. At the same time, journalism prepares itself for rare events. The White House press corps covers the president as close to round-the-clock as it can, not because the president is so endlessly important or fascinating but because his assassination or heart attack would be. This may be ghoulish but it organizes journalistic effort.

Covering a tornado or a flood or an assassination brings individual reporters career advancement and garners individual newspapers or broadcast stations major journalism prizes. Most news is routine news but the ideology of American journalists focuses insistently on exploits and challenges that arise when routines fail. It is not easy to accommodate this feature of journalism any more than it is easy for historians to know how to make sense of the assassin's bullet in Sarajevo or in Dallas that through no particular logic influenced the course of history. But somehow a sociology of journalism has to find a way to do this.

The membrane of the journalistic field, permeable in relation to the market or state, is relatively resistant to influence from other groups. Eric Klinenberg's example of youth media (chapter 9) is a case of one important group – young people – who have occasionally organized to influence how members of their group are portrayed in the news. They have an uphill battle. Academic experts who hope their views will be taken seriously in the media are often rudely rebuffed. In the United States, journalists typically seek out only certain kinds of experts to comment on politics – those who are or have been close to government and who are facile at talking the talk of policy options and predictions. Authorities who might want to stand a bit further back from the "inside Washington" perspective and offer views on, say, the history of a conflict or the morality of a policy, are unlikely to get a hearing from a journalist on deadline.[9]

So what degree of autonomy should one seek for journalism? A democrat should not want journalism to be as self-enclosed and separated from outside pressures as mathematics or poetry. At least in an American view of journalism, that I share, journalism is not supposed to be a set of individual thinkers and explorers in search of truth but a set of energetic and thoughtful communicators who try to keep a society attuned to itself. Journalism, as the primary circulator of meanings in society, the realm in which the ideas and values of other fields and other lands come to the same page before a wide array of readers and viewers, should be dependent to a degree – a degree difficult to define – on the market. The market here is an imperfect proxy for the general public, but of course there are different markets and market segments and accordingly different publics and elements of the public so represented.

Journalists should also be particularly attuned to the state – and dependent on the state to a degree – for the sake of democracy. An argument can be made, in terms of democratic theory, that journalism should be significantly occupied with the task of relaying the views of elected governmental officials. Who, after all, are the journalists to determine what information, what history, and what context is appropriate for citizens who want to know about political life? Why should a democracy trust in the intellectual currents autonomously ruling journalists at a particular moment rather than trusting to the dynamic of forces that is pushing or pulling politicians? Perhaps journalism, consistent with representative democracy, should concentrate on reporting back to citizens what their elected representatives say and do, allowing citizens as voters to assess leaders after they have acted.[10] This, I think, would narrow the role of political news too much. Journalists should not deny themselves the avenues of analysis and criticism. They should be active in opening up the political windows and airing out the public sphere, even when politicians are content to stay in stuffy rooms. But at the same time, journalists can and should give disproportionate space and attention to the people's elected representatives. They can and should seek to articulate a place for journalism in democracy that calls on journalists to be serious and valiant but appropriately modest.

If journalism is sufficiently decentralized and varied in the viewpoints it presents; if journalists are recruited from different walks of life and promote different points of view; if journalism is institutionally self-critical in ways that guarantee variety and change in the news; if, in a word, journalism is a pluralistic institution, then journalistic autonomy may be good not only for journalists, who of course appreciate the freedom to write what they please, but good for a democratic society. Pluralism inside media organizations helps open a space for what Herbert J. Gans a generation ago called "multiperspectival news."[11] Honest observers can differ over how pluralistic the journalism of the United States or France or anywhere is – and may differ, too, over how degrees of pluralism may be measured. But only if journalism is relatively pluralistic, and only if journalism is relatively vulnerable to the assaults of government sources, marketplace competition, and the surprises of daily events, can we anticipate that news will not be captive to an insular professional elite.

These observations raise more questions than they answer. Let me close by restating the questions. First, does journalistic autonomy from the commercial and political field mean a journalism that takes only its own narrow opinions seriously? What structures of journalistic ownership, recruitment, culture, and organization can keep the field open to alternative opinions? Second, does journalistic dependence on both state and market afford in different ways an appropriate or valuable place for democratic sentiment and democratic values to enter into news production? If so, is it possible to define a point of dependence on state or market that reduces the value of the media to democratic values?

In the end, journalistic autonomy cannot be a value for its own sake. Journalism can do many things but one thing it is obliged to do by its history, its traditions, its highest values, and sometimes its legal license, is to serve democracy. When the autonomy of journalism conflicts with the best practices of democratic government, journalistic autonomy has to be challenged.

Notes

1 Does Bourdieu actually use the concept of field to genuinely break from deterministic thinking? Or is "field" only a kind of screen for an underlying reductionism? In a spirited, highly critical assessment of Bourdieu's work, Jeffrey C. Alexander argues that Bourdieu never finally escaped determinism. See Jeffrey C. Alexander, *Fin de Siècle Social Theory* (Verso, London, 1995), esp. pp. 157–64.
2 Daniel C. Hallin, *The "Uncensored War": The Media and Vietnam* (Oxford University Press, New York, 1986), p. 78.
3 Hallin, *The "Uncensored War"*, p. 70.
4 W. Lance Bennett, "Toward a Theory of Press-State Relations," *Journal of Communication*, 40 (1990), pp. 103–25.
5 In the essay by Bourdieu in the present volume, he describes journalism as a "very weakly autonomous field" and judges politics "very strongly independent" of voters and "more and more inclined to close in on itself" (see pp. 33–4).
6 See Michael Schudson, *The Sociology of News* (W.W. Norton, New York, 2003), p. 122.
7 *Miami Herald Publishing Company* v. *Tornillo* 418 US 241 (1974), p. 260.
8 On the cult, see Stanley Schachter, *When Prophecy Fails* (University of Minnesota Press, Minneapolis, MN, 1956) and on science, see Thomas S. Kuhn, *The Structure of Scientific Revolutions* (University of Chicago Press, Chicago, 1962).

9 Janet Steele, "Experts and the Operational Bias of Television News: The Case of the Persian Gulf War," *Journalism and Mass Communication Quarterly*, 72 (1995), pp. 799–812.
10 John Zaller, "Elite Leadership of Mass Opinion: New Evidence from the Gulf War," in *Taken by Storm*, eds. W. Lance Bennett and David Paletz (University of Chicago Press, Chicago, 1994), pp. 186–209, esp. 201–2.
11 Herbert J. Gans, *Deciding What's News* (Vintage, New York, 1980 [Pantheon, 1979]).

12

Field Theory, Differentiation Theory, and Comparative Media Research

Daniel C. Hallin

One of the principal virtues of the media sociology that has emerged in France out of the tradition of Bourdieu's field theory is the fact that it is focused on understanding the media as an institution within a wider social formation. In this it contrasts with much research on the media, which has avoided the system level of analysis and tended to analyze the media in isolation from society as a whole. This focus makes field theory particularly useful for historical and comparative analysis of the media. In this chapter I would like to consider field theory in relation to another perspective which also has attempted to understand media as part of the social system as a whole: the systems model or "differentiation theory" tradition derived from the work of Talcott Parsons.

The perspective of differentiation theory is implicit in much of the conventional wisdom about the relation of media and society, and for this reason is quite useful for illuminating what is distinctive about Bourdieu's field theory. In the first section of this chapter I outline the differentiation theory of Jeffrey Alexander, who has advanced what is probably the most developed contemporary application of this perspective to media studies. I then introduce the media research carried out from the perspective of Bourdieu's field theory as a possible alternative framework, and summarize the strengths and weaknesses of these two perspectives. I also discuss the relation of both perspectives to the work of Jürgen Habermas and to the tradition of "critical political economy" which developed in Anglo-

American media studies during the 1970s. I will not attempt here to deal in any systematic way with the underlying theoretical differences between differentiation theory and Bourdieu's field theory, but will focus specifically on their contrasting analyses of the relation of media to other social institutions.

Differentiation Theory

In the 1960s systems theory had enormous influence on media scholarship in the United States. This was manifested particularly in the "communication and development paradigm," which defined "modernization" of the media in terms of the notion of differentiation which Parsons had taken from the work of Emile Durkheim. In *Communications and Political Development*, Lucien Pye wrote:

> In any society only a small fraction of political communication originates from the political actors themselves, and this proportion tends to decrease with modernization as increasing numbers of participants without power join the communications process. In a fundamental sense modernization involves the emergence of a professional class of communicators . . . The emergence of professionalized communicators is . . . related to the development of an objective, analytical and nonpartisan view of politics.[1]

According to structural-functionalist systems theory, societies tend to evolve toward increasing functional differentiation of institutions. Social structures which at one time served multiple functions tend to disintegrate and to be replaced by more specialized structures. The communication and development paradigm argued that communication institutions tended to become differentiated from political structures, and also to become increasingly central to the social and political system, since differentiation increased the importance of their role in the process of social integration. As political parties, interest groups, religious institutions, administrative apparatuses, etc., become increasingly differentiated from one another, the media, which become increasingly differentiated from all of these, play an increasing role in coordinating their interactions. The communication and development paradigm also placed strong emphasis on the notion of professionalization. Structural functionalists often pointed to professionalization as evidence against the Marxist argument that capitalist societies "left remaining no other nexus between man and man than naked self-interest, than callous 'cash payment.'"[2] The communication and development perspective took the version of journalistic professionalism which emerged most strongly in the United States – centered around the notion of "objective journalism" – as the epitome of modernity in the field of communication.

The communication and development paradigm died out without leaving a particularly large body of empirical research. Much of it had been developed in political science, which lost interest in the media until the 1980s to 1990s. Differentiation theory is not often used explicitly in contemporary media studies. It is, however, implicit in much contemporary literature, and in some sense lies behind the common assumption that the Anglo-American model of journalism is the norm toward which media systems naturally tend to evolve. It is implicit, certainly, in what the British often call the Whig interpretation of media history, which holds that "the increasing value of newspapers as advertising mediums allow[ed] them gradually to shake off government or party control and to become independent voices of public sentiment."[3] The development of commercial media markets in the nineteenth century, according to this interpretation, permitted the differentiation of the media from political structures, and their reconstitution as independent structures increasingly central to the process by which public opinion was formed.

One contemporary theorist who does make explicit use of differentiation theory is Niklas Luhmann, whose work on the mass media is built around the distinction between "attention rules" and "decision rules."[4] According to Luhmann, it is the function of public opinion, organized around the structures of the media system, to draw attention to social problems, while the state and more broadly the political system has the function of making decisions. Jeffrey Alexander also makes an unusual attempt to sketch out a comparative analysis of the evolution of the news media based on differentiation theory, in his 1981 article, "The Mass News Media in Systemic, Historical and Comparative Perspective."[5] Much of his analysis is focused on the contrasting cases of the United States and France, and I will focus primarily on his account here. The heart of Alexander's analysis is the idea that the "possibility of flexible normative production is dependent on the autonomy of news media from control by groups and institutions in other social subsystems," among which he includes the state, parties, the university, the church, and social classes.

> The emergence of a more independent news media can be interpreted as the creation of an "autonomous regulatory mechanism" for the integrative dimension of society in the same manner that the emergence of

> representation, party formation and constitutionalism indicates the development of regulatory mechanisms in the political sphere. . . . [T]he differentiation of mass news media can be regarded as the generalization of normative resources, a development that provides society with an enormously increased flexibility in responding to changing events.[6]

The movement toward greater differentiation of the news media is driven, where it does occur, by the same social forces that "create differentiation in other social spheres."[7] Alexander lists three such forces: "demands for more universalistic information that oppressed groups make in the course of their demands for societal inclusion and support,"[8] the growth of professional norms and self-regulation, driven in part by journalists' own struggle for status and autonomy, and the more general development of social norms of universalism.

For many years I have been engaged in a series of comparative analyses of US and European news media, together with Paolo Mancini of the University of Perugia.[9] Repeatedly we have been drawn back to Alexander's article as a point of comparison, in part because it is such a rare attempt to do a comparative and historical analysis of the development of media institutions in relation to processes of social change at the system level. Alexander's analysis seems to us to be correct in many important ways, and misleading in others; we have found Bourdieu's field theory a useful alternative perspective against which to contrast Alexander's structural-functionalism.

Differentiation of media from parties and organized social groups

The history of the news media in the West clearly does involve a process of differentiation from political parties and from organized social groups rooted in religious, class and other forms of community. From the time of the Thirty Years War in Northern and Central Europe, newspapers began to evolve as means of expression for social groups engaged in conflict and ideological competition with one another. These kinds of ties were strengthened as political parties and trade unions, often with strong mass bases, began to develop. In much of Europe, the news media evolved in a context in which religious and ideological communities and the organizational structures they developed fused together many social functions. This is most obvious in the case of the Dutch "pillars." The Catholic, Protestant, socialist and liberal communities into which Dutch society was once divided maintained a wide variety of institutions – schools, hospitals, social clubs, welfare organizations, and, not least important, newspapers and eventually broadcast organizations – and carried out a wide range of social functions, including the production of symbolic meaning, the "aggregation of interests" and organization of political decision making, the organization of leisure time, provision of social welfare and more. The Catholic and Communist subcultures in Italy similarly organized wide areas of social, political, and cultural life, as did similar subcultures, often in less dramatic form, in other European countries. In Southern Europe, fusion of social structures and functions often resulted from clientelism: clientelist networks tied together the worlds of politics, business, religion and journalism, reducing the autonomy of actors in the separate spheres and binding those actors in common relationships of power, interdependence and affinity.[10]

Newspapers commonly served as means of organization and expression for these kinds of social groups, whose internal cohesion they helped to secure, and whose voice they projected into the wider public sphere. They were organizationally tied to them, often subsidized by them and distributed through their organizational networks. The connection of newspapers with these groups was reflected in their content, which expressed the ideological orientations of the different groups. It was reflected in newspaper markets, which were divided according to the boundaries among social groups. And it was reflected in the career paths of journalists, who tended to work in newspapers belonging to their own social groups, and often to move back and forth between journalism and other forms of organizational, particularly political party work. In the 1970s, for example, high percentages of Scandinavian journalists still served as party functionaries and office holders.

Over the course of the twentieth century, western societies have become increasingly "secularized." Citizens have come to see themselves as individual consumers and voters rather than as members of social groups, and the institutions once fused within the subcommunities defined by these groups have become separated and often "professionalized," run by specialists whose identity is rooted in their socialization within a particular sector rather than their ideological and group commitments. The party press has declined dramatically, replaced by "omnibus" commercial newspapers which appeal to individual consumers across ideological and group boundaries. Journalism has become professionalized, with journalists gaining greater autonomy in important ways as well as developing a distinct identity rooted in technical training and a common peer culture. Distinctive journalistic routines have largely replaced ideological frameworks as guides to the presentation of news. As Italian scholar Gianpietro Mazzoleni puts it, a distinctive media logic has replaced the political logic that once governed the behavior of the media and the circulation of public information more generally.[11] Italian television is an excellent example of the change. Through the 1980s it was governed by a logic of proportional representation, with the three channels of public broadcasting divided among the political parties. Journalists and other personnel were appointed to a significant degree on the basis of political representation, and the news was essentially a presentation of the comments of party spokesmen on the major events and issues of the day. Today, though political influences are still greater in Italy than in many systems, news increasingly follows the "media logic" of creating narratives that will appeal to a mass audience.

Also consistent with differentiation theory, the media have become increasingly central to political and much of social life. In part, this results from the growing autonomy of the media from the political actors that once controlled them. As they are increasingly organizationally and economically independent of political institutions, and as journalists develop separate identities, career tracks, and modes of practice, the independent influence of the media increases. Other institutions that once performed functions of socialization and production of meaning, meanwhile, have weakened, and the media often fill the vacuum of power. Finally, as political parties become separated from churches, trade unions, and other social groups – as well as from portions of the state they may once have controlled (an increasingly professionalized judiciary, for example) – they increasingly must depend on the media to establish ties with individual voters and other social actors. In general, according to differentiation theory, a differentiated society relies on media to connect actors and institutions no longer connected by more direct ties.

These processes of change started at different times in different societies. They started earliest in the United States, where commercial media began weakening the ties between media and organized social groups as early as the 1830s, when the commercial penny press developed. Tocqueville wrote eloquently of the strength of connections between newspapers and "associations" in America; but he wrote at a time when this connection was beginning to be disrupted by the beginning of commercialization. In most of Europe, and in many other parts of the world, the differentiation of media from parties and organized social groups dates mainly from the post-World War II period. The process has gone farther in some systems than others, and the degree of differentiation of the media from the party system and from other systems of political representation is clearly an important variable in comparative analysis.

Bourdieu and the Critique of Differentiation Theory

There are, at the same time, many problems with differentiation theory as an approach to understanding the development of media systems. It seems doubtful that media history anywhere in the world can be understood as an essentially unilinear move toward greater differentiation: there are important processes of de-differentiation at work simultaneously. Here the perspectives of Bourdieu's field theory, as developed by the contributors to this volume, are quite useful for developing an alternative interpretation.

Field theory shares much of the problematic of differentiation theory. It is centrally concerned with the development of fields as autonomous "social universes," with distinctive forms of practice, conceptions of their social role, and standards for judging cultural production and assigning status to cultural producers. The work that has come out of this tradition so far has been marked by detailed, nuanced empirical studies of the development of the profession of journalism, with its ethical codes, role-conceptions and status hierarchies, and, very centrally, its varying degrees of autonomy in relation to other fields and their actors and logics. Like differentiation theory, field theory involves a normative preference for the autonomy of fields. As Rodney Benson puts it:

> In Bourdieu's model total domination exists when one field dominates all others and there exists only one acceptable "definition of human accomplishment" for the entire society. A field's autonomy is to be valued because it provides preconditions for the full creative process proper to each field and ultimately resistance to the "symbolic violence" exerted by the dominant system of hierarchization.[12]

When fields lose their autonomy in relation to one another, society loses diversity of creative resources, and presumably – consistent with Alexander's argument – flexibility.

Field theory does not, however, assume an evolutionary process of development toward greater differentiation; for this reason it seems to me a potentially more open framework for understanding change in the relations of media to other social structures. Fields, in Bourdieu's theory, change through a process of struggle among the agents working within them, and there is no reason to assume that change will result in greater rather than lesser autonomy of fields. In the case of journalism, Champagne argues that its history "could well be in large part the story of an impossible autonomy – or, to put it in the least pessimistic way, the unending story of an autonomy that must always be re-won because it is always threatened" (p. 50). The history of journalism is not, in other words, a "natural history" that moves inevitably toward the autonomy of journalism from other fields. It is an uncertain and changeable process, in which parts of the field of journalism (it is notable that the papers in this volume insist on the importance of disaggregating the field of journalism, and remembering that its component parts are not all similarly positioned) have sometimes won relative autonomy in relation to other fields, often then losing it again, or sometimes winning it in one direction while they simultaneously lose it in another. Bourdieu and those who have used field theory in analyzing the French media have argued, more specifically, that the media have in recent years become increasingly de-differentiated in relation to the economic system. This seems to me to be clearly correct, and here the contrasting argument of Bourdieu and other field theorists captures a key ambiguity and ultimately a key failing of differentiation theory as articulated by Alexander, and as it is implicitly developed in much media theory.

The journalistic field and the economic field

Alexander argues that modernization of the media requires that "there must be differentiation from structures in the economic dimension, particularly social classes."[13] The main meaning he gives to the differentiation of media from "economic structures" has to do with ties of media to class-linked parties and organizations: he argues that trade-union-linked papers are historically a hindrance to professionalization and differentiation, though he also mentions highly partisan bourgeois papers in nineteenth-century Germany. He does not address the role of the *market* in detail, nor that of private media owners. He makes only one comment about media economics, in discussing US media history: "This transition in content [away from partisanship] coincided with the birth of journalistic professionalization and the emergence of newspapers as big business. By the turn of the twentieth century, the notion of the news media as a 'public institution' was, then, beginning to be institutionalized."[14] Clearly this implies that commercialization contributed to or at least was in harmony with differentiation and professionalization, though Alexander does not elaborate on the point, and leaves the development of commercial media markets out of his list of three forces that underlie the drive toward greater differentiation of the media system. In discussing the differences between the media history of France and the United States, Alexander focuses on political polarization in France, and does not mention the fact – heavily stressed by Jean Chalaby – that the French newspaper did not develop as a cultural industry the way the American newspaper did.[15] In a more recent book, Alexander has harshly criticized Bourdieu as a reductionist, arguing that despite the stated intent to analyze fields as relatively autonomous spheres of action, Bourdieu treats all fields as dominated in the end by the logic of the economic.[16] Surely, though, we cannot make the opposite mistake of ignoring the obvious fact that most media institutions are deeply rooted in the market.

If Alexander is largely silent about markets, the same cannot be said about the "whig" interpretation of Anglo-American media history, which does stress the argument that the development of commercial media markets played a key role in the differentiation of media from political institutions. And in important ways this is clearly correct. Where media markets have been weakly developed, the mass media have frequently been "dominated" (in Bourdieu's terms) by the state and political parties. As Italian scholar Bechelloni notes:

> In Italy . . . all cultural undertakings were economically fragile, requiring, with some exceptions, help from the state or from private patrons in order to survive. This had two important consequences: there never were many economically self-sufficient cultural or journalistic enterprises, and intellectuals and journalists . . . always lived in a state of financial uncertainty and hence enjoyed little autonomy. The state, which was in control of this situation, always had ample opportunities for maneuver and interference.[17]

In Britain and in North America, on the other hand, and somewhat later in other parts of Europe, the development of strong media markets gave the mass media an economic base of their own, which reduced their need for subsidies from the state and political parties, and increased their role as an independent actor. The size of media organizations, moreover, something which is clearly connected to their growth as commercial enterprises, had much to do with the growth of a journalism as a distinct occupational category. Competition for readers and for advertisers, meanwhile, often encourages media to seek audiences across subcultural boundaries, as well as leading to a process of concentration which disrupts older patterns of association between media and social groups, and enhances the power and independence of the large surviving media organizations. C. Edwin Baker makes a strong argument that the development of the "objectivity norm" so central to journalistic professionalization in the United States was driven above all by the growth of advertising markets and the concentration of the newspaper industry that resulted from it.[18]

But there is another side to the relation between commercialization and media system differentiation. Professional autonomy in the news media, though it developed in a commercial context in many cases,[19] has by no means developed in total harmony with commercialization. It involved differentiation of the journalistic field from the economic as well as from the political fields. Journalistic professionalization has in most cases meant not only separation of journalists from partisan connections or connections to the state, but also from economic entanglements. In the US case, agitation for professionalization came against the background of corruption and sensationalism in the nineteenth century, and codes of ethics emphasized the avoidance of economic conflicts of interest. Professionalization also involved a form of differentiation that takes place within news organizations, as journalists assert the integrity of journalistic criteria *against* purely commercial ones, and their own autonomy against the intervention of owners, marketers and advertising sales staff. In the United States, this is part of the dual meaning of the "separation of church and state" that is one of the key principles of professionalism (the other meaning has to do with separation of news from editorial opinion). In the French case, parts of the elite press achieved a significant degree of autonomy in the post-World War II period, manifested in the fact that *Le Figaro* at one time had a dual organization structure separating the business and editorial sides of the paper, while *Le Monde* was – and to some degree still is – owned by journalists, who have the right to elect its director.

One of the most dramatic changes in the media systems of the advanced capitalist countries has been a general shift toward the dominance of commercial logic. In the United States, the media have been primarily commercial in character since the mid-nineteenth century; nevertheless commercial pressures have intensified with deregulation of broadcasting and changes in ownership patterns that have brought newspapers under the influence of Wall Street, and the autonomy of journalism as a profession has declined in important ways.[20] Similar changes are clearly under way to varying degrees throughout Europe, most dramatically in the sphere of broadcasting.

Here it is worth going back to Mazzoleni's distinction between media logic and political logic. "Media logic" has become increasingly differentiated from "political logic" and increasingly dominant over the latter. Story selection, for example, is increasingly determined not by political criteria – like principles of proportional representation – but by journalistic or media-based criteria of what is a "good story." It is important to recognize, however, that this "media logic" which has emerged in the late twentieth century is a hybrid logic. Here the insistence in the chapters in this volume on seeing journalism as a complex field and not as a single homogeneous institution or profession is very relevant. "Media logic" can be said to be rooted in two developments that overlapped historically, and were intertwined in important ways, but are also distinct: one is the growth of commercial cultural industries; the other is the growth of journalistic professionalism. Champagne refers to the strictly professional logic of journalism as an "intellectual" logic; the use of the word "intellectual" to refer to journalists may seem strange to Americans, for in the United States the journalistic and academic fields are much more strongly differentiated than in France. (*Le Monde* used to have footnotes – obviously something unknown in an American newspaper!) Nevertheless, the underlying point is clearly correct, that during the twentieth century, in all Western countries, journalists developed criteria of cultural production that were distinct from either the discourse of party politics or the commercial logic of the cultural industries.

Here I would like to make a brief digression on the subject of the emphasis in field theory on the struggle for distinction among the agents of a field. "One of the general properties of fields is that there are struggles within fields for the power to impose the dominant vision of the field," Bourdieu writes in the lecture reproduced in this volume (p. 36). In response to passages like this, Alexander argues that Bourdieu reduces all forms of action to a paradigm based on the economic, that strategic action becomes the only form of human action, and interest the only form of motivation. Champagne's insistence that the logic of the journalistic field is an *intellectual* logic obviously conflicts with Alexander's charge that field theory is reductionist. But the emphasis on the position agents occupy within the "game" that constitutes the field of journalism is potentially distorting and indeed potentially reductionist. This is a common way to understand journalism in popular discourse: people will say that journalists cover a story in a certain way because they want to get a scoop, to make themselves journalistic stars. Certainly there is an important element of truth in this; journalists and news organizations do compete for distinction within the field. And the applications of this perspective in the research presented in this volume are often quite interesting, as when Darras discusses the competition between news organizations for star political guests, or when Champagne and Marchetti discuss the efforts of health journalists to increase the prestige of their specialty within journalism. Nevertheless, competition by itself will in most cases explain little of the actual content of what journalists do; and it is important to keep in mind that there are other modes of interaction. Journalism is a "game," but it is also an "interpretive community,"[21] and even as a game it is not always competitive. To a large extent, for example, the routines of journalism allow easy cooperation among journalists. Bourdieu is aware, of course, that there is a "fundamental complicity among the members of a field," but this does appear more as background than foreground in many of the discussions of field theory – even in the use of the term "complicity," which seems to imply that the noncompetitive side of the logic of the field somehow lacks legitimacy and cannot be acknowledged.

The central point I want to make here, however, is that the distinctive "media logic" that has developed during the twentieth century is in fact a complex hybrid influenced by both commercial and strictly "professional" or "intellectual" influences; these two are in many ways in tension with one another; and the balance is shifting toward the commercial. "Media logic as professional logic" fits the story told by differentiation theory much better than "media logic as commercial logic." The growth of infotainment as a hybrid form of programming is a good illustration. Luhmann argues that the differentiation of mass media content into three genres – news and current affairs, advertising, and entertainment, each with distinct social functions, is "the most important internal structure of the system of the mass media."[22] Commercialization undercuts this form of differentiation, not only by blurring the boundaries between news and entertainment, but also those between advertising and the other two, as product placement increases in entertainment and as news is used to cross-promote other products of media conglomerates. Alexander, meanwhile, links the commercialization of media, the professionalization of journalism, and the "notion of the news media as a 'public institution.'"[23] But the recent commercialization of the media seems to undercut this idea, at least insofar as we consider the "public" to have a meaning apart from the aggregation of consumers in media markets.

Many would argue that the commercialization of media is part of a more general tendency toward de-differentiation in contemporary society: that with the shift toward neoliberalism market logic tends to dominate wide swaths of society, including politics, which increasingly resembles marketing, and also education, leisure, social services, etc. If an increasingly commercialized media are growing more central to social life they may be an important agent of this broader process of de-differentiation. This is part of Bourdieu's argument in *On Television*: there he agrees with differentiation theorists that the media have increasing centrality in society, but goes on to argue that the increased centrality of commercial media threatens the differentiation of other forms of cultural production: "The journalistic field tends to reinforce the 'commercial' elements at the core of all fields to the detriment of the 'pure.' It favors those cultural producers most susceptible to the seductions of economic and political powers, at the expense of those intent on defending the principles and the values of their professions."[24] At one point he speaks of "media intrusion – or, rather the intrusion of economic pressure as relayed by the media – even in the 'purest' science."[25]

The argument of *On Television* is exaggerated and simplistic in many ways – hence the need for Neveu's *apologia* published in this volume. For one thing, despite the repeated use of quotation marks in phrases like "pure" science – suggesting that a more sophisticated analysis is needed – the book depends for much of its rhetorical force on a naïve view of the separation of scientific knowledge from society. This is ironic given Alexander's charge of reductionism, but here the normative preference of Bourdieu's theory for autonomy of fields seems to take an unproductive form, and we lose sight of a very interesting set of issues about the balance between autonomy and accountability of social institutions and the question of whether "pure" professional autonomy is in fact desirable. Neveu is right, however, that it makes more sense to ask what Bourdieu's core work on cultural production can tell us about the media, than to focus on the one slight essay he published directly on the subject. And the point that commercial media may in many cases be transmitters of the influence of the market into other areas of social life – and hence an agent of de-differentiation – seems quite cogent.

Here it is worth mentioning the parallel with Habermas, who has also argued that the history of the media and of society in general is characterized in important ways by de-differentiation. Habermas's initial argument in *The Structural Transformation of the Public Sphere* was that the media, which were originally rooted in the emerging public sphere, were eventually absorbed into the market and the arena of political power. In his later work, he analyzes this in terms of the "colonization of the life world" by the systems of economics and political power. His analysis of the historical development of the news media is far too simplistic, once he gets past the eighteenth century: it is a bit like systems theory stood on its head – instead of a unilinear trend toward greater differentiation, Habermas claims the reverse. The underlying point though, that cultural institutions like the media or education are quite vulnerable to "colonization" by the social systems that concentrate economic and political resources and power, seems correct.[26]

I would like to close this section by addressing the issue of social classes and stratification. In the passage quoted at the beginning of this section, Alexander argues that media systems must be differentiated from "structures in the economic dimension, particularly social classes." He seems to assume, though he does not argue directly, that the status of media organizations as privately-owned businesses does not compromise their differentiation from social classes. This assumption is based on the idea that professionalization involves the development by the media of a network of connections with a variety of parties, social groups and sectors of society – not organizational connections, which tend to die out as the media become commercialized, but relations of influence and exchange of information. And indeed it is true that commercial media in general have tended to distance themselves from earlier narrow connections to conservative parties and to broaden and blur their political identities, as they have sought to capture readers from the party press of the left.

But the degree of this independence is hotly contested. This is one of the central arguments of the "critical political economy" school in Anglo-American media studies against the "Whig" interpretation of journalism history. The critical political economy school is one part of the legacy of the British cultural studies tradition, and as Neveu observes it has much in common with the work of Bourdieu, including the desire, noted at the beginning of this chapter, to analyze the media as part of a wider social formation. One of the key arguments of this perspective is that commercialization placed the media in the hands of business owners and led to a significant bias toward the parties and ideologies of the right. That tendency has been modified historically by a number of factors, including the professional autonomy of journalists (whose personal political orientations tend in most countries somewhat to the left), the continued existence of media subsidized by parties and associations, and public broadcasting. If commercialization undercuts all of these countervailing forces, however, the kind of link between media and social class that is central to the perspective of the critical political economy school may become increasingly important. This issue seems to me understressed in the work on journalism that has come out of the Bourdieu tradition – surprisingly given the emphasis in Bourdieu's sociology on social stratification, and ironically given Alexander's contention that Bourdieu sees the logic of all fields as ultimately determined by stratification. Instead, one finds in the study of the media a tendency to focus on the question of power in the relation of one field to another, or in the relations of the different – essentially elite – agents who make up the journalistic field, more than on the question of how the development of the journalistic field affects the representation of different social interests in public discussion.

The journalistic field and the political field

I would like to close with a briefer discussion of the relation between the media and the field of politics. Earlier in this chapter, I argued that there was a strong tendency for the media to become differentiated from certain political institutions, particularly parties and organized social groups like trade unions. Whether it is a positive development for democratic political systems is subject to some debate. Alexander assumes that it is, though he does acknowledge that the media system of the United States might be criticized for a lack of diversity in the political discourse it offers to the public. He argues that this results not from characteristics of the media system, but from lack of differentiation of the American political party system. Jean Chalaby, James Curran, and others have argued that promotion and representation of organized social groups is an important function of a media system, and that commercialized media systems tend to perform this function poorly.[27] In any case, it is clearly true that there is a historical tendency in this sense for media to become differentiated from political institutions.

But the political field is complex, and it may be that there are tendencies to de-differentiation as well as to differentiation in the relation of media to politics, as there are in the relation of media to the economic field. If, for example, we turn our attention from parties and social groups to the structures of the state, a more complicated picture begins to emerge. Alexander accepts the "watchdog" theory of the American media's political role. The media, he argues, "confront the state as the populist counterpart to rational-legal social control."[28] He acknowledges near the end of his paper that a tendency for journalists to become so close to their sources that the independence of their judgment comes into question is a "structural strain" of the journalists' role. He does not regard it, however, as raising any fundamental question about the differentiation of the media in relation to the state. There are, certainly, important tendencies toward differentiation of the media from the state. In the French case, television was fully integrated into the state apparatus until the 1980s, when it became substantially more independent. The US press was often subsidized by the state until the second half of the nineteenth century. In both countries, as in many others around the world, there was a tendency in the 1970s to 1980s toward the development of a kind of "critical professionalism" that often involved more adversarial relations with state actors.

But this is by no means the complete story. For the United States, there is a large body of literature which emphasizes the integration of the news media into the political process as a sort of "fourth branch of government."[29] The paper by Darras in this volume underscores the conclusions of that literature and shows the essential similarity here between the United States and France. None of this research suggests complete de-differentiation of the news media in relation to the state. The state is itself institutionally differentiated, for one thing, and the news media could not mediate among its different parts if they did not themselves have a significant degree of autonomy, nor would they have the legitimacy to be useful to political actors as a means of shaping public opinion. Nevertheless, in the US case the professional model of journalism coincided historically with a movement toward greatly increased interdependence between the news media and the state – particularly during the period running from the New Deal through World War II to the Cold War (the phrase, "fourth branch of government," comes from a 1958 book by Douglass Cater[30]). That interdependence was connected in the American case with the consolidation of rational–legal authority and the national security state, and also with the decline of partisanship in journalism. It was certainly modified by the growth of critical professionalism; nevertheless the interdependence remains great enough that here, too, we can not tell the story of journalism as a unilinear evolution toward greater differentiation.

Bourdieu, meanwhile, puts forward a formulation in *On Television* and in the lecture reproduced in this volume that seems just as problematic as Alexander's argument that the media have moved in a simple way toward differentiation from the sphere of politics. Journalism, he says, is "structured on the basis of an opposition between . . . those who are 'purest,' most independent of state power, political power and economic power, and those who are most dependent on these powers and commercial powers . . . [T]he journalistic field is increasingly subject to the constraints of the economy and of politics" (p. 41, this volume). This formulation essentially collapses the economic and political fields, introducing the assumption that political and economic "heteronomy" necessarily go hand in hand, and positing an essentially unilinear process of de-differentiation of the media. No doubt it is true that commercialization in many cases does have the effect of aligning the media with dominant political actors; this is also the argument of the "critical political economy" school. Thus Darras outlines some reasons why economic pressures may contribute to the dominance of political elites in the kinds of talk shows he analyzes, though he goes on to consider other factors that also contribute to this result. But it is too simplistic to assume that economic and political power are always in perfect alignment, and it contradicts other points Bourdieu makes about the complexity of the fields themselves. Many of the essays in this volume suggest that more complex dynamics are at work, as for example in Champagne and Marchetti's analysis of the contaminated blood scandal, which points to the increasingly aggressive attitude of journalists toward official sources, something rooted in part in the development of a consumerist culture in the field of medicine. This seems to me one of the most central issues that needs to be developed from the perspective of field theory: the nature of the relation between the political and economic fields, and the intersection of journalism with these fields.

Conclusion

Differentiation theory has been a fundamental point of view in media studies since the end of World War II. It has not been developed in a systematic and explicit way in recent years, but for those interested in historical and comparative analysis of media systems, a dialogue with differentiation theory is essential. In many ways, differentiation theory is illuminating. But it involves many blindspots and mistaken assumptions as well, most fundamentally the assumption of a unilinear trend toward greater differentiation. Bourdieu's field theory and the media research derived from this model share many of the underlying theoretical questions that motivate differentiation theory, but address those questions in quite different ways, and provides an important alternative framework for understanding historical change in the relation of media to the social system. Field theory is closer in many ways to the "critical political economy" tradition in the central importance it gives to the embedding of the contemporary media in the market. It is also potentially more open than differentiation theory, in the sense that it doesn't make any particular assumption about whether media move over time toward differentiation or de-differentiation. It does need to free itself from some of the more simplistic formulations that Bourdieu himself popularized in *On Television*. And there is also clearly a need for greater clarification within the field theory tradition on a number of issues, including the relation between competition among journalistic agents and the formation of common standards within the journalistic community, and the relation between the political and journalistic fields.

Notes

1 Lucien W. Pye, ed., *Communications and Political Development* (Princeton University Press, Princeton, NJ, 1963), p. 78. See also Richard Fagen, *Politics and Communication* (Little, Brown and Company, Boston, 1966).
2 Karl Marx, "Manifesto of the Communist Party," in *The Revolutions of 1848*, ed. D. Fernbach (Vintage, New York, 1974).
3 Richard D. Altick, *The English Common Reader: A Social History of the Mass Reading Public, 1800–1900* (Ohio State University Press, Columbus, OH, 1957), p. 322.
4 Niklas Luhmann, *The Reality of the Mass Media* (Stanford University Press, Stanford, CA, 2000).
5 Jeffrey C. Alexander, "The Mass News Media in Systemic, Historical and Comparative Perspective," in *Mass Media and Social Change*, eds. E. Katz and T. Szecskö (Sage, Beverly Hills, CA, 1981), pp. 17–51.
6 Alexander, "The Mass News Media in Systemic, Historical and Comparative Perspective," pp. 23–4.
7 Alexander, "The Mass News Media in Systemic, Historical and Comparative Perspective," p. 25.
8 Alexander, "The Mass News Media in Systemic, Historical and Comparative Perspective," p. 25.
9 See Daniel C. Hallin and Paolo Mancini, "Speaking of the President: Political Structure and Representational Form in US and Italian TV News," *Theory and Society*, 13 (1984), pp. 829–50, and *Comparing Media Systems: Three Models of Media and Politics* (Cambridge University Press, New York, 2004). Parts of this article are adapted from the latter text, and much of the argument about differentiation and de-differentiation of media systems is developed at greater length there.

10 Daniel C. Hallin and Stylianos Papathanassopoulos, "Political Clientelism and the Media: Southern Europe and Latin America in Comparative Perspective," *Media, Culture and Society*, 24, 2 (2002), pp. 175–95.
11 Gianpietro Mazzoleni, "Media Logic and Party Logic in Campaign Coverage: The Italian General Election of 1983," *European Journal of Communication*, 2, 1 (1987), pp. 81–103.
12 Rodney Benson, "Field Theory in Comparative Context: A New Paradigm for Media Studies," *Theory and Society*, 28 (1999), pp. 463–98.
13 Alexander, "The Mass News Media in Systemic, Historical and Comparative Perspective," p. 24.
14 Alexander, "The Mass News Media in Systemic, Historical and Comparative Perspective," p. 24.
15 Jean K. Chalaby, "Journalism as an Anglo-American Invention: A Comparison of the Development of French and Anglo-American Journalism, 1830s–1920s," *European Journal of Communication*, 11, 3 (1996), pp. 303–26.
16 Jeffrey C. Alexander, *Fin de Siècle Social Theory: Relativism, Reduction and the Problem of Reason* (Verso, London, 1995).
17 Giovanni Bechelloni, "The Journalist as Political Client in Italy," in *Newspapers and Democracy*, ed. A. Smith (MIT Press, Cambridge, MA, 1980), p. 234.
18 C. Edwin Baker, *Advertising and a Democratic Press* (Princeton University Press, Princeton, NJ, 1994).
19 In *Comparing Media Systems*, Mancini and I argue that professionalization also developed within noncommercial contexts, including much of the party press and public broadcasting. Commercialism is not *necessary* to the professional differentiation of journalism, any more than it is to the professional differentiation of the civil service or judiciary.
20 Daniel C. Hallin, "Commercialism and Professionalism in the American News Media," in *Mass Media and Society*, eds. J. Curran and M. Gurevitch (Arnold, London, 2000), pp. 218–37.
21 Barbie Zelizer, *Covering the Body: The Kennedy Assassination, the Media, and the Shaping of Collective Memory* (University of Chicago Press, Chicago, 1992).
22 Luhmann, *The Reality of the Mass Media*, p. 24.
23 Alexander, "The Mass News Media in Systemic, Historical and Comparative Perspective," p. 31.
24 Pierre Bourdieu, *On Television* (The New Press, New York, 1998), p. 70.
25 Bourdieu, *On Television*, p. 60.
26 See Jürgen Habermas, *The Structural Transformation of the Public Sphere* (MIT Press, Cambridge, MA, 1989, originally published in Germany in 1962) and *The Theory of Communicative Action*, vol. I (Beacon Press, Boston, 1984).

27 Jean K. Chalaby, *The Invention of Journalism* (Macmillan, London, 1998); James Curran, "Rethinking the Media as a Public Sphere," in *Communication and Citizenship: Journalism and the Public Sphere in the New Media Age*, eds. P. Dahlgren and C. Sparks (Routledge, London, 1991), pp. 27–57.
28 Alexander, "The Mass News Media in Systemic, Historical and Comparative Perspective," p. 25.
29 Timothy E. Cook, *Governing with the News: The News Media as a Political Institution* (University of Chicago Press, Chicago, 1998).
30 Douglass Cater, *The Fourth Branch of Government* (Vintage, New York, 1958).

Select Bibliography

Albert, Pierre. 1990 and 1998. *La Presse française*. Paris: La Documentation française.

Alexander, Jeffrey. 1981. "The Mass News Media in Systemic, Historical and Comparative Perspective." In *Mass Media and Social Change*, eds. E. Katz and T. Szecskö. Beverly Hills, CA: Sage.

——. 1995. *Fin de Siècle Social Theory*. London: Verso.

Åsard, Erik and Lance W. Bennett. 1997. *Democracy and the Marketplace of Ideas: Communication and Government in Sweden and the United States*. Cambridge: Cambridge University Press.

Bagdikian, Ben. 1992. *The Media Monopoly*, 4th edition. Boston: Beacon Press.

Baker, C. Edwin. 1994. *Advertising and a Democratic Press*. Princeton, NJ: Princeton University Press.

——. 2002. *Media, Markets, and Democracy*. Cambridge: Cambridge University Press.

Benson, Rodney. 1999. "Field Theory in Comparative Context: A New Paradigm for Media Studies." *Theory and Society*, 29, 463–98.

——. 2002. "The Political/Literary Model of French Journalism: Change and Continuity in Immigration Coverage, 1973–1991." *Journal of European Area Studies*, 10(1), 49–70.

——. 2004a. "Bringing the Sociology of Media Back In." *Political Communication*, 21, 275–92.

——. 2004b. "La Fin du *Monde*? Tradition and Change in the French Press." *French Politics,Culture & Society*, 22(1), 108–26.

Bourdieu, Pierre. 1984. *Distinction*. Cambridge, MA: Harvard University Press.

——. 1988. *Homo Academicus*. Stanford, CA: Stanford University Press and Cambridge: Polity.

——. 1991. *Language and Symbolic Power*, ed. John Thompson. Cambridge, MA: Harvard University Press.

——. 1992. *The Logic of Practice*. Stanford, CA: Stanford University Press and Cambridge: Polity.
——. 1993. *The Field of Cultural Production*. New York: Columbia University Press and Cambridge: Polity.
——. 1995. *The Rules of Art*. Stanford, CA: Stanford University Press and Cambridge: Polity.
——. 1996. *The State Nobility*. Stanford, CA: Stanford University Press and Cambridge: Polity.
——. 1998a. *On Television*. New York: New Press [1996. *Sur la télévision*. Paris: Liber].
——. 1998b. "Social Space and Symbolic Space." In *Practical Reason*. Stanford, CA: Stanford University Press and Cambridge: Polity.
Bourdieu, Pierre and Loïc J.D. Wacquant. 1992. *An Invitation to Reflexive Sociology*. Chicago: The University of Chicago Press.
Calhoun, Craig. 1992. "Introduction." In *Habermas and the Public Sphere*, ed. C. Calhoun. Cambridge, MA: MIT Press.
Chalaby, Jean. 1996. "Journalism as an Anglo-American Invention: A Comparison of the Development of French and Anglo-American Journalism, 1830s–1920s." *European Journal of Communication*, 11(3), 303–26.
——. 1998. *The Invention of Journalism*. London: Macmillan.
Champagne, Patrick. 1990. *Faire l'opinion*. Paris: Minuit.
——. 1999. "The View from the Media." In *The Weight of the World*, ed. P. Bourdieu. Stanford, CA: Stanford University Press [2000] and Cambridge: Polity.
Cook, Timothy E. 1998. *Governing with the News: The News Media as a Political Institution*. Chicago: The University of Chicago Press.
Couldry, Nick. 2003. "Media Meta-Capital: Extending the Range of Bourdieu's Field Theory." *Theory and Society*, 32, 653–77.
Devillard, Valérie, Marie-Françoise Lafosse, Christine Leteinturier, and Rémy Rieffel. 2001. *Les journalistes français à l'aube de l'an 2000: Profils et parcours*. Paris: Panthéon-Assas.
Gans, Herbert. 1980. *Deciding What's News*. New York: Vintage.
Garnham, Nicholas and Raymond Williams. 1980. "Pierre Bourdieu and the Sociology of Culture: An Introduction." *Media, Culture and Society*, 2, pp. 209–23.
Gitlin, Todd. 1980. *The Whole World is Watching: Mass Media in the Making and Unmaking of the New Left*. Berkeley, CA: University of California Press.
Habermas, Jürgen. 1989. *The Structural Transformation of the Public Sphere. An Inquiry into a Category of Bourgeois Society*. Cambridge, MA: The MIT Press.
Hallin, Daniel C. 1994. *We Keep America on Top of the World: Television Journalism and the Public Sphere*. London: Routledge.
Hallin, Daniel C., and Paolo Mancini. 1984. "Speaking of the President: Political Structure and Representational Form in US and Italian News." *Theory and Society*, 13, 829–50.

——. 2004. *Comparing Media Systems: Three Models of Media and Politics*. Cambridge: Cambridge University Press.
Klinenberg, Eric. 2002. *Heat Wave: A Social Autopsy of Disaster in Chicago*. Chicago: The University of Chicago Press.
Kuhn, Raymond. 1995. *The Media in France*. London and New York: Routledge.
Kuhn, Raymond and Erik Neveu, eds. 2002. *Political Journalism: New Challenges, New Practices*. London: Routledge.
Luhmann, Niklas. 2000. *The Reality of the Mass Media*. Stanford, CA: Stanford University Press.
Marchetti, Dominique and Denis Ruellan. 2001. *Devenir journalistes: Sociologie de l'entrée dans le marché du travail*. Paris: La Documentation française.
Martin, John Levi. 2003. "What is Field Theory?" *American Journal of Sociology*, 109, 1–49.
Mohr, John. 2000. "Introduction: Structures, Institutions, and Cultural Analysis." *Poetics*, 27, 57–68.
Neveu, Erik. 2001. *Sociologie du journalisme*. Paris: La Découverte.
Padioleau, Jean-G. 1976. "Systèmes d'interaction et rhétoriques journalistiques." *Sociologie du travail*, 3, 256–82.
——. 1985. *Le Monde et le Washington Post*. Paris: PUF.
Pedelty, Mark. 1995. *War Stories: The Culture of Foreign Correspondents*. London: Routledge.
Powell, Walter W. and Paul J. DiMaggio, eds. 1991. *The New Institutionalism in Organizational Analysis*. Chicago: University of Chicago Press.
Schlesinger, Philip. 1990. "Rethinking the Sociology of Journalism: Source Strategies and the Limits of Media-Centrism." In *Public Communication: The New Imperatives*, ed. M. Ferguson, pp. 61–83. London: Sage.
Schudson, Michael. 1994. "The 'Public Sphere' and its Problems: Bringing the State (Back) In." *Notre Dame Journal of Law, Ethics & Public Policy*, 8, 529–46.
——. 2000. "The Sociology of News Production Revisited (Again)." In *Mass Media and Society*, eds. J. Curran and M. Gurevitch, pp. 175–200. London: Arnold.
——. 2003. *The Sociology of News*. New York: W.W. Norton.
Sparrow, Bartholomew H. 1999. *Uncertain Guardians: The News Media as a Political Institution*. Baltimore, MD: The Johns Hopkins University Press.
Swartz, David. 1997. *Culture and Power: The Sociology of Pierre Bourdieu*. Chicago: The University of Chicago Press.
Thelen, Kathleen, and Sven Steinmo. 1992. "Historical institutionalism in comparative politics." In *Structuring Politics: Historical Institutionalism in Comparative Analysis*, eds. S. Steinmo, K. Thelen, and F. Longstreth. Cambridge: Cambridge University Press.

Thogmartin, Clyde. 1998. *The National Daily Press of France*. Birmingham, AL: Summa.
Tunstall, Jeremy. 1971. *Journalists at Work*. London: Constable.
——. 1996. *Newspaper Power: The New National Press in Britain*. Oxford: Oxford University Press.

Index